IMAGES
of America

LOST MINDEN

On the Cover. Abraham Dow migrated to Minden from his home in Syria shortly after 1900. His store on what was commonly called "Back Street" served both the black and white communities for nearly seven decades. The store was torn down in 1970 as part of the construction of the Minden Civic Center and City Hall Complex. This image, taken in the early 1920s, shows Dow (center with no hat) and customers. (Author's collection.)

IMAGES
of America

LOST MINDEN

John A. Agan

ARCADIA
PUBLISHING

ISBN 978-1-4671-1319-9

Published by Arcadia Publishing
Charleston, South Carolina

Printed in the United States of America

Library of Congress Control Number: 2014942567

For all general information, please contact Arcadia Publishing:
Telephone 843-853-2070
Fax 843-853-0044
E-mail sales@arcadiapublishing.com
For customer service and orders:
Toll-Free 1-888-313-2665

Visit us on the Internet at www.arcadiapublishing.com

To my parents, J.C. Agan Jr. and Juanita Murphy Agan, for their many years of support, encouragement, and love

Contents

Acknowledgments

I began researching local history as a high school student in the 1970s, and it has become both a vocation and an avocation for me. I would have not been able to pursue that passion and produce research and publications without the help of so many people. I want to acknowledge a few of them here. The first would be my maternal grandmother, Louannie Longino Murphy, and her daughter, my mother, Juanita Murphy Agan, who inspired me with a love of history as a small child and were my partners in this work so long as they were both alive. I thank my teachers, from the earliest years through my college training, who taught me so much about the value of history and how to preserve and protect our heritage. My gratitude goes to my employers, both at the Webster Parish Library and Bossier Parish Community College, who have allowed me the freedom to research and produce such projects as this book.

This work would not have been possible without the aid of the Dorcheat Historical Association Museum, its executive director, Schelley Francis, and its president, Thad Andress. Schelley and Thad have been my friends for years, but their support went a long way toward making this book a reality. Over the years, I have been given images by so many citizens of Minden that I hesitate to list names, fearing omission, but I want to thank the following folks who have been so helpful: Frank Griffith, Craig Farley, Clair Moore, the families of Grace Turner Watson and George Turner, the family of Lillian Life Willis, Joan Wiley Luck, and Meg McCowen. The collections of the Webster Parish Library and the Archives and Special Collections of Noel Memorial Library of Louisiana State University in Shreveport (LSUS) were vital to completing this work. Particularly, thanks go to library director Beverly Hammett at the Webster Parish Library and Shawn Bohannon at LSUS. I also was assisted by staff at the National Archives at Fort Worth, Texas, in obtaining some of the images used in this book. Finally, I am so very grateful to Julia Simpson, my acquisitions editor at Arcadia Publishing on this project, who tolerated my lack of technical skill and blurred deadlines to bring this book to fruition.

Introduction

Minden, Louisiana, was founded in 1835 by Charles Veeder, a German American entrepreneur. In the more than 180 years since that time, the town has experienced times of triumph and tragedy like most communities in our country. Each of these events in some way changed the landscape, personality, and character of the town. While progress has been fairly stable in Minden, progress always implies change. In those changes, things are invariably lost. The title of this book, *Lost Minden*, reflects those things—both physical structures and individuals—that have been lost during those years of growth but have also shaped the community and are still remembered today.

When the original plat for Minden was designed, it was in the form of a parallelogram, and the town developed with the two long sides of that shape becoming two parallel streets with a middle ground in between. Those two streets have borne different names over the years. Today, the northern street is Main Street, and the southern street is Broadway, but for most of our history, locals knew them as "Front Street" to the north and "Back Street" to the south. The middle ground between those two streets was broken into two large portions. The eastern portion was home to businesses, while the western section was originally common green space. After Minden became a parish seat with the creation of Webster Parish in 1871, the green space was converted to public use. Eventually, three different Webster Parish courthouses would be built in that green space, along with a large section where, at the start, horses and buggies were hitched. Beyond that lot, a large Civic Park was created in the early 20th century. Today, the hitching lot is a parking lot, and the third Webster Parish Courthouse sits on what was the park. Many memories of good times in the old park remain, of those who experienced it before it was replaced in the early 1950s.

The eastern end of the middle ground with the businesses is a unique aspect of Minden life, particularly during the years of Jim Crow. Under segregation, white residents almost exclusively shopped the stores on the north side of Front Street. While there were black businesses in the largely black sections of Minden, the stores on Back Street became the black business district. The stores in the middle ground with front doors on Front Street and back doors on Back Street accepted customers both white and black, each using the "appropriate" door. For a terrible period, any black person seen on Front Street without apparent justification risked arrest or, at the very least, harassment. From the 1890s to the 1960s, these two communities were a living embodiment of "separate but equal" with all that entailed—the mores of segregation extended into the economic life of the community. The images in chapter 1 largely focus on the business structures along the parallelogram, thus the title "The Parallelogram and Beyond."

Minden has always been a city of churches and an active community, with its citizens being enthusiastic participants in civic events. In the early years, downtown was dotted with the churches of several denominations, and even today, at least five churches remain active in the downtown area. Beyond the spiritual implications of these congregations, the unique architecture of the churches left lasting memories. In terms of community cohesion, the populace embraces causes for the public good. For example, Minden gives more per capita to St. Jude's Research

Hospital than any community in the United States; its annual February telethon produces more than $1,000,000 in donations. The St. Jude's project is only the most modern expression of the community spirit present in our town. A major part of this community spirit has been driven by religion. In fact, an editorial writer in 1901 stated that, in Minden, "the shadows of a spire are athwart the hearthstones of each home." Community-sponsored athletics, entertainment, and celebrations were the norm in Minden and left indelible marks on the heritage of the town. So, the images that focus on that religious and community spirit give chapter 2 the title "Shadows of Spires athwart the Hearthstones."

Although Minden was not formally incorporated until 1854, the community made its first foray into local government years earlier, and that attempt focused on a very specific role of government. In 1838, three years after Minden was founded, Mindenites attempted to stimulate public education in the town. Minden residents, led by Charles Veeder, persuaded the Louisiana legislature to grant the town $1,500 for the purpose of "erecting a building for academic purposes." They created the Minden Academy, one of the first public schools in the state of Louisiana, and cemented the marriage between government and education that has always been prevalent in Minden. When a change in the Louisiana constitution forced the school to alter its policy of providing free tuition to needy students, a private male academy and female college emerged in 1850 to replace the original academy. In the first quarter of the 20th century, E.S. Richardson was hired as superintendent of Webster Parish Schools. Under his leadership, the school system was modernized and become a model copied across the nation. Within a period of 15 years, Minden, after having never built a public school since the 1830s, erected two modern brick facilities with public funding. Minden's founder had intended the town to be a parish seat, and while it was never achieved while he lived in Minden, the creation of Webster Parish in 1871 made Minden the seat of government for the parish. This status entailed the construction of government buildings over time. Because of this close relationship between education and its government sponsor, the chapter on education and government, chapter 3, is titled "Erecting a Building for Academic Purposes."

I hope this book helps keep the readers' "lost" memories of Minden alive.

One

The Parallelogram and Beyond

Business and Commerce

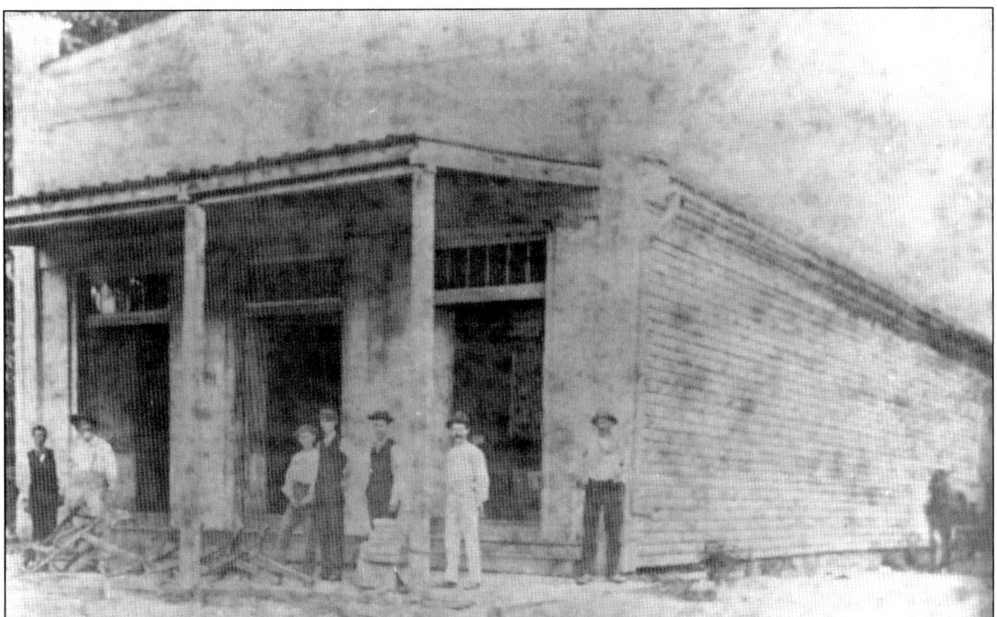

Drake's Store, shown in a post–Civil War image, was founded in the late 1830s and served as the midpoint when Minden's original one-mile-square town limits were laid out in 1854. It was also used as a headquarters by the Union forces that occupied Minden at the conclusion of the Civil War in 1865. (Courtesy of Clair Drake Moore.)

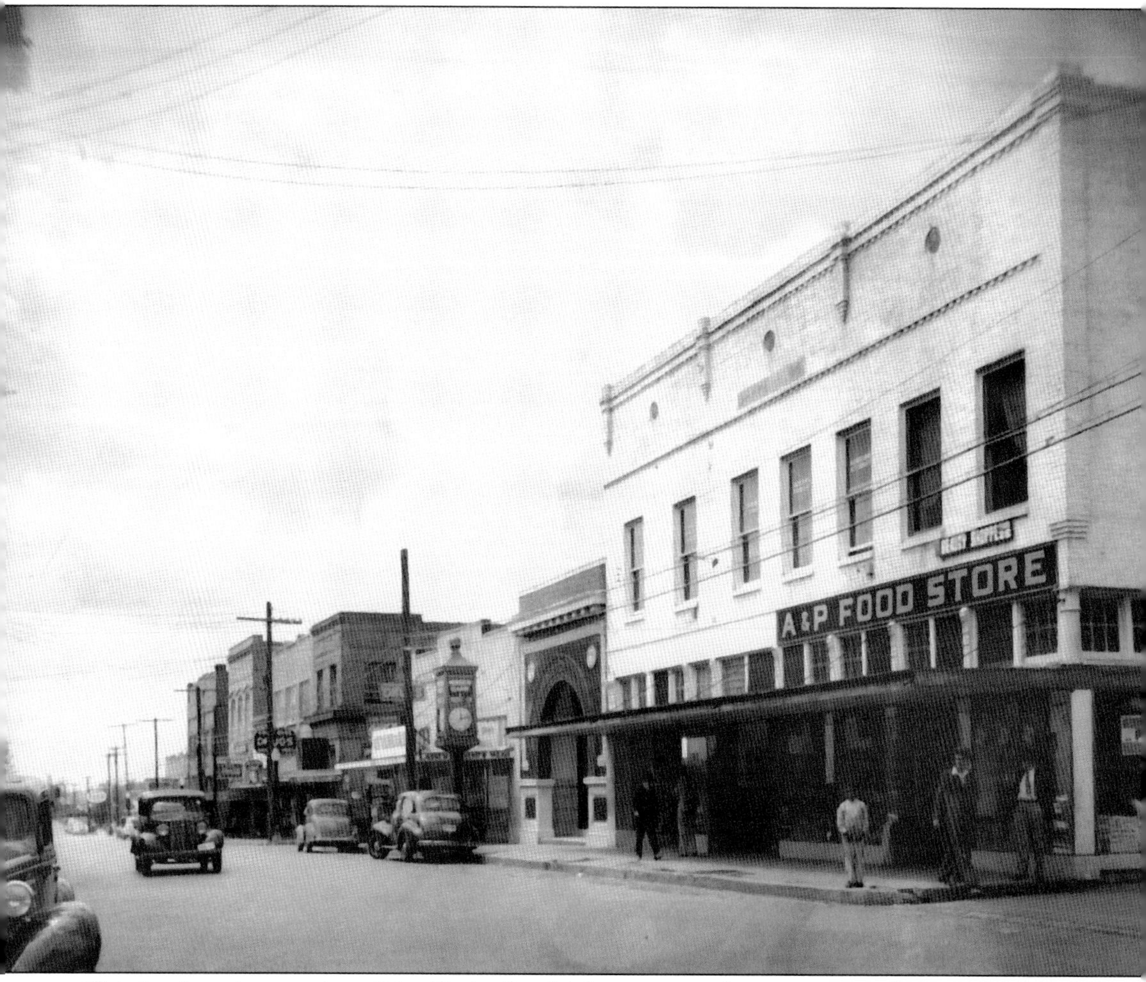

This is a later incarnation of the Drake family's business on the same site as the original store. The Drake Building (the white structure on the right) was erected in the 1890s and is still in use today. Over the years, many different firms operated in the street-level storefronts while the upstairs provided office space for attorneys, physicians, and other businesses. The Drake Building still has functioning commercial offices upstairs, which are rather unique for downtown Minden. When this image was taken around 1940, the largest storefront was occupied by the A&P grocery store. A&P would later relocate to two other sites in Minden before closing in the 1970s. Another major national retailer, Sears, Roebuck and Co., would open its Minden catalog store in that space in the Drake Building in the 1960s. This image also gives a good view of Minden's brick Main Street. The bricks were laid in 1917–1918 and remain today. (Author's collection.)

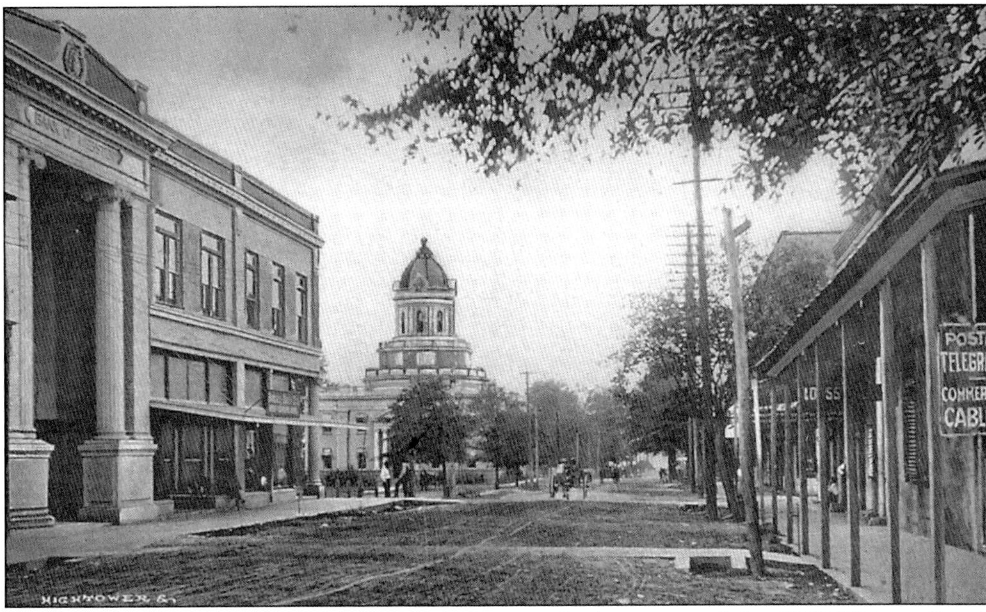

Minden's c. 1908 Main Street is pictured in a view looking toward the 1905 Webster Parish Courthouse on the left. The Bank of Webster Building in the left foreground had been erected about 1903 on part of the property that had been home to the first business constructed in Minden in 1835, Charles Veeder's Rock Inn. (Author's collection.)

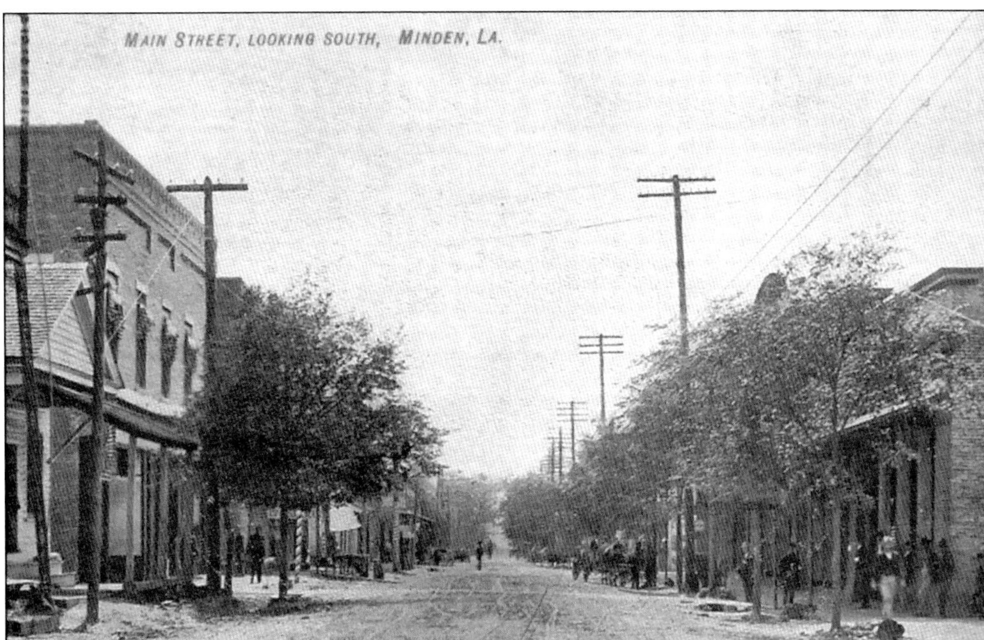

The view in this postcard from the first decade of the 20th century looks west (despite the card's caption) from the modern intersection of Fogle and Main Streets in Minden. The building in the right foreground is Goodwill's Store, built by pioneer settler Alfred Goodwill, great-grandfather of former Louisiana governor Mike Foster. (Author's collection.)

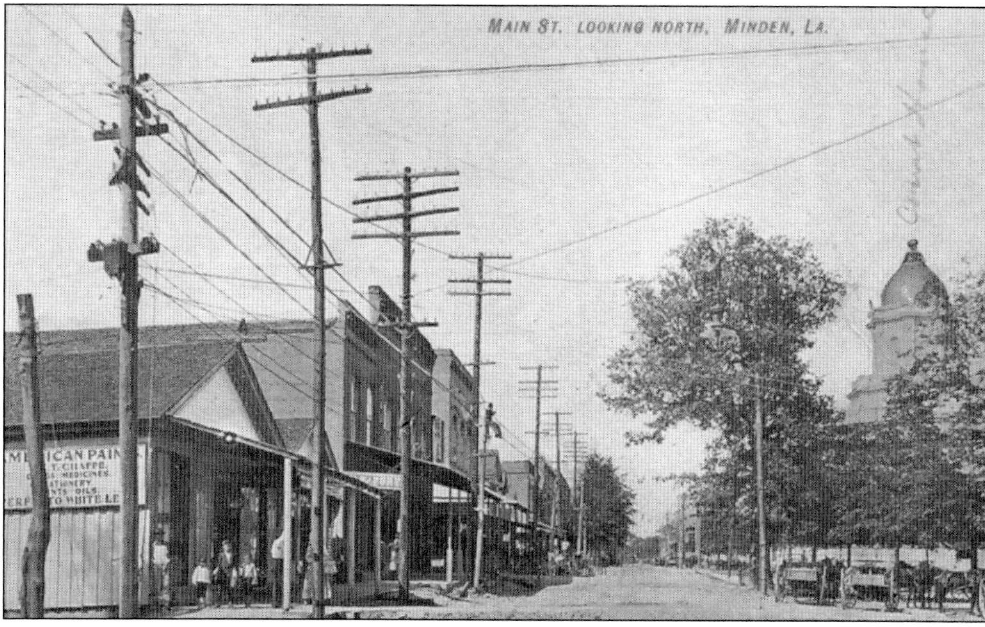

From the same series, this postcard view looks east (not north) from the intersection of Main and Pine Streets in Minden. The 1905 Webster Parish Courthouse is prominent in the left side of the picture as is the "hitching lot" in the left foreground. That space has been used for parking—from horse-drawn buggies to cars—since the founding of Minden until today. (Author's collection.)

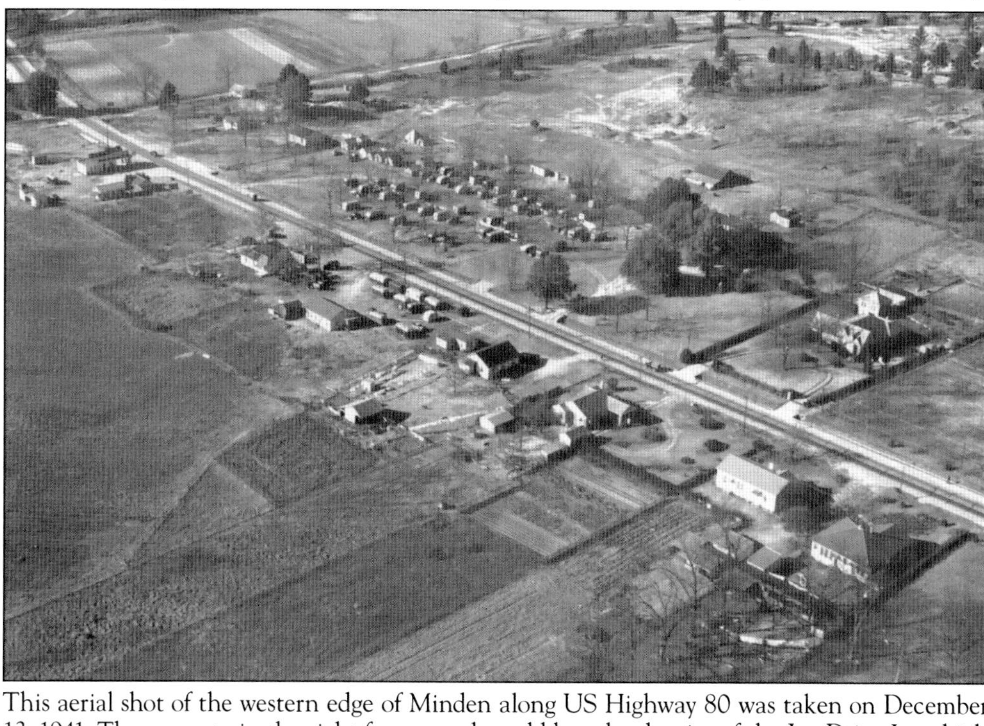

This aerial shot of the western edge of Minden along US Highway 80 was taken on December 13, 1941. The property in the right foreground would later be the site of the Joy Drive-In, which entertained Minden from the late 1940s until the 1970s and even hosted a performance by Elvis Presley in 1955. (Courtesy of the Webster Parish Library.)

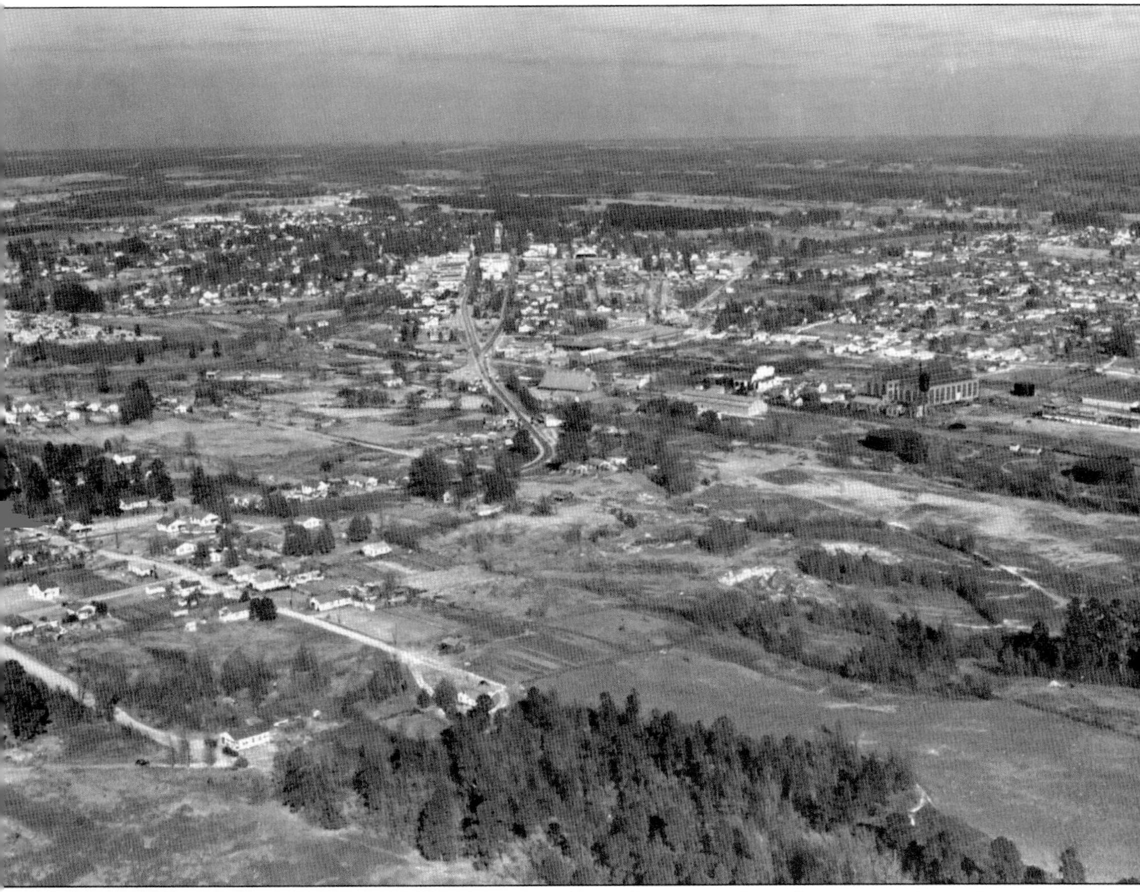

Another image from the December 1941 series shows downtown Minden as seen from the west. Clearly visible are the shops of the Louisiana & Arkansas (L&A) Railway along the eastern side of the railroad tracks. Other prominent landmarks include the 1905 Webster Parish Courthouse in the middle block between Main Street (more commonly known as Front Street) and Broadway (Back Street). These parallel streets created two business districts—one for blacks and the other for whites. There were a few stores that catered to both races. In the right center of the picture is the Ferguson Memorial Tabernacle of the First Baptist Church, looking rather like an aircraft hangar at first glance. On the cusp of World War II, Minden was also on the edge of a transformation as the massive Louisiana Ordnance Plant, located west of Minden, was nearing completion. (Courtesy of the Webster Parish Library.)

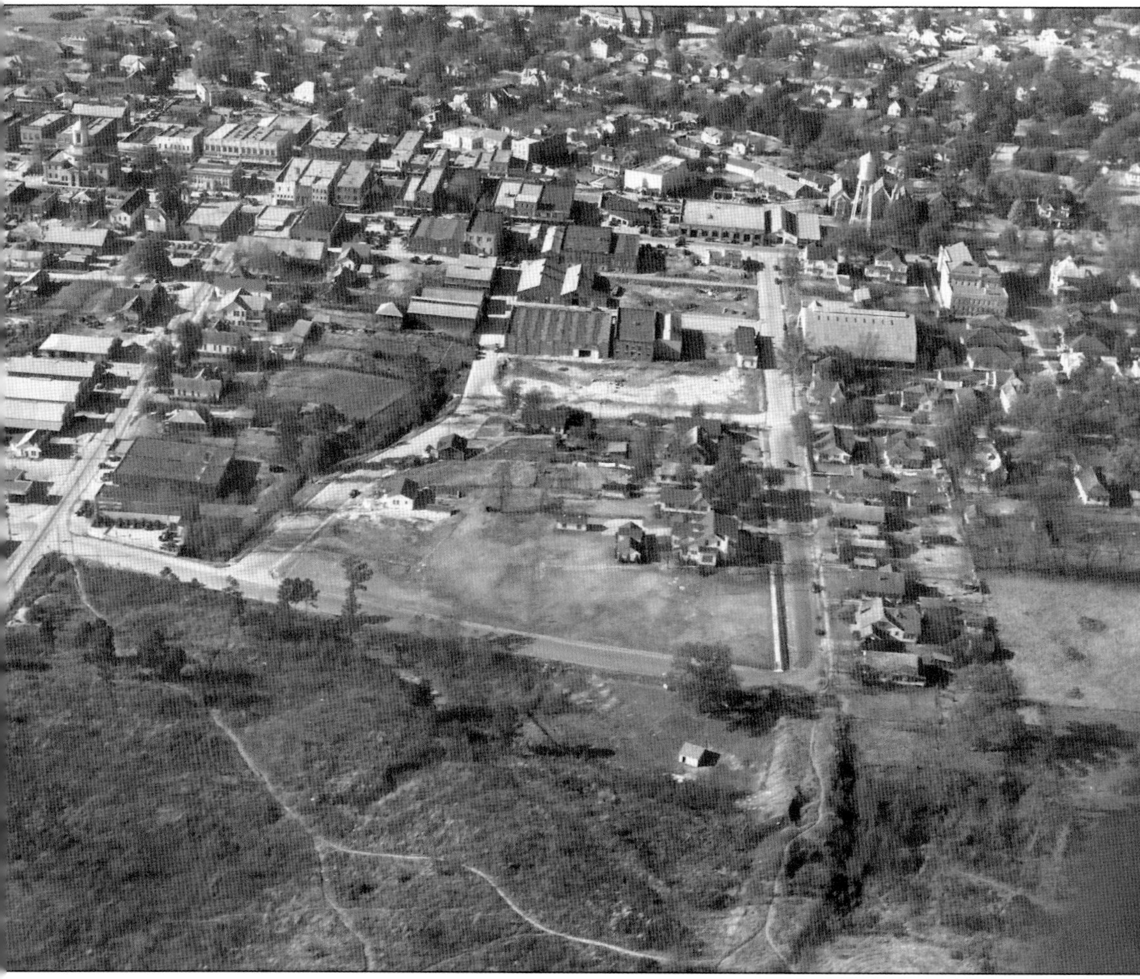

This third image from December 1941 gives a closer look at downtown Minden from the air. Again the Webster Parish Courthouse is prominent, and just to its right is the Minden Post Office, built in 1916. While many of the buildings in this picture remain today, the area around and south of the courthouse is completely changed. Nearly everything in that area was torn down and replaced by the Minden Civic Center in 1970. Toward the right edge of the image is the Ferguson Tabernacle of First Baptist Church. Across the boulevard from the Baptist church to the north is the First Methodist Church of Minden. At the extreme top of the picture is the 1910 Minden public school building, which, by 1941, was serving as the grammar school, with the newer 1924 high school building located to its west. (Author's collection.)

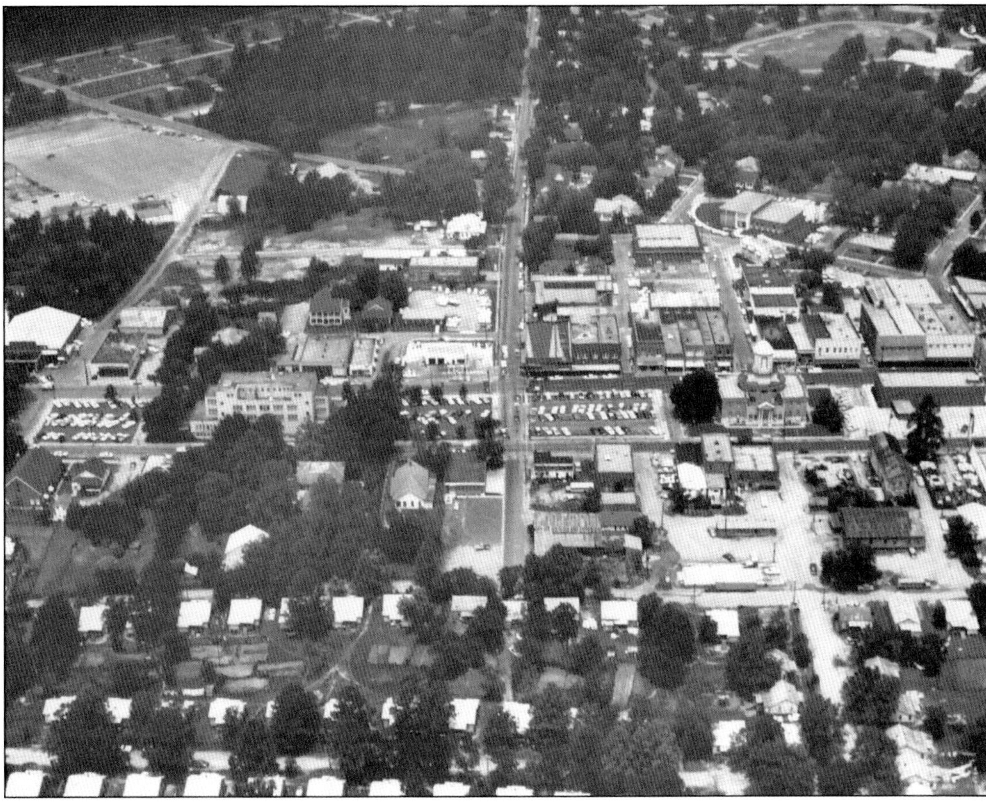

These two photographs, taken in 1969, show the area around the 1905 Webster Parish Courthouse shortly before its demolition. The structure was then serving as the Minden City Hall since a new courthouse had replaced it in 1953. The newer courthouse is the first building to the west (left) of the 1905 building, across two parking lots. Also by this point, the US post office had been torn down and replaced by a bank. The newer 1960 post office is seen two blocks north of the 1905 courthouse in the image above. The image below gives a good view of the block of businesses directly south of the 1905 courthouse. (Both, author's collection.)

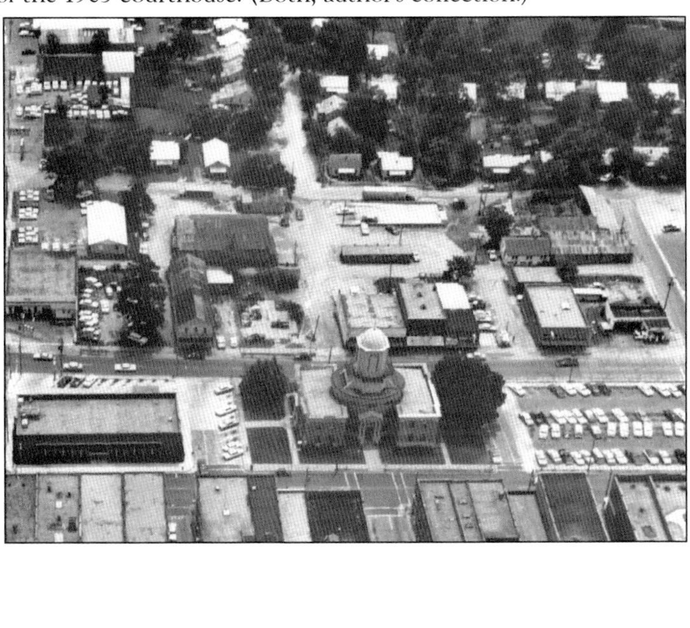

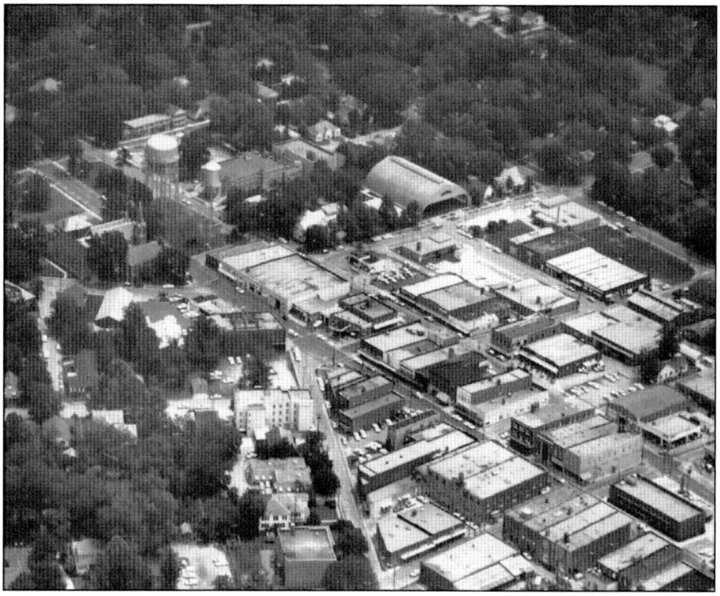

This 1969 image shows the Ferguson Tabernacle, which, in 1977, was torn down in a church expansion project. The photograph gives a better perspective of the location of the First Baptist and First Methodist Churches, for many years the two largest church congregations in Minden, across the boulevard from each other. (Author's collection.)

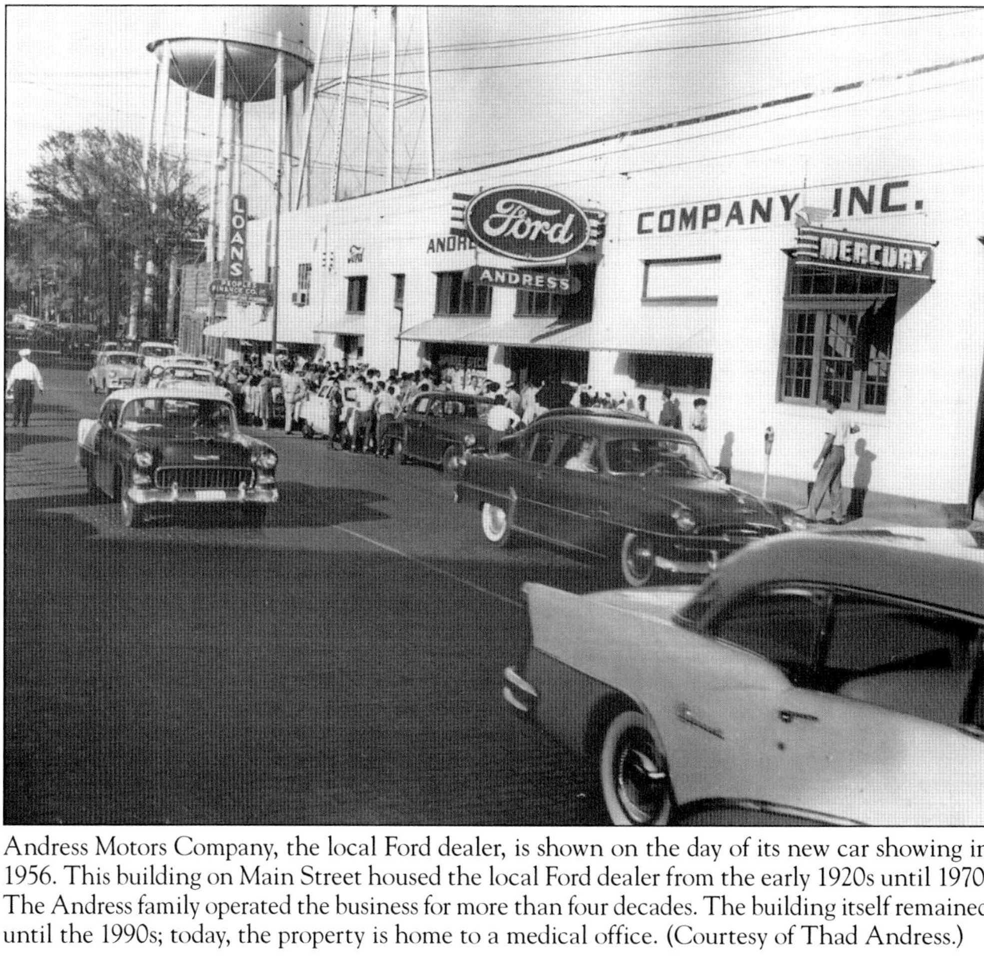

Andress Motors Company, the local Ford dealer, is shown on the day of its new car showing in 1956. This building on Main Street housed the local Ford dealer from the early 1920s until 1970. The Andress family operated the business for more than four decades. The building itself remained until the 1990s; today, the property is home to a medical office. (Courtesy of Thad Andress.)

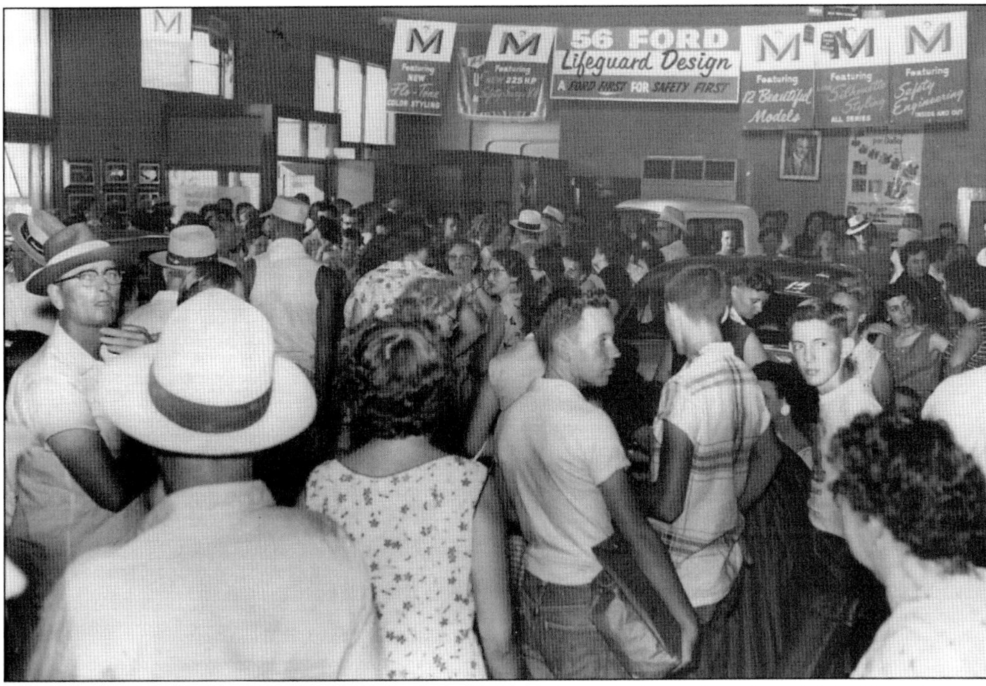

This is an inside view of Andress Motors' new car show, held in October 1956. The changed designs of the new cars were such a secret in those years that, as shown by the crowd, the chance to see the new vehicles brought out lots of local residents. (Courtesy of Thad Andress.)

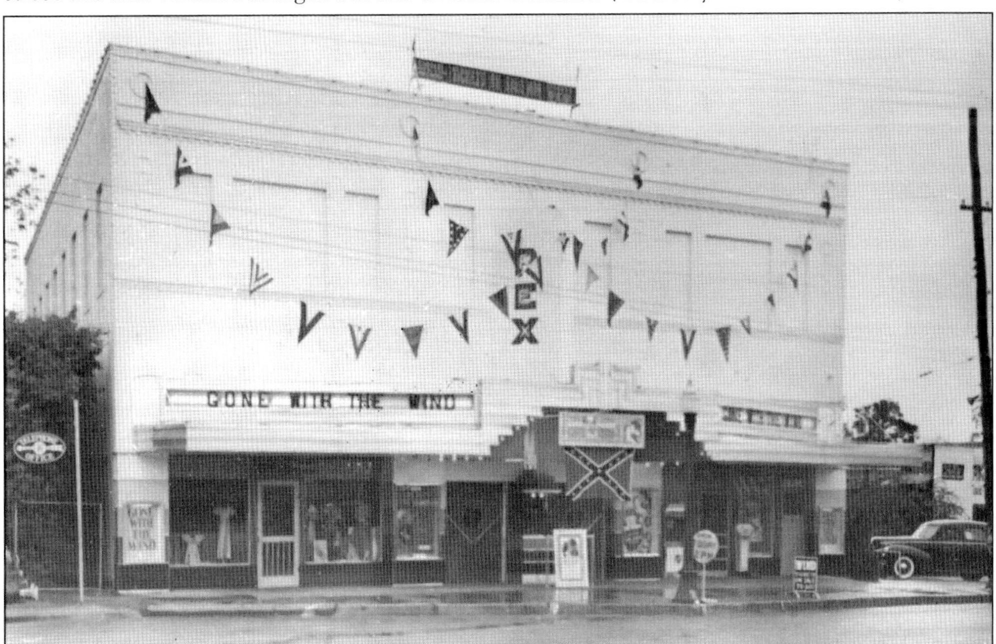

Minden had its first movie theater in 1915 and, over the years, had as many as four operating at the same time. Probably the best remembered is the Rex, located in the remodeled building constructed by the First Baptist Church in 1902. In this image, the Rex is decorated for the local premiere of *Gone with the Wind* in 1940. (Author's collection.)

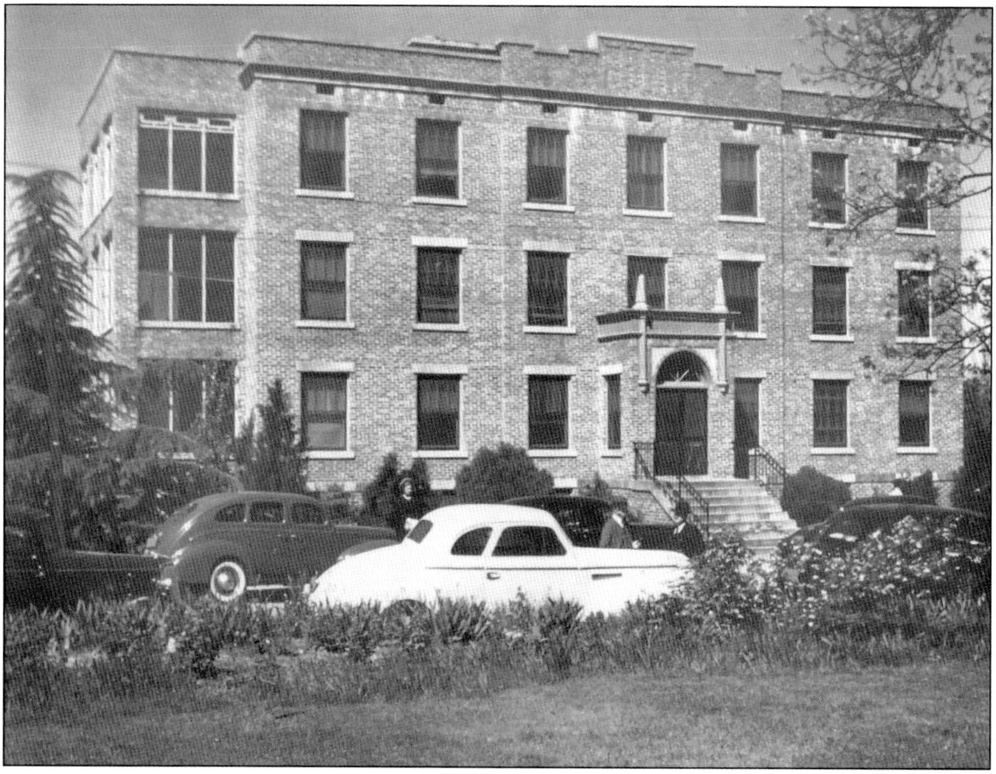

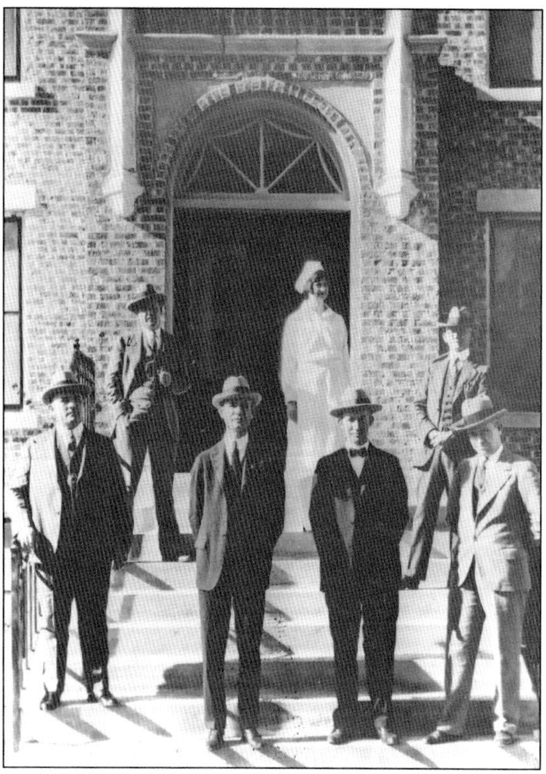

In 1927, a group of doctors formed a corporation and established the Minden Sanitarium, bringing a hospital to the community for the first time. Although local ownership no longer possesses the enterprise, this original building is still actually at the core of today's Minden Medical Center. (Author's collection.)

The original staff members of the Minden Sanitarium are shown in front of the hospital at the time of its opening. The hospital was somewhat unique for the area of Northwest Louisiana in that, although segregated, it did take black patients, who were housed in the basement of the building. (Author's collection.)

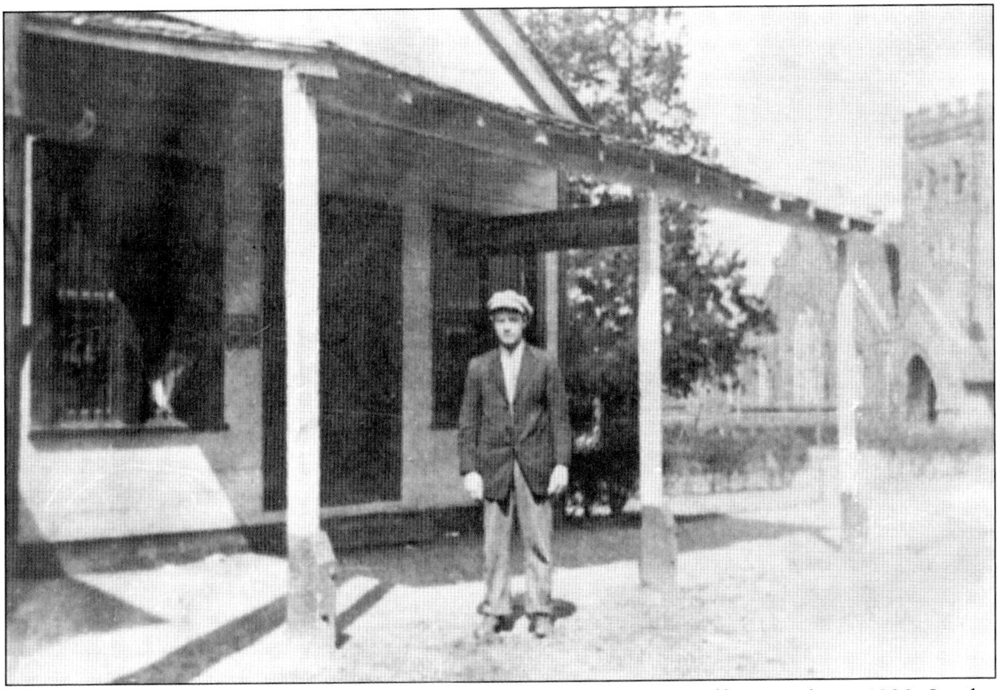

A telegraph boy is shown in front of the local Western Union office in about 1920. In the background is the First Baptist Church's 1902 building that was later converted to the Rex Theater. (Author's collection.)

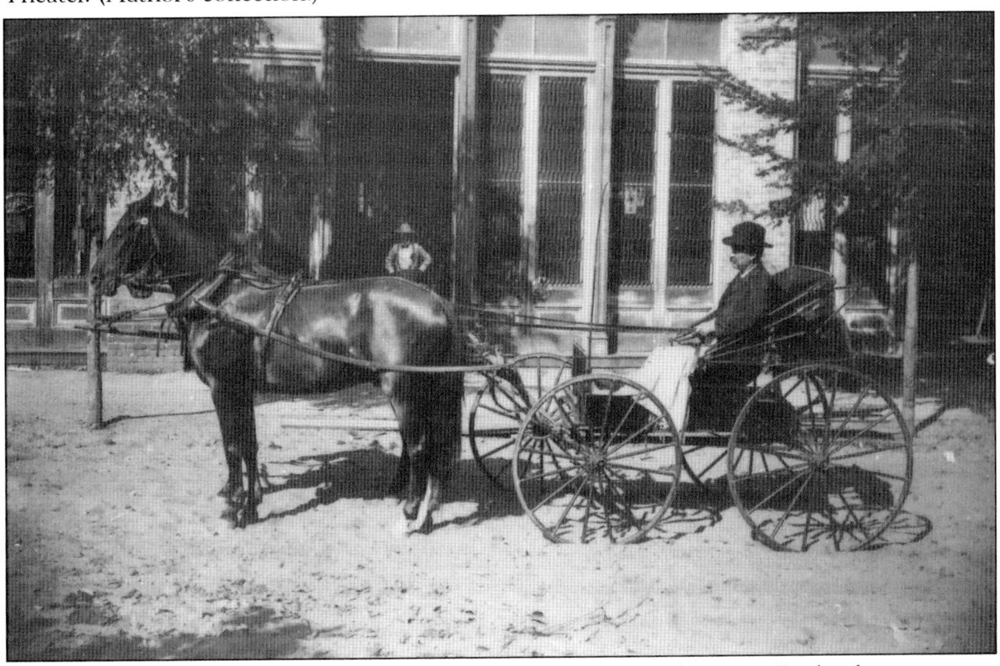

In 1880, Alfred Goodwill, who had come to Minden from his home in England as a teenage orphan, built a store in downtown Minden that was one of the largest in the state of Louisiana. This image, taken in the mid-1890s, shows Goodwill, seated in the buggy, in front of that store. (Courtesy of the Webster Parish Library.)

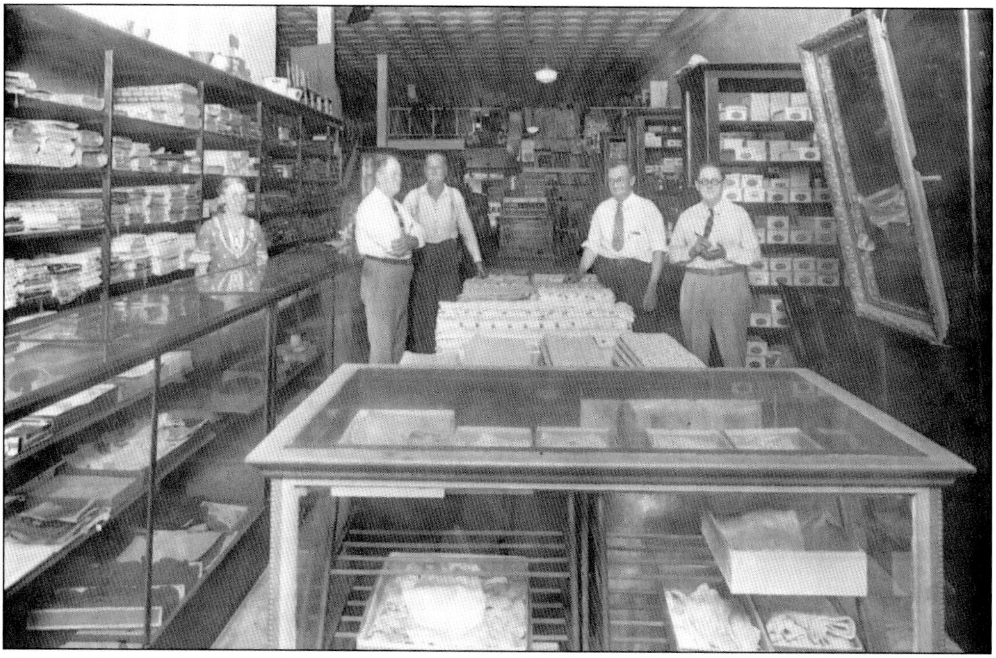

The employees of Minden Mercantile, owned by the Turner brothers, are shown in the store, located in downtown Minden in the 1930s. The Turner family owned and operated several businesses, which were largely connected to the timber industry in the Minden area. (Courtesy of George Turner.)

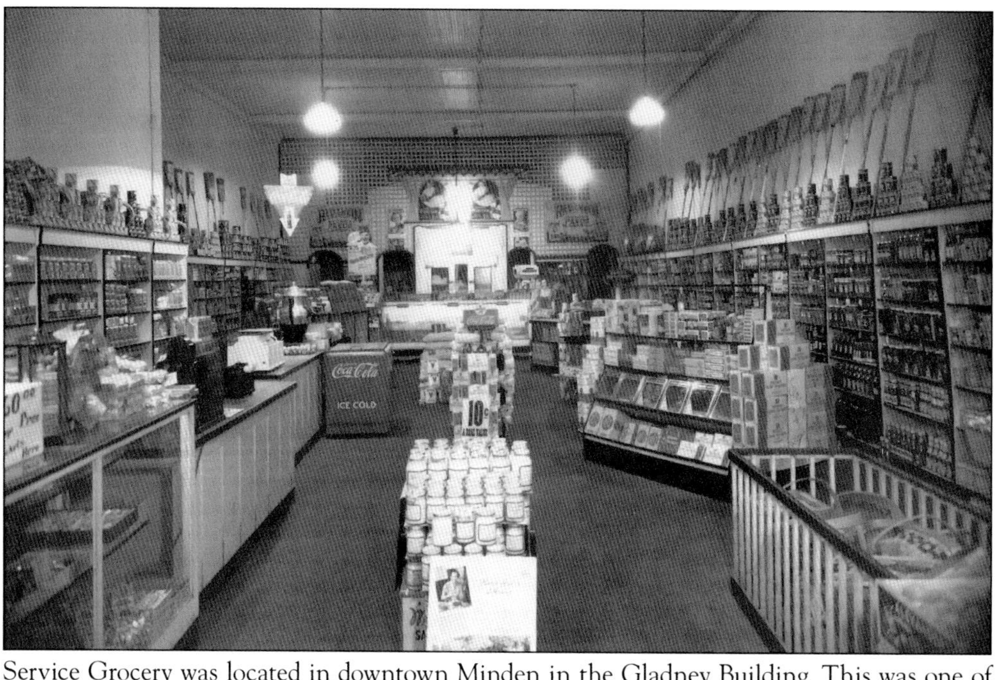

Service Grocery was located in downtown Minden in the Gladney Building. This was one of nearly 40 grocery stores operating in Minden in 1930. A Piggly Wiggly had first been located in this building, but self-service groceries were slow to catch on in Minden, and local full-service firms dominated for years. (Author's collection.)

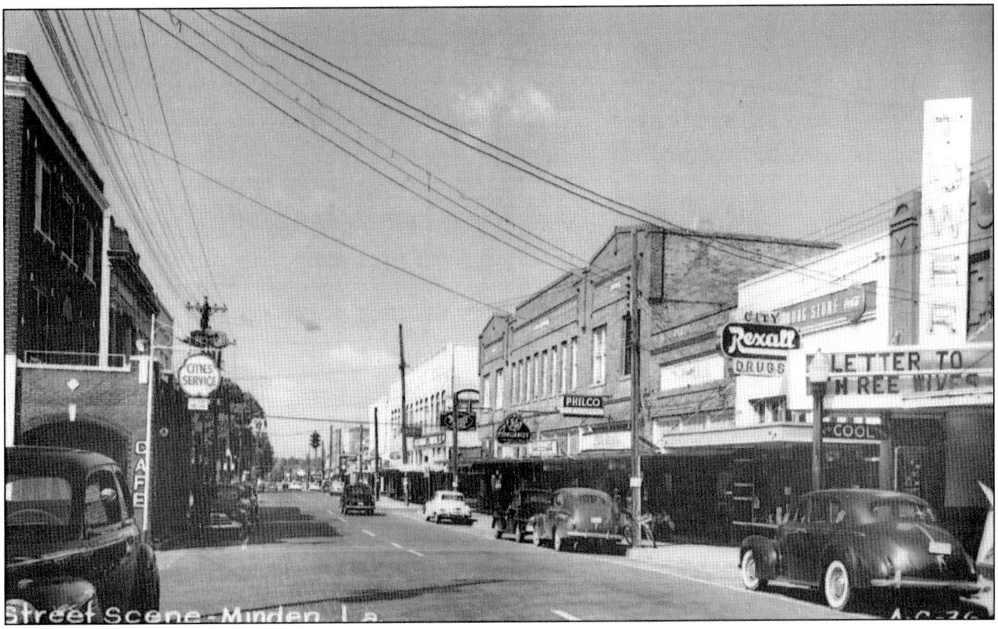

This 1949 photograph is of the 600 block of Main Street in Minden. The marquee at the Tower Theater indicates the film being shown is *Letter to Three Wives*, which is key to dating the image. The large building with a GE Appliances sign at the center left is the Miller Building, which houses many local offices on its upper floor. (Author's collection.)

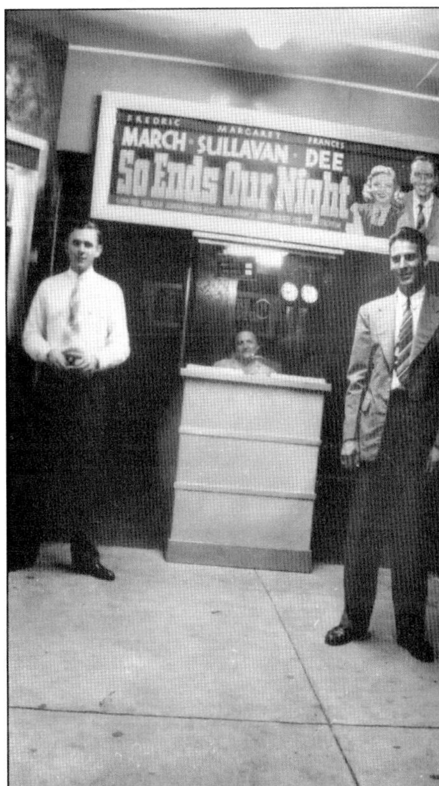

The Tower Theater had first been opened under the name Scout Theater. The owner of that theater was Rollin Williams, who also owned the City Drugstore next door to the theater. This image comes from the Scout years at the theater. After the theater closed, the building housed a skating rink, and today, there is a jewelry store. (Courtesy of LSU-Shreveport Archives and Special Collections, Noel Memorial Library.)

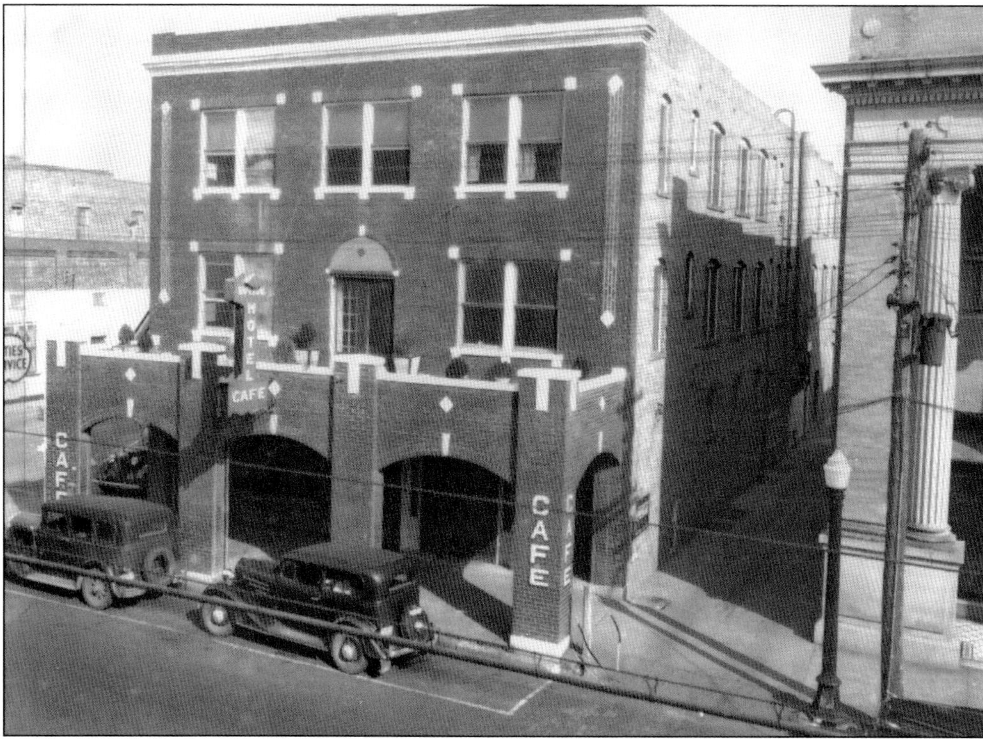

The Imperial Hotel was the first "modern" hotel built in Minden after World War I. It became the meeting place for most civic clubs in town and any outside events, like the two education conferences held in Minden between 1920 and 1950. (Author's collection.)

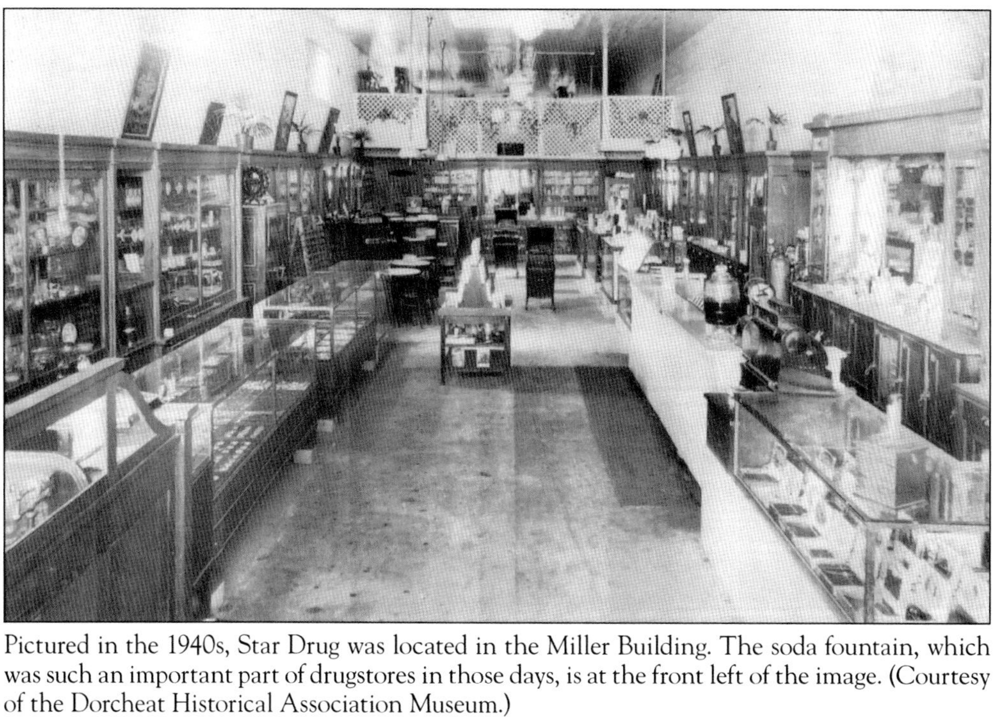

Pictured in the 1940s, Star Drug was located in the Miller Building. The soda fountain, which was such an important part of drugstores in those days, is at the front left of the image. (Courtesy of the Dorcheat Historical Association Museum.)

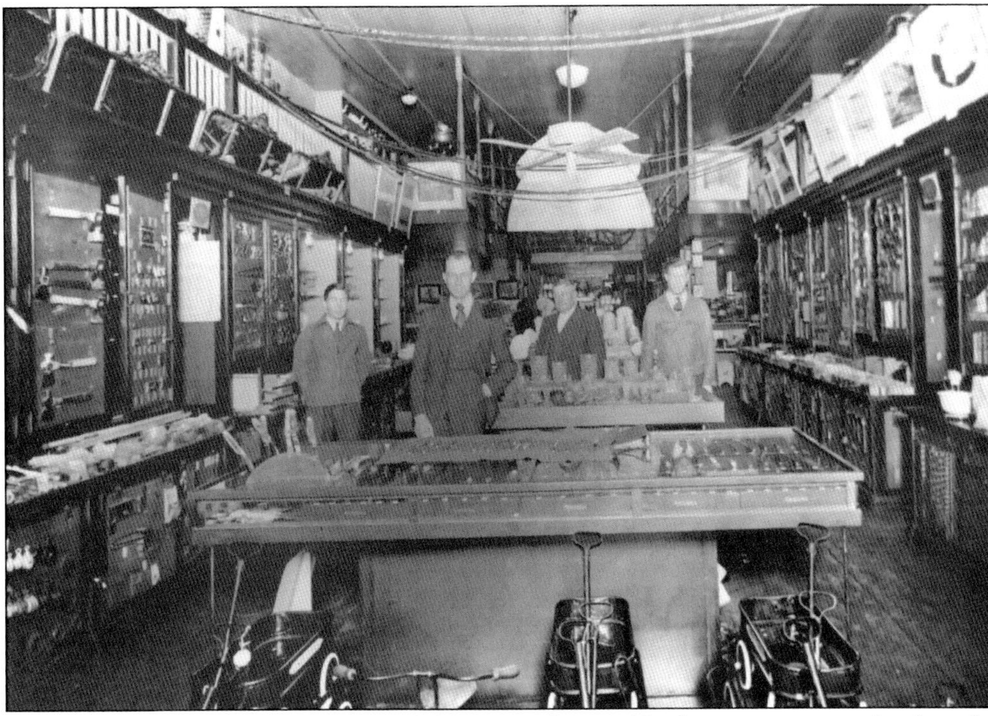

Webb Hardware is pictured here. Founded by Samuel G. Webb, the store was owned and run by Will Life for most of its 80 years of operation. (Courtesy of Lillian Life Willis.)

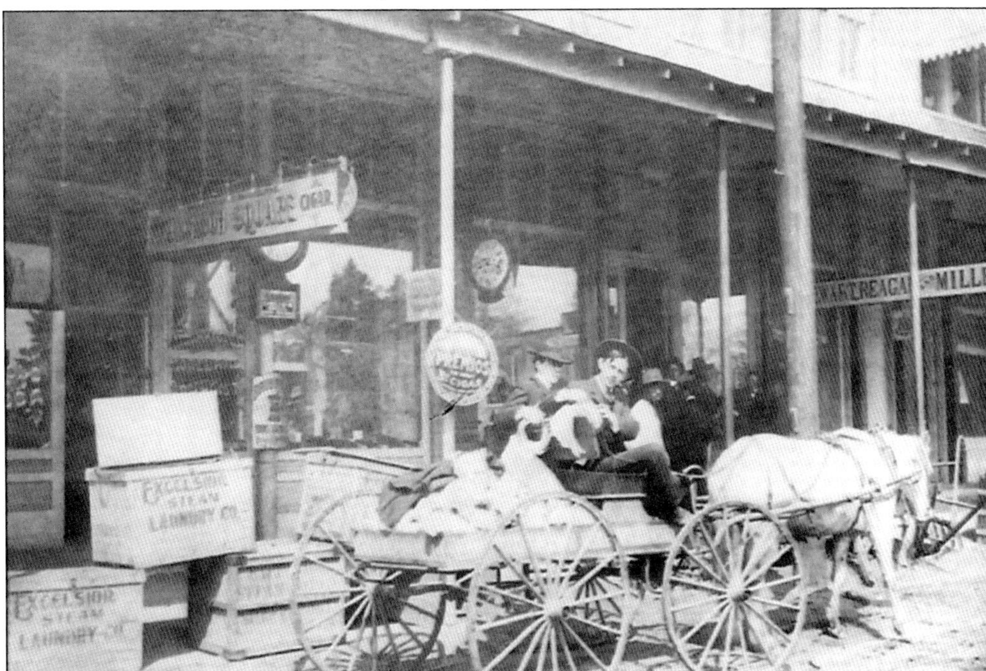

This image shows a Shreveport laundry wagon making pickups and deliveries to Minden in the early years of the 20th century. The contrast of the new with the old in this picture shows a time of transition being experienced in Minden. (Courtesy of the Major De Pingre.)

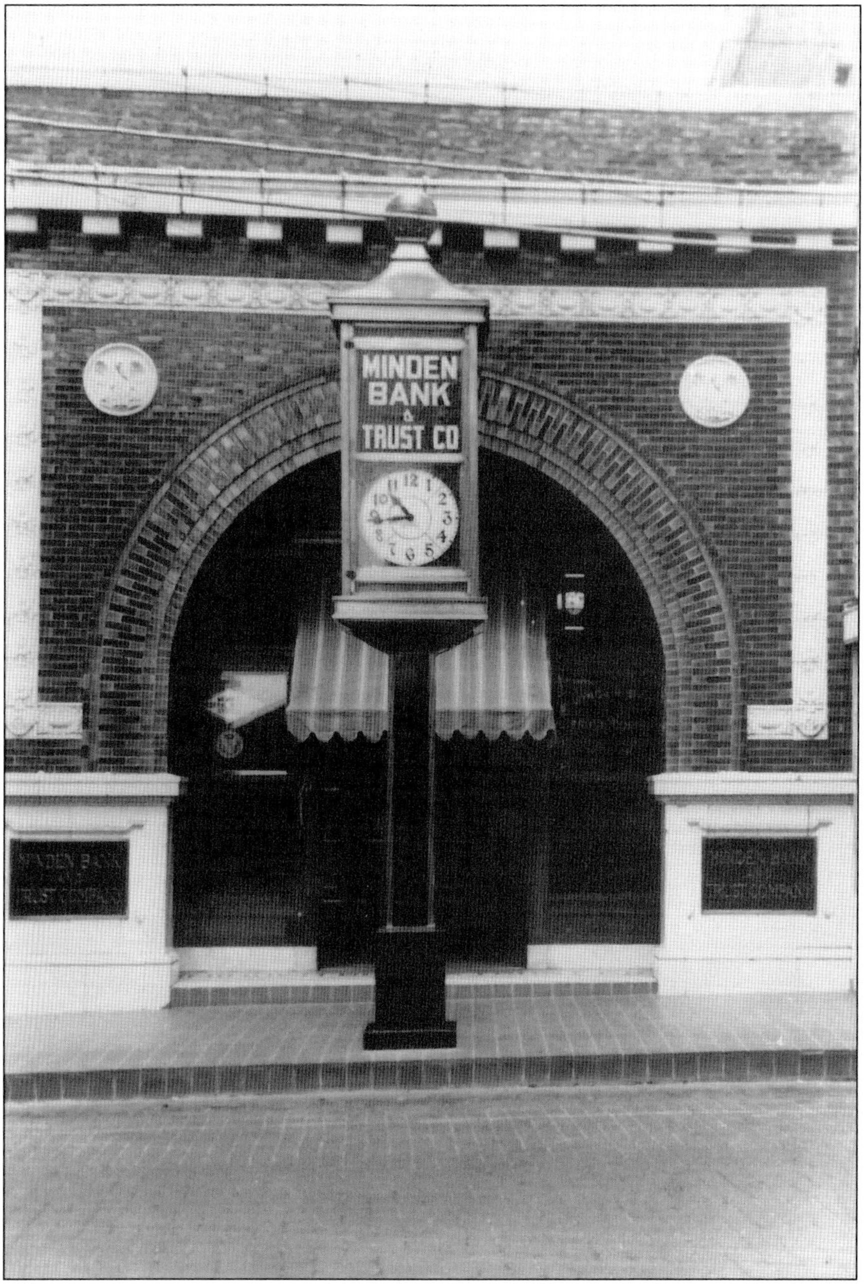

The Bank of Minden was founded in 1890 and moved into this unique tile-front building in about 1905. It was the largest and oldest bank in the community until it failed in April 1933 during the Great Depression. That failure disrupted the Minden community as it came less than two months after a major downtown fire and two weeks before the devastating tornado of May 1, 1933. After reorganization characterized by a community-wide drive to regain confidence and support, the bank reopened as Minden Bank and Trust in December of that year. The McCullough clock tower was added to the bank in May 1939. Downtown had been without any visible clock since the courthouse dome was remodeled in 1933, and the new clock was a sensation. Today, it remains a landmark in downtown Minden, although it has not functioned in years. (Author's collection.)

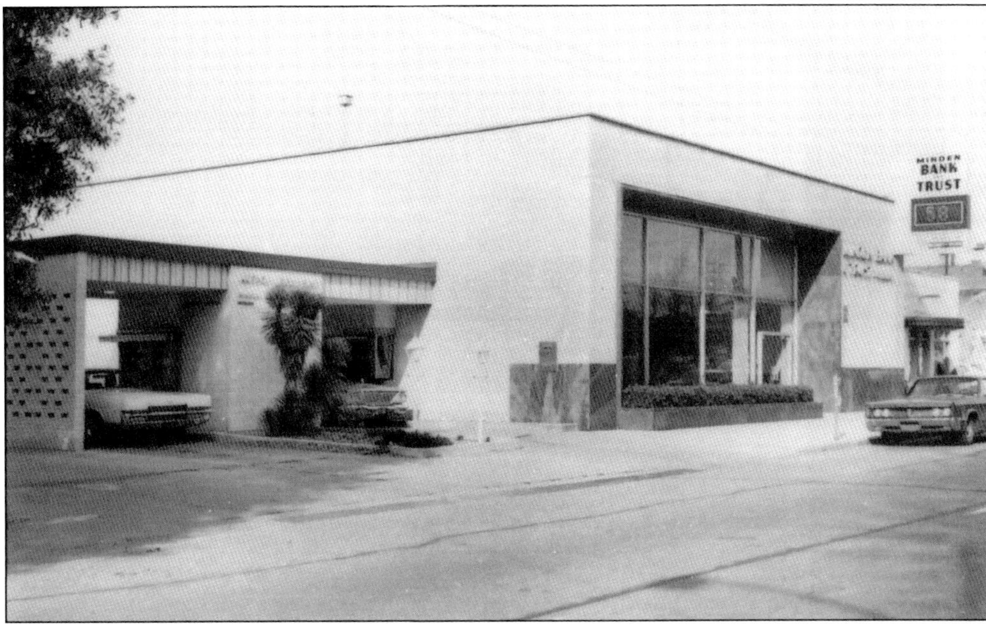

Minden Bank moved to this new location in 1954, and eventually, out-of-state banking interests purchased the bank and changed its name. The new owners continued to use this building until the early 1980s, when a newer structure replaced this one after a little more than 30 years of usage. (Courtesy of LSU-Shreveport Archives and Special Collections, Noel Memorial Library.)

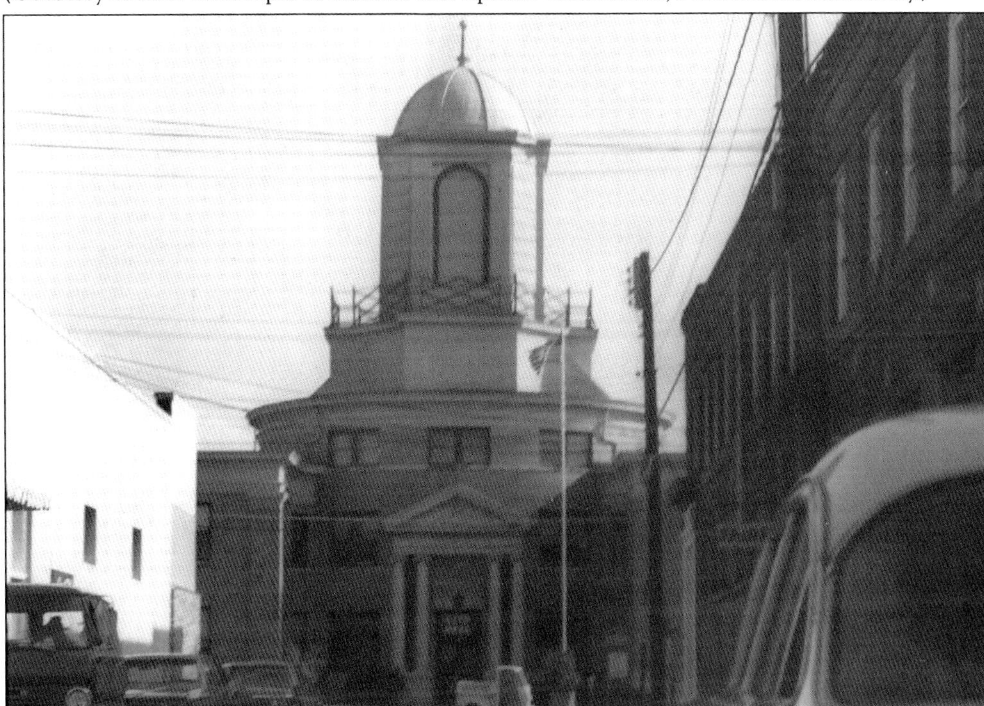

The view in this image from the 1960s looks south on Pearl Street toward Main Street and the 1905 Webster Parish Courthouse. By this time, the old courthouse was serving as Minden City Hall after the construction of a new courthouse in 1953. (Author's collection.)

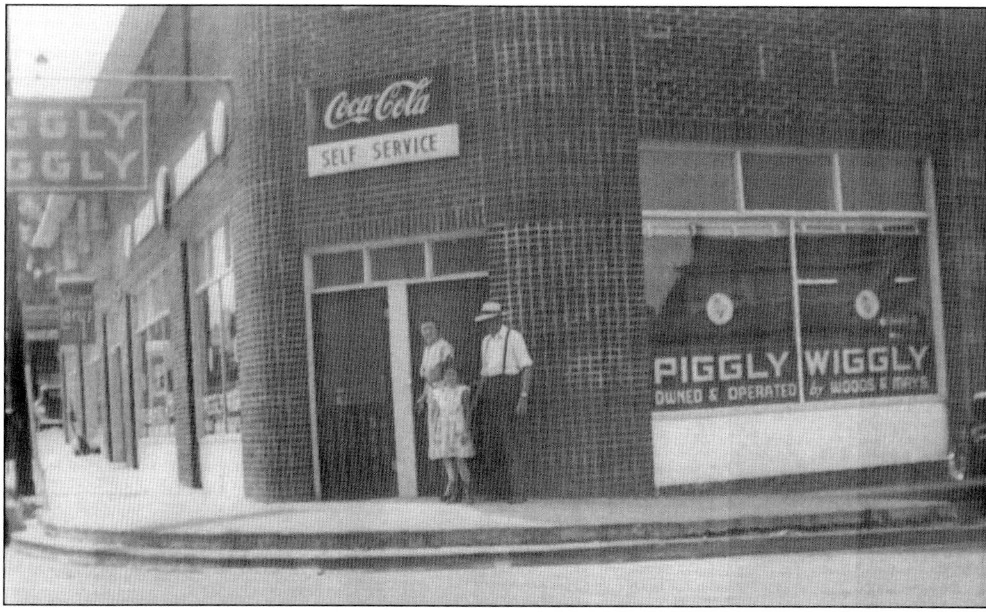

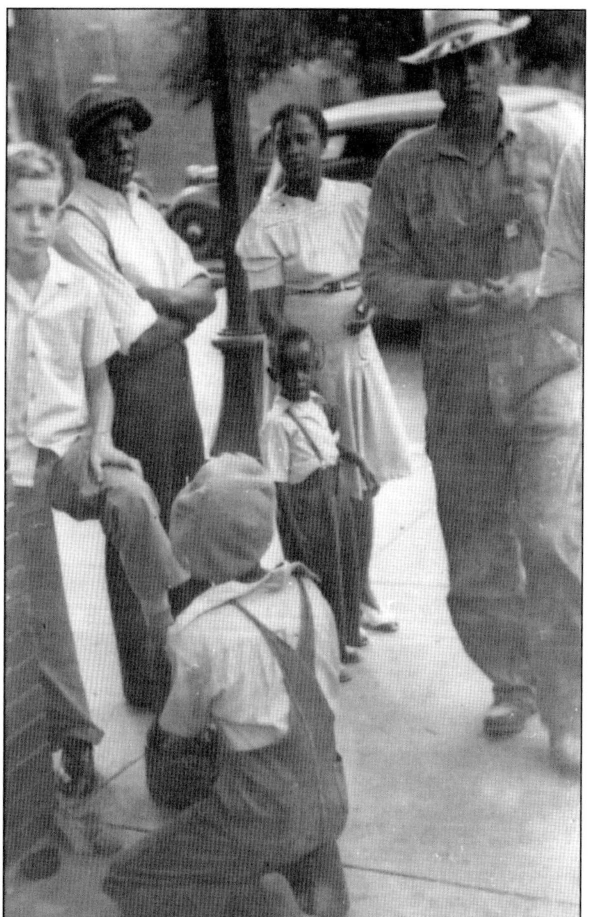

Piggly Wiggly was the first self-service grocery to open in Minden in 1925 and closed after a brief time. After World War II, this Piggly Wiggly franchise opened at the corner of Pearl and Monroe Streets in Minden. The franchise would later move to at least three other locations in the community, with two separate stores operating for many years. (Courtesy of Ann Mays Harlan.)

This 1940s street scene displays an enterprise that would probably be illegal today due to street vending and child labor laws. This is a shoeshine boy practicing his trade at the corner of Pearl and Main Streets in downtown Minden, across the street from the Webster Parish Courthouse. (Courtesy of LSU-Shreveport Archives and Special Collections, Noel Memorial Library.)

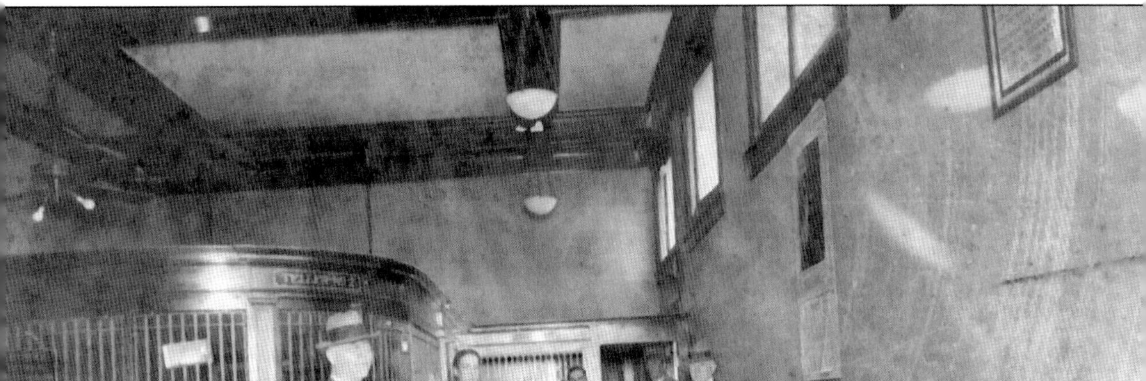

First National Bank operated in Minden from 1914 until 1931, when the Bank of Webster absorbed it. This picture shows former Webster Parish sheriff B.F. Griffith (far left) in the bank. After the bank closed, the building was first home to a cotton firm and then a discount grocery store. As it was right across the street from the Webster Parish Courthouse, lawyers seeking to be close to the seat of justice usually occupied the offices upstairs. For the next two decades, the former bank space served as a drugstore before spending three decades as a women's clothing store. Originally constructed by Dr. Luther Longino, the building then became a beauty salon for many years. Today, that building is being remodeled to become a restaurant, and the only legacy of the days as a bank are the seals that still remain in place on the facade of the structure. (Courtesy of the Frank Griffith.)

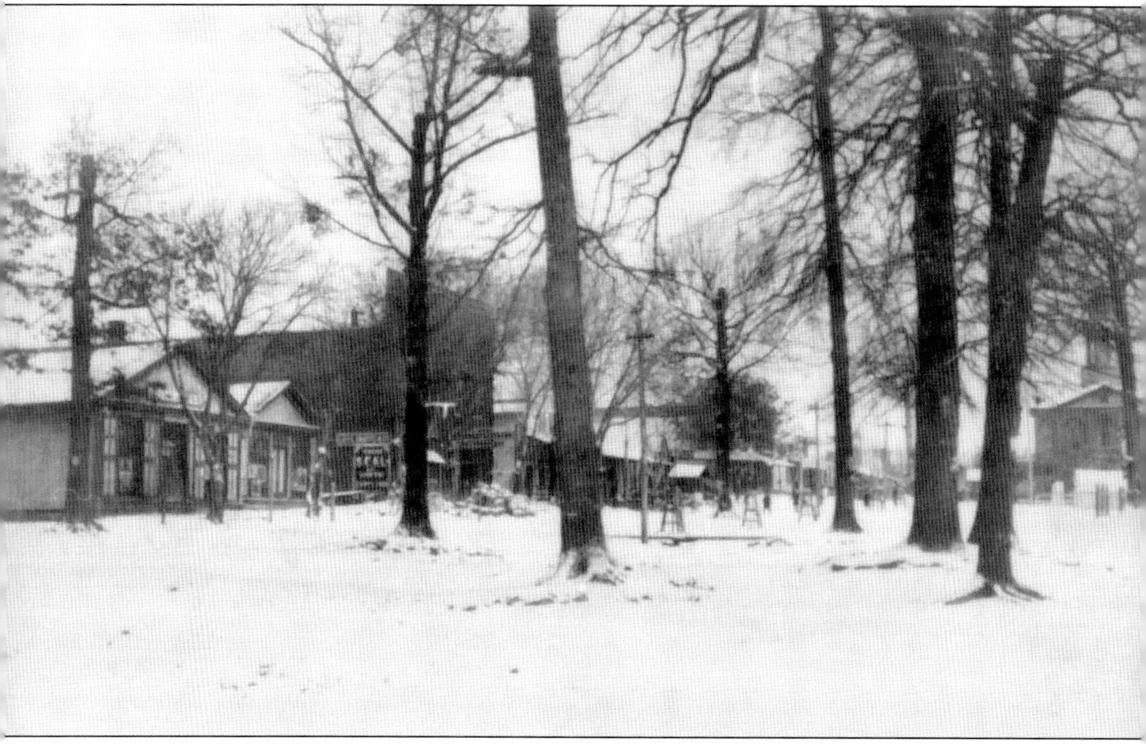

Taken during the 1890s, this image shows the 500 block of Main Street in Minden during a rare snowfall in Minden. Minden averages one or two snows a year and even fewer that stick for more than a day. This scene emphasizes how the area between Front and Back Streets truly was a wide-open area of green space in those days. Realistically, in this section of town, it was hard to see two distinct streets prior to middle ground being occupied with businesses. One outside observer even commented on the area as a single wide street with wagons and horses tied in the middle of the street. Visible in the right background is the 1872 Webster Parish Courthouse. In the right foreground is the hitching lot, an area used to park vehicles since the days of horses and wagons. (Courtesy of LSU-Shreveport Archives and Special Collections, Noel Memorial Library.)

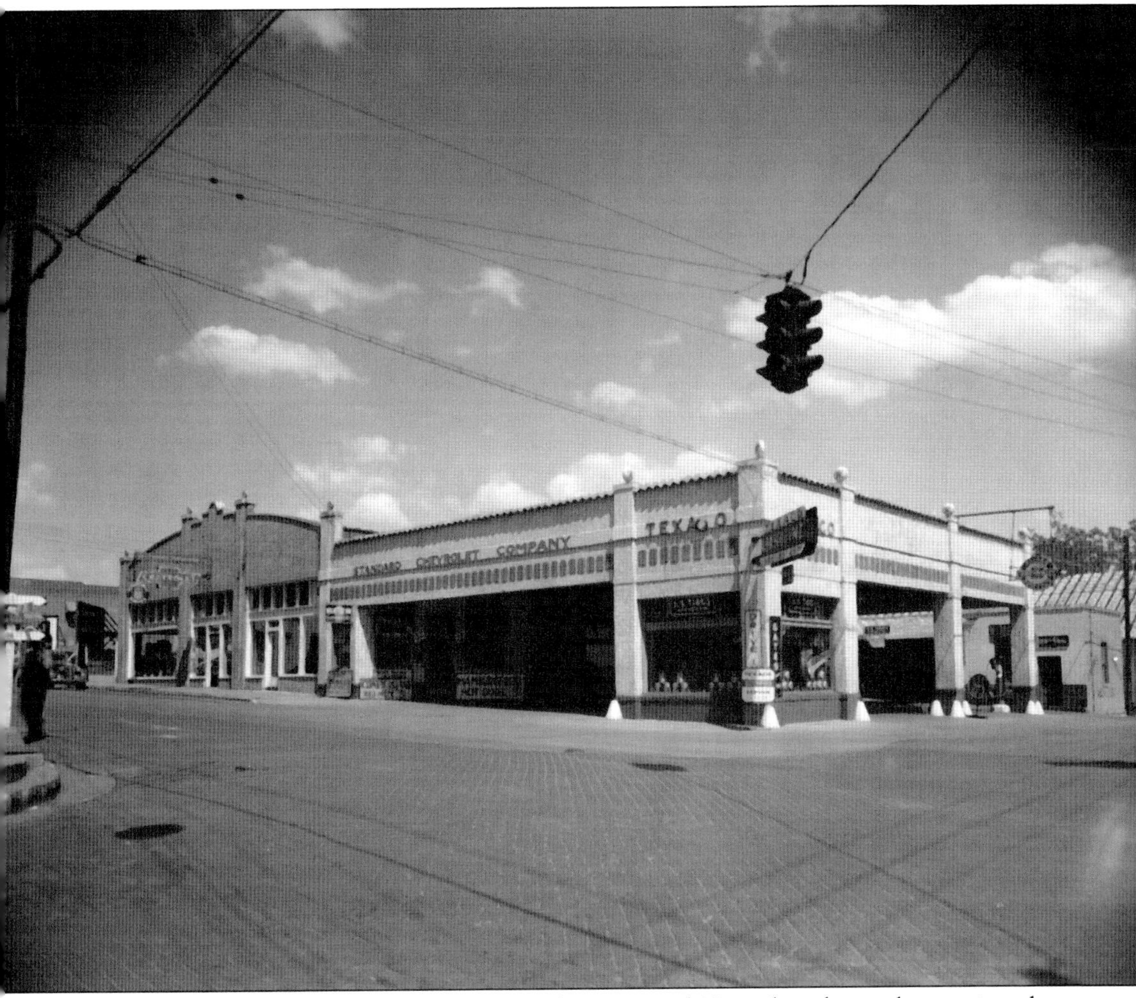

This building on the southeast corner of US Highways 79 and 80 combined a gasoline station, the local Chevrolet automobile dealership, and a café. The beer sign on the café dates the photograph to the 1930s. Between 1893 and 2004, the only time such sales were legal in Minden was a period from 1933 to 1939. A local election in August 1893 banned all sales of alcohol in Minden. The national end of Prohibition caused all state and local laws against alcohol sales to be invalidated, making the sale of alcohol legal in Minden. A local option election in December 1938 would restore Minden's dry status. That would remain the status quo until a special law passed by the state legislature and another local election in 2003 made sales of alcohol in restaurants legal again beginning in 2004. So, few images exist showing alcohol advertising signs in the community. (Author's collection.)

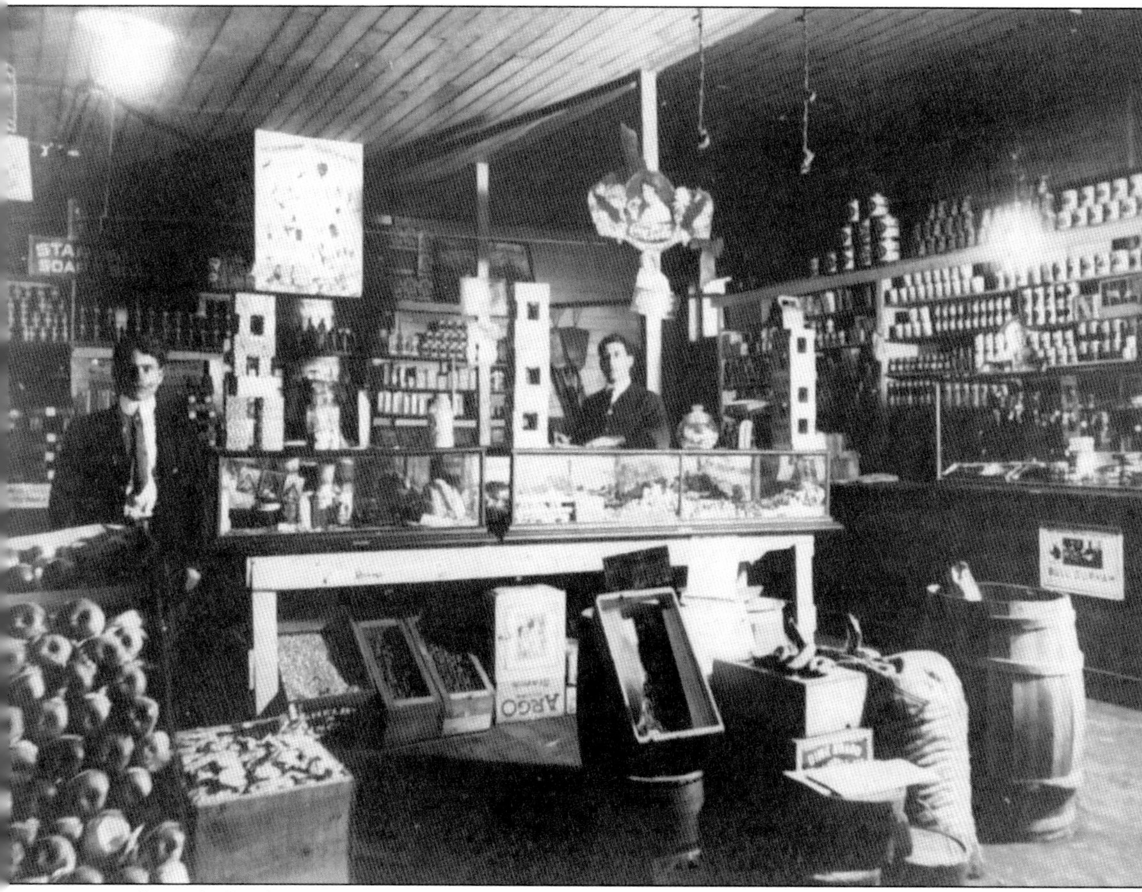

Matching the book's cover image, this is another photograph of the interior of Dow's Store in Minden in around 1920. With so many immigrant families owning stores along Back Street, Minden felt, perhaps, more cosmopolitan than one might have expected. Beyond the Dow's business, in this part of town, there were the Minden Café of Gus Kirkikis, an immigrant from Greece, and the store of the Elzen family from Syria. The Mourad and Michael families in other areas of town were also first-generation Americans. So while this was still the segregated South, a miniature United Nations of sorts was present in parts of town. Shoppers remember that Dow hung merchandise on strings and attached them to the ceiling. Although there is not much hanging in this image, one can see the strings dangling from the ceiling. (Author's collection.)

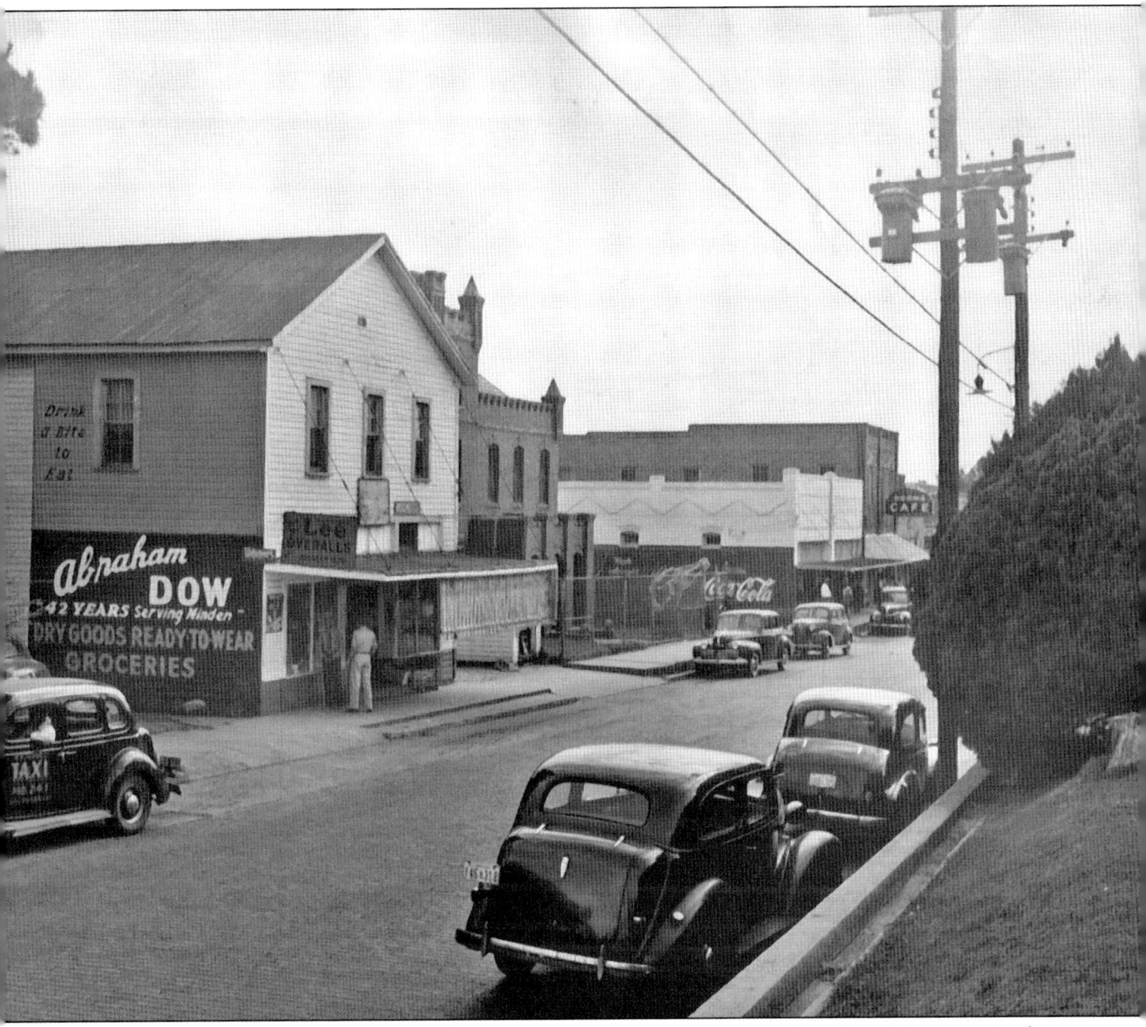

This look at the stores on Broadway (Back Street) dates from August 1946. Dow's Store is in the left foreground, with the Webster Parish Jail just beyond it to the west. Economically at this point, Minden was still enjoying the postwar boom, and these businesses were doing well. Back Street was part of US Highway 80, and in those years before the construction of the interstate, traffic on this street increased as Americans became more prosperous and more mobile as many families had a car. Reaching Front Street required getting off the main route, so this was the memory many cross-country travelers would have of Minden. (Courtesy of the National Archives.)

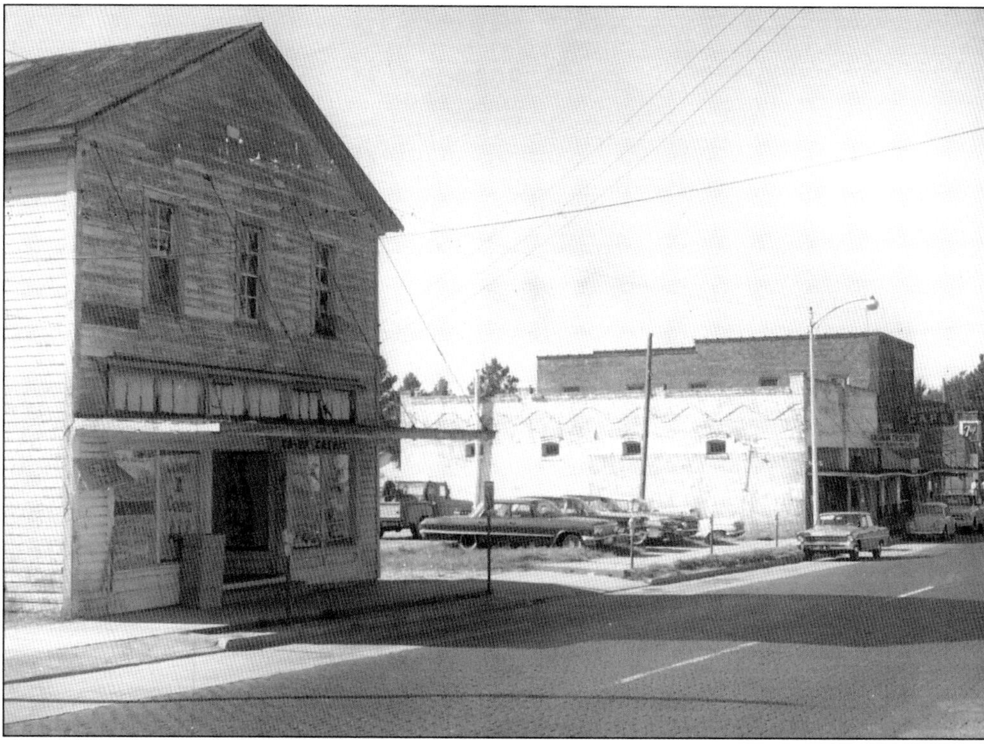

By 1969, times had changed, and this nearly identical view as the previous image has the former Dow's Store at the left foreground vacant and crumbling and less than a year from demolition. Like in many small communities, the business center shifted from downtown. (Author's collection.)

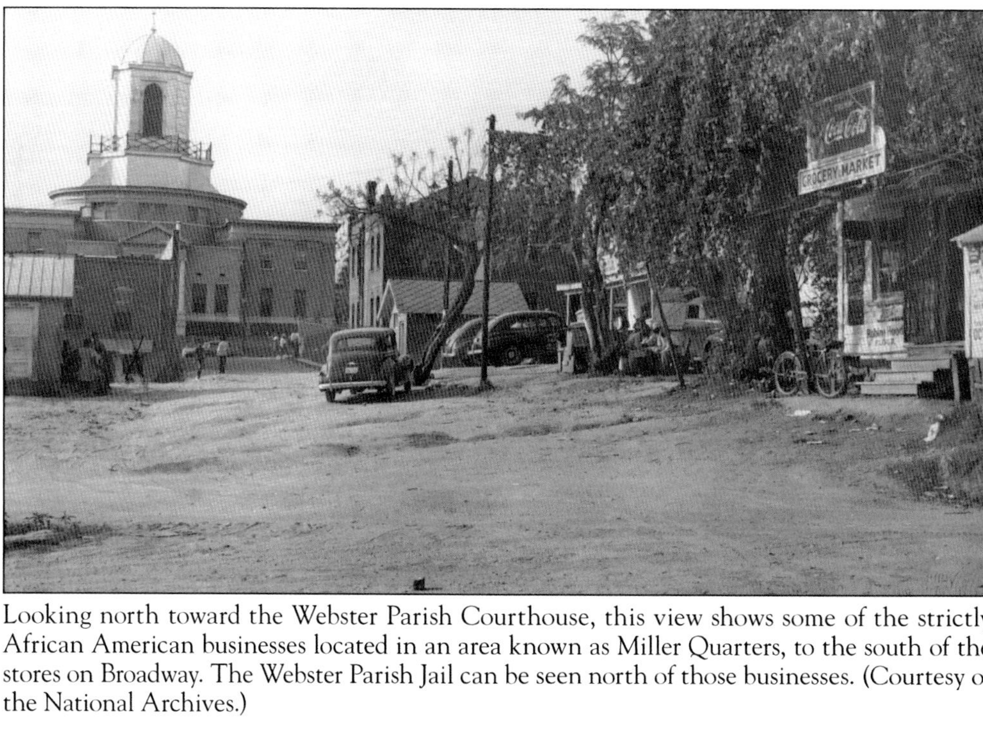

Looking north toward the Webster Parish Courthouse, this view shows some of the strictly African American businesses located in an area known as Miller Quarters, to the south of the stores on Broadway. The Webster Parish Jail can be seen north of those businesses. (Courtesy of the National Archives.)

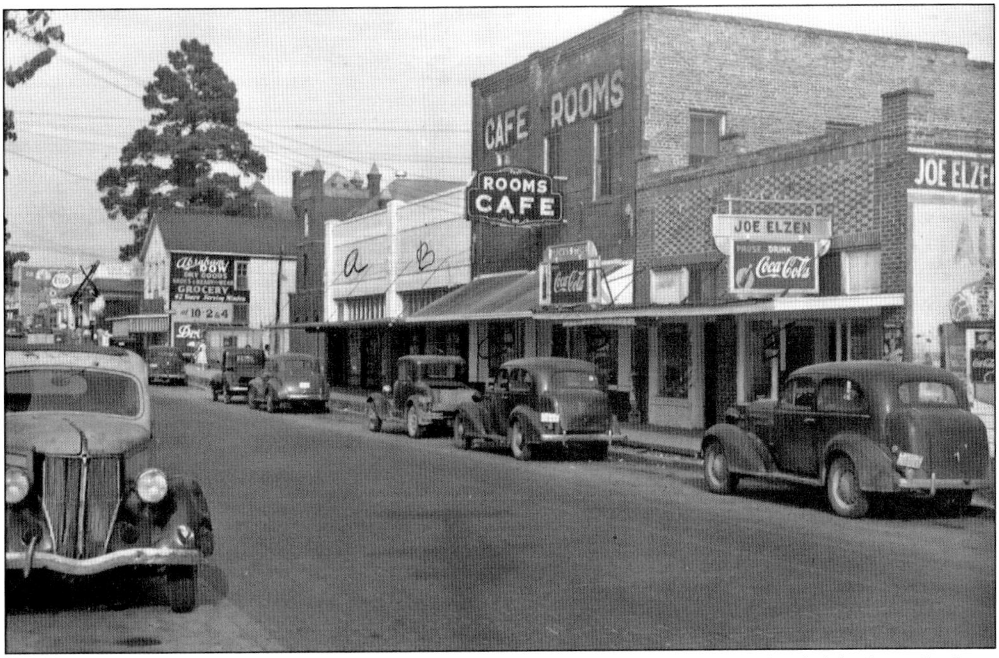

Pictured are some of the local stores on Broadway that were open to both black and white shoppers. Families who had immigrated to the United States and to Minden during the early 20th century, such as the Elzen and Kirkikis families, operated many of these businesses. (Courtesy of the National Archives.)

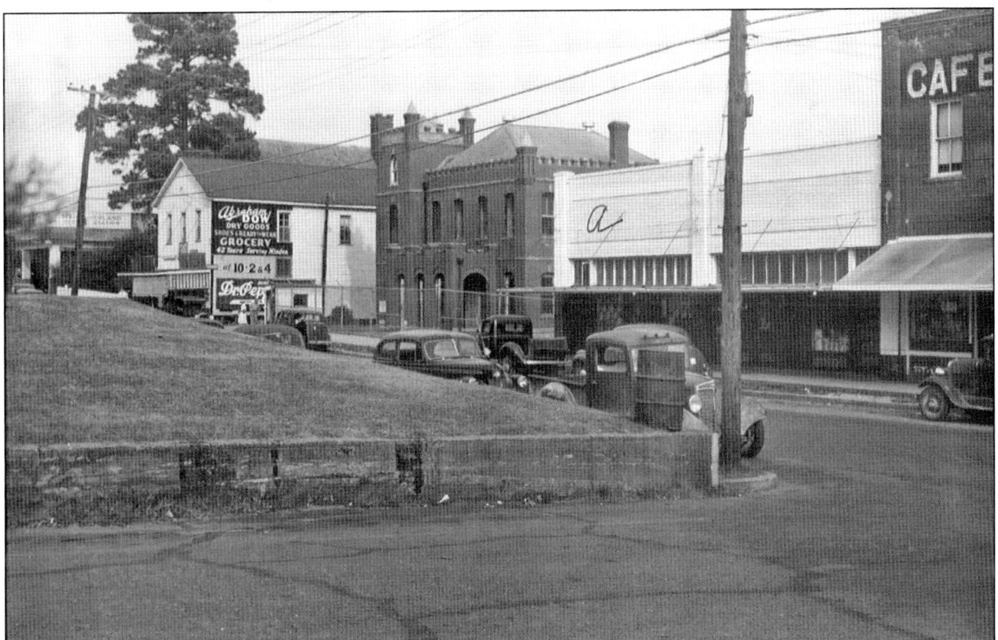

Here is another view of the Back Street businesses, showing the edge of the lawn of the Webster Parish Courthouse at the left foreground. Just beyond Dow's Store, one can see the Dixie-Overland Station, named for the Dixie-Overland Highway, today's US Highway 80. (Courtesy of the National Archives.)

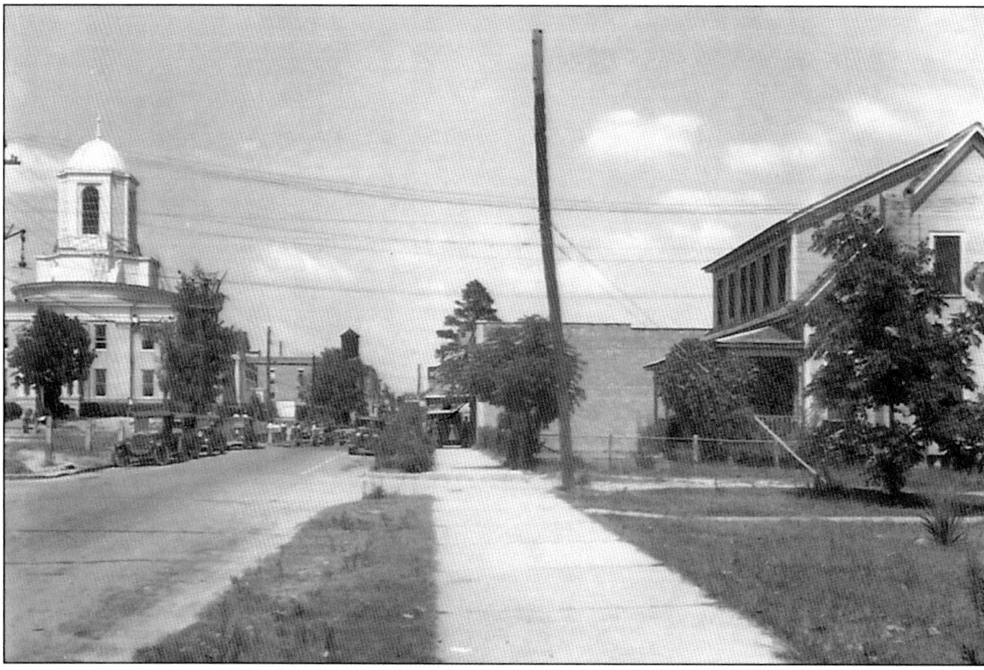

This 1930s image of the Back Street businesses shows the Webster Parish Courthouse after the 1933 tornado, which caused damage and led to the replacement of the original courthouse dome and clock with this larger version with glass windows. (Author's collection.)

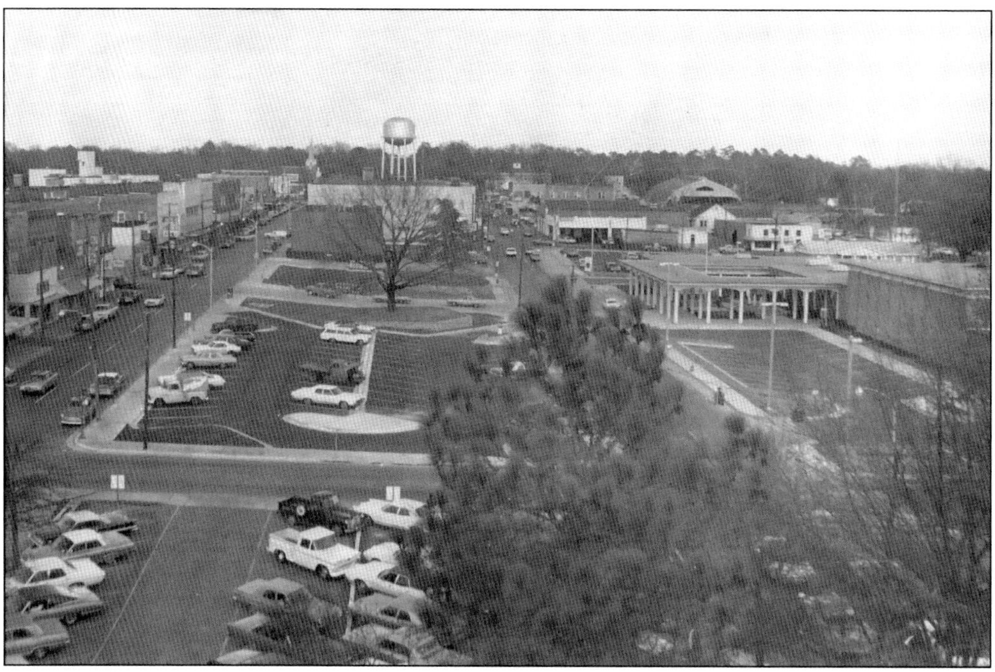

By 1970, the landscape of downtown had changed. The 1905 Webster Parish Courthouse was gone, and the new Minden Civic Center and City Hall Complex had replaced the businesses along Back Street. The old hitching lot had become a modern striped parking lot for cars. (Author's collection.)

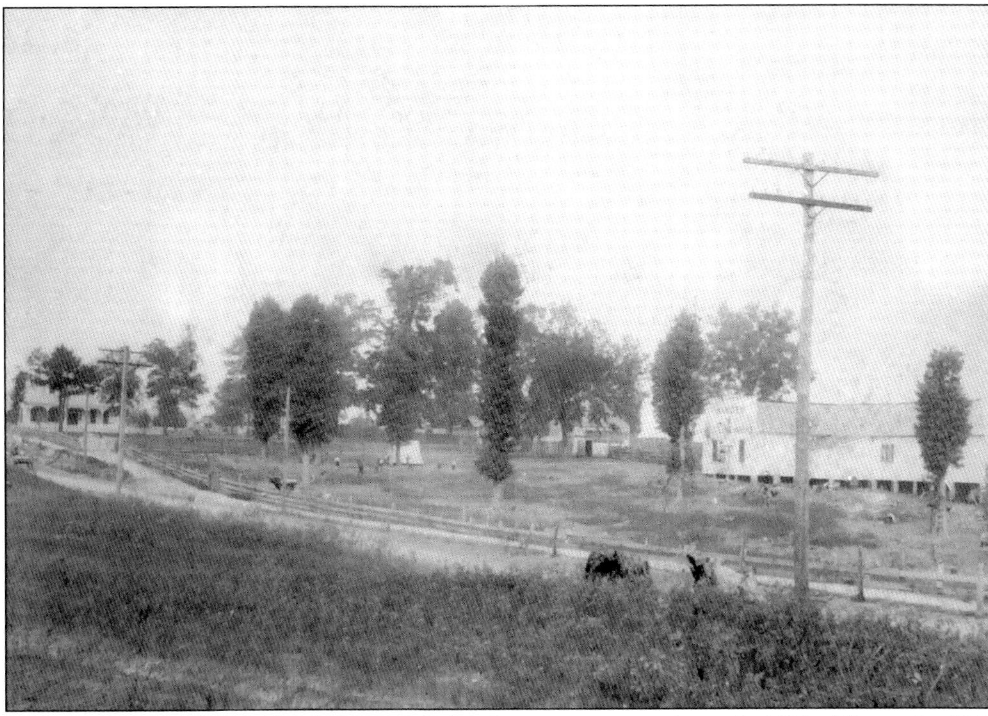

W.S. Hunter founded the local Coca-Cola bottling company in the early 1900s. This is the 1901 location of the company when it was known as the Minden Bottling Company, which was before it housed the region's Coca-Cola franchise. (Courtesy of LSU-Shreveport Archives and Special Collections, Noel Memorial Library.)

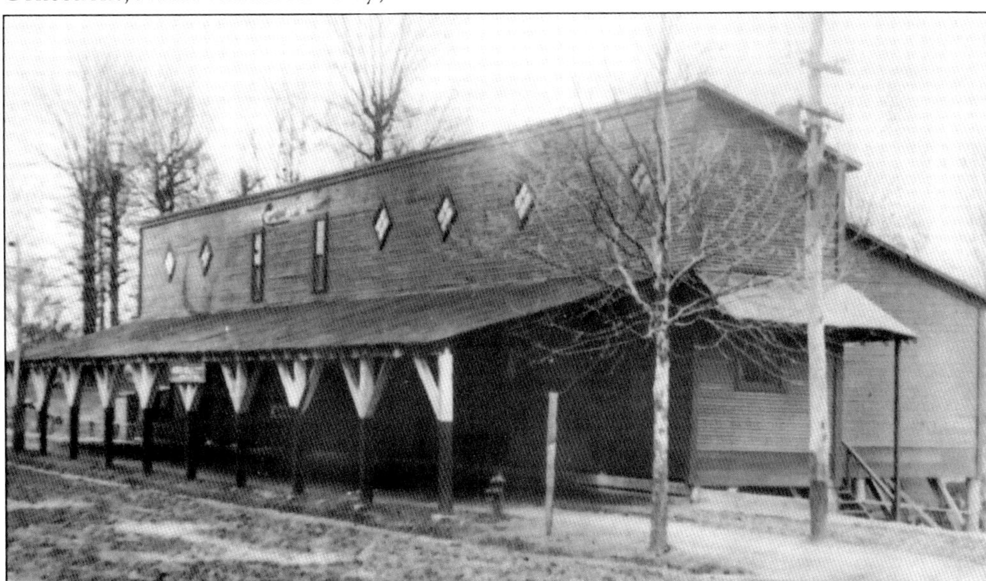

As the Hunters' business grew, by 1914, the name of the firm had been changed to the North Louisiana Bottling Works, and the company was bottling Coke. At that point, it was located in this building in Minden, which is still the location of the company today. (Courtesy of Ben Hunter.)

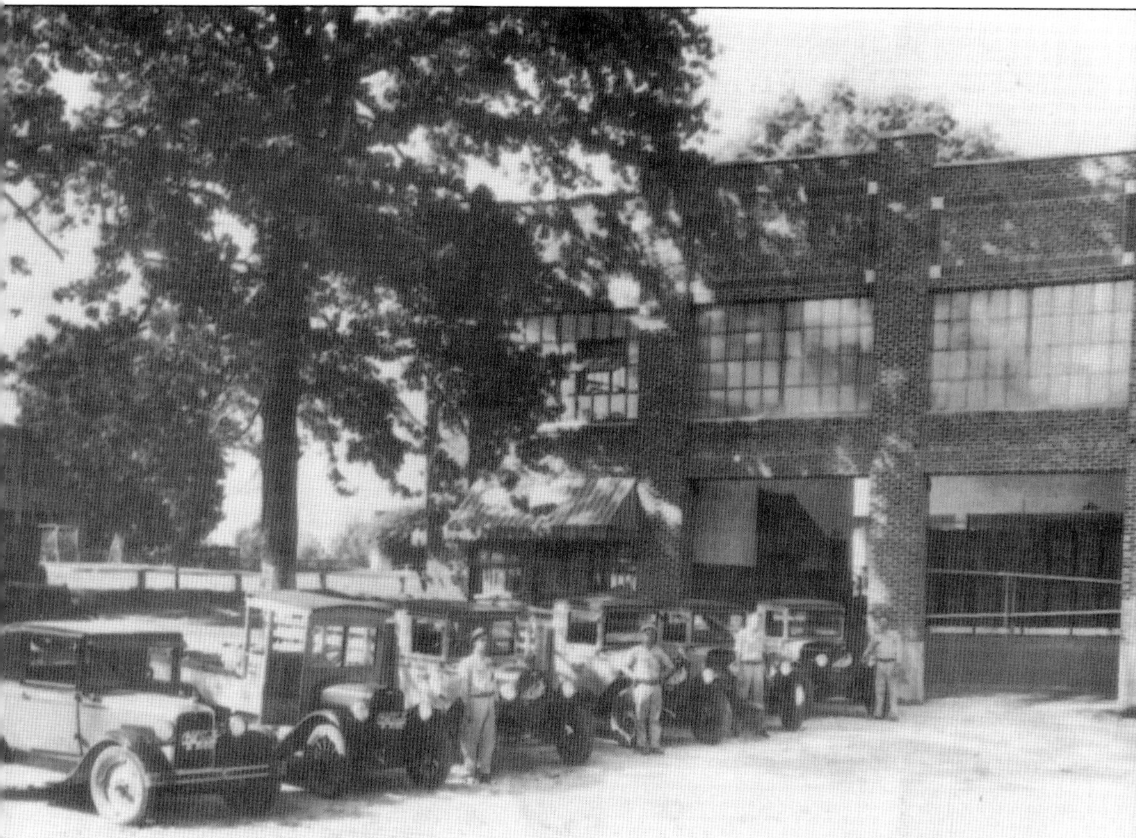

By 1926, when this picture was taken, the Minden Coca-Cola Bottling Company was under the control of Larry Hunter, son of founder W.S. Hunter, and had moved into a new building and into the modern era with trucks to distribute its beverages. The contributions of the Hunters to Minden went so far beyond their business that it is difficult to describe. Single-handedly, the family started a recreation program, including summer baseball and swimming for the city. For many years, they allowed the city to use family-owned facilities for $1 per year. The family sponsored the local American Legion baseball team, paying for the squad to travel all across the country to compete, and they also provided the first home for the Minden Redbirds semiprofessional baseball team. Beyond the area of recreation, Larry Hunter's wife, Gladys Hunter, was the first woman to serve on the Webster Parish School Board. (Courtesy of Ben Hunter.)

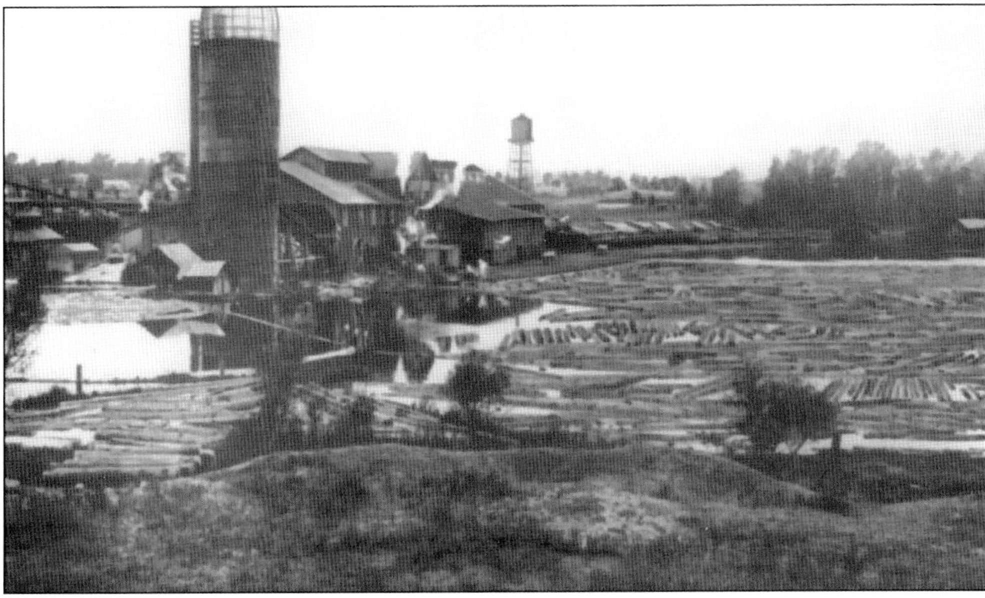

The Minden Mill of the Bodcau Lumber Company came to town in 1900 and changed the way of life. Beyond being the town's major employer, the business also brought electric and natural gas utilities to Minden. At its peak, the mill was among the largest in the world. A fire destroyed the mill in May 1918, and the loss was devastating to the community. The city was left without electricity for months, and only the addition of the L&A Railway a few years later restored economic prosperity. (Above, author's collection; below, courtesy of David Parker.)

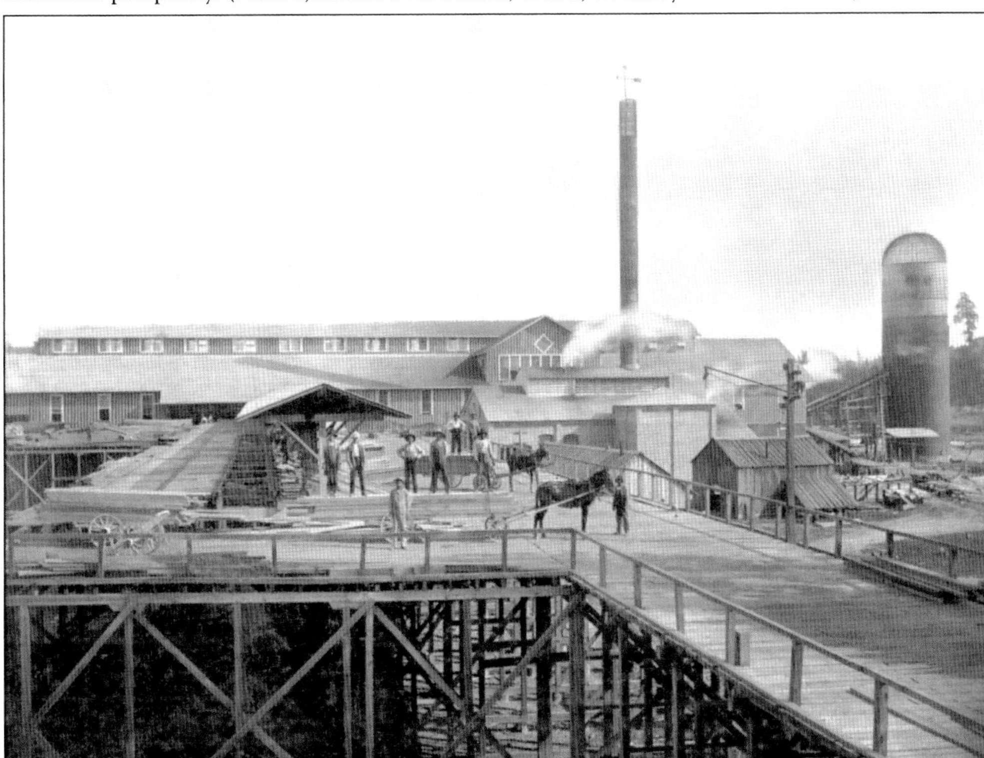

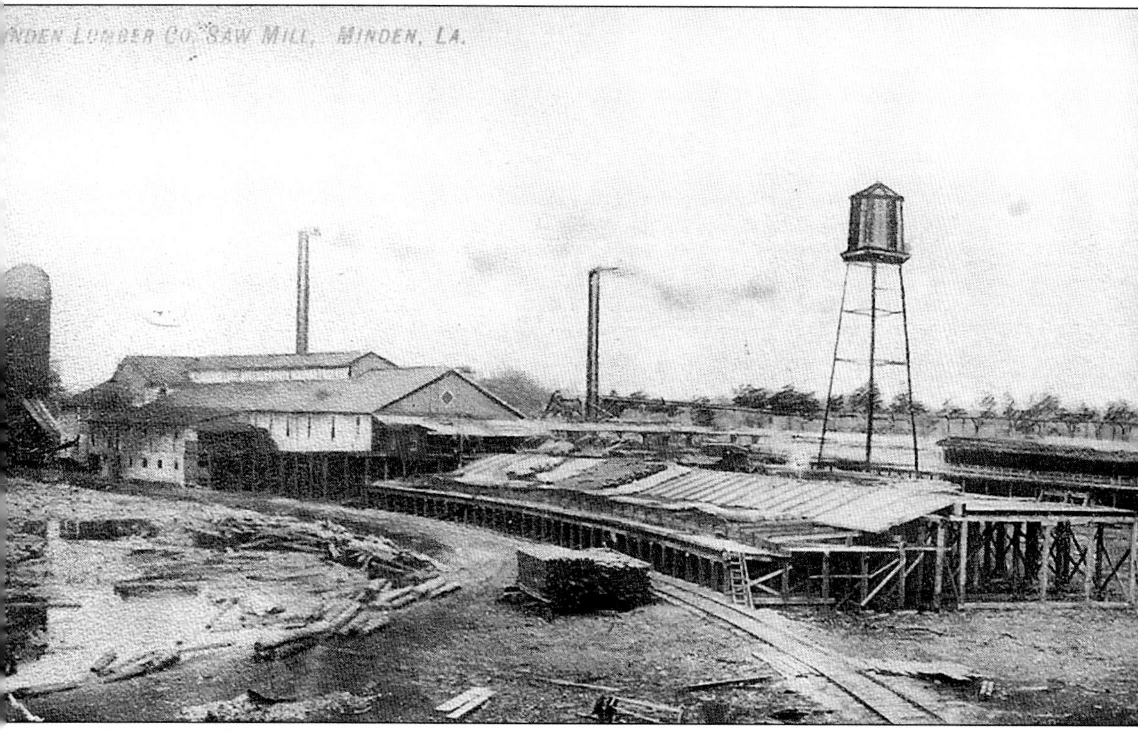

This postcard image of the Minden Lumber Mill gives an idea of the size and complexity of the operation. The mill was easily the largest employer in the town and changed aspects of the landscape of Minden. Several of the millponds remain in place today and are a legacy of the Bodcau Company's presence. The mill quarters were torn down after the mill closed, and the property was deeded to the city. It was converted into an expansion of the Minden Cemetery, and the lumber company built the streets in use in that part of the cemetery today. Since the mill was involved in producing lumber for the military shipbuilding industry, rumors were spread that the fire that destroyed the mill was sabotage, but no evidence of that claim ever emerged. (Author's collection.)

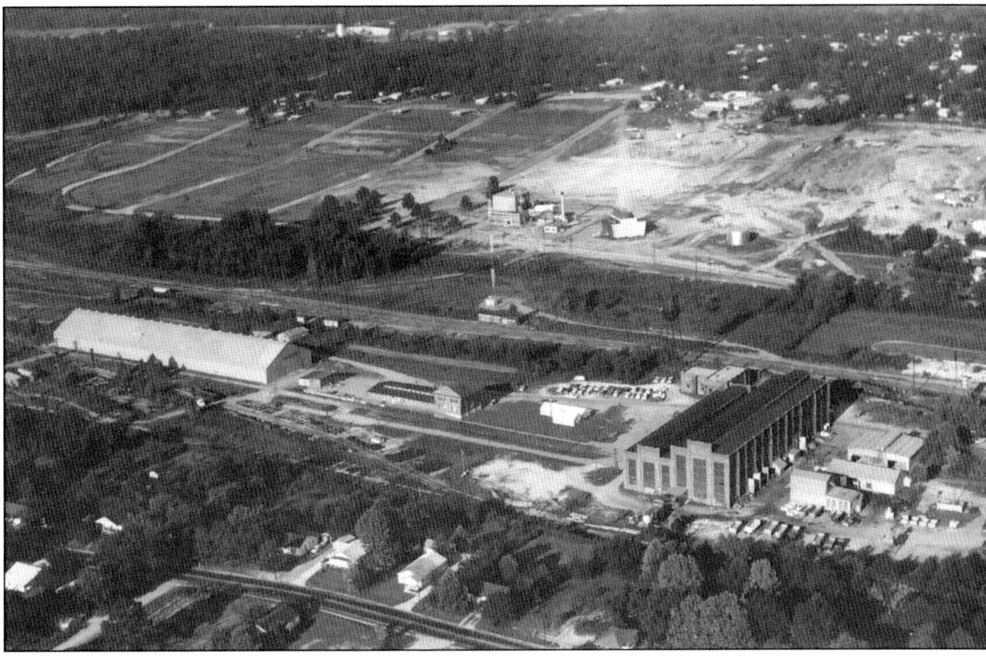

After the loss of the lumber mill, William Buchanan, who owned the Bodcau Company, restored Minden by moving the railroad shops of his Louisiana & Arkansas Railway to Minden in 1923. Those shops are shown in this image. Some years, one in three families in town had a member working for the L&A. (Author's collection.)

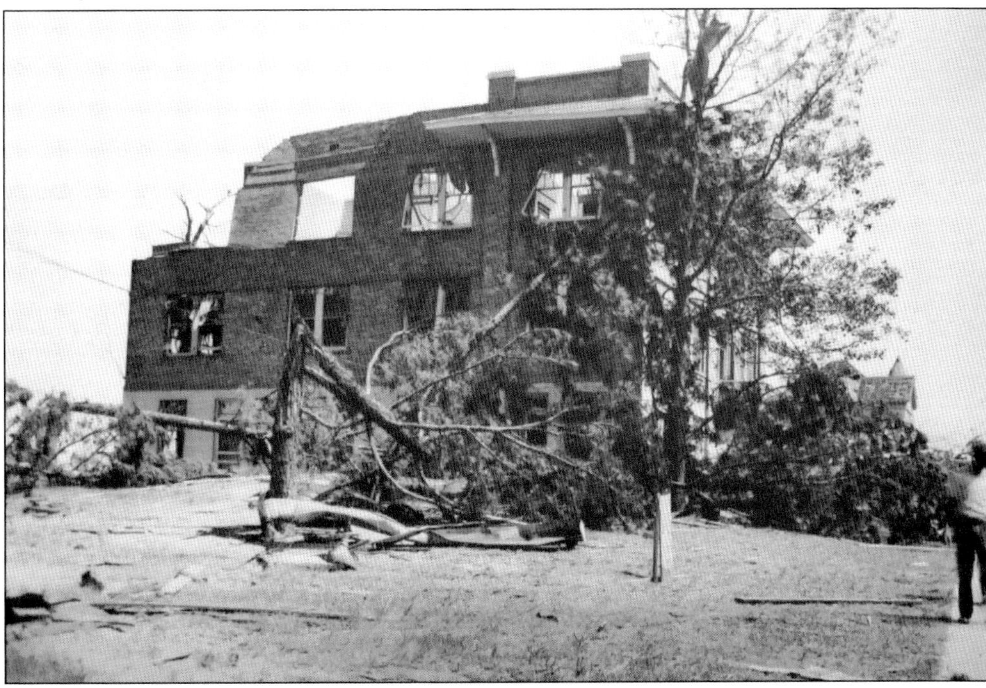

In 1926, the Buchanan family moved the office of the L&A to Minden. This image of the office building was taken after the tornado of May 1, 1933, but the structure was rebuilt and stood in Minden long after the railroad left town in the 1940s. (Author's collection.)

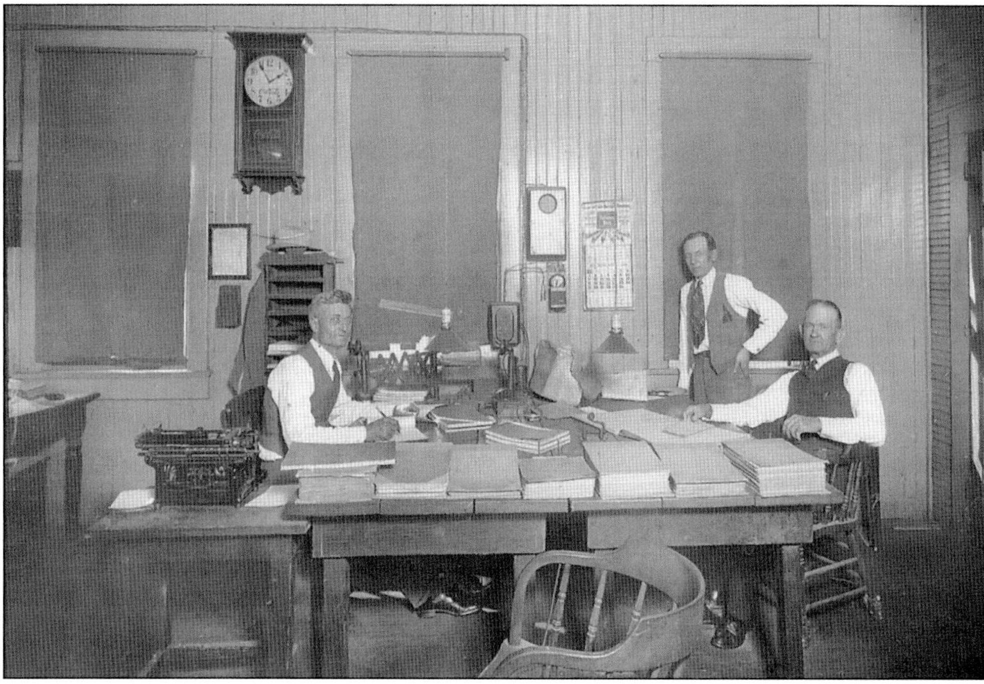

In this image is the freight office of the L&A Railway during the 1920s. The area along the railroad tracks surrounding the depot became home to many businesses and was particularly devastated by the 1933 tornado. (Author's collection.)

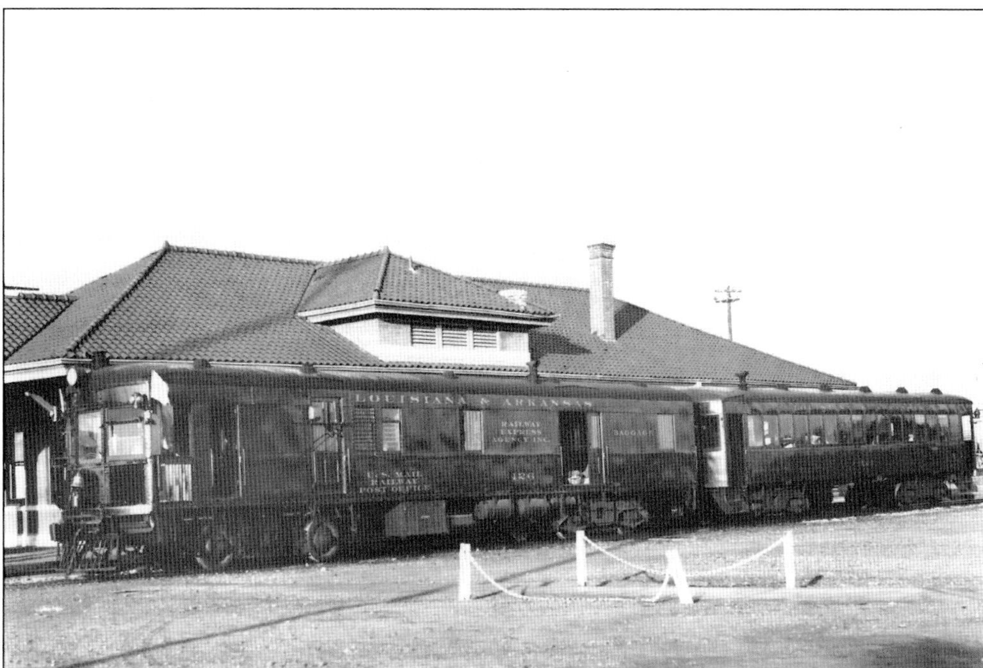

This was the Minden depot of the L&A Railway. This building was used from about 1915 until 1955, when a new, smaller passenger depot was built as the L&A ceased operations in Minden. This depot was torn down after attempts to use it for city purposes failed. (Author's collection.)

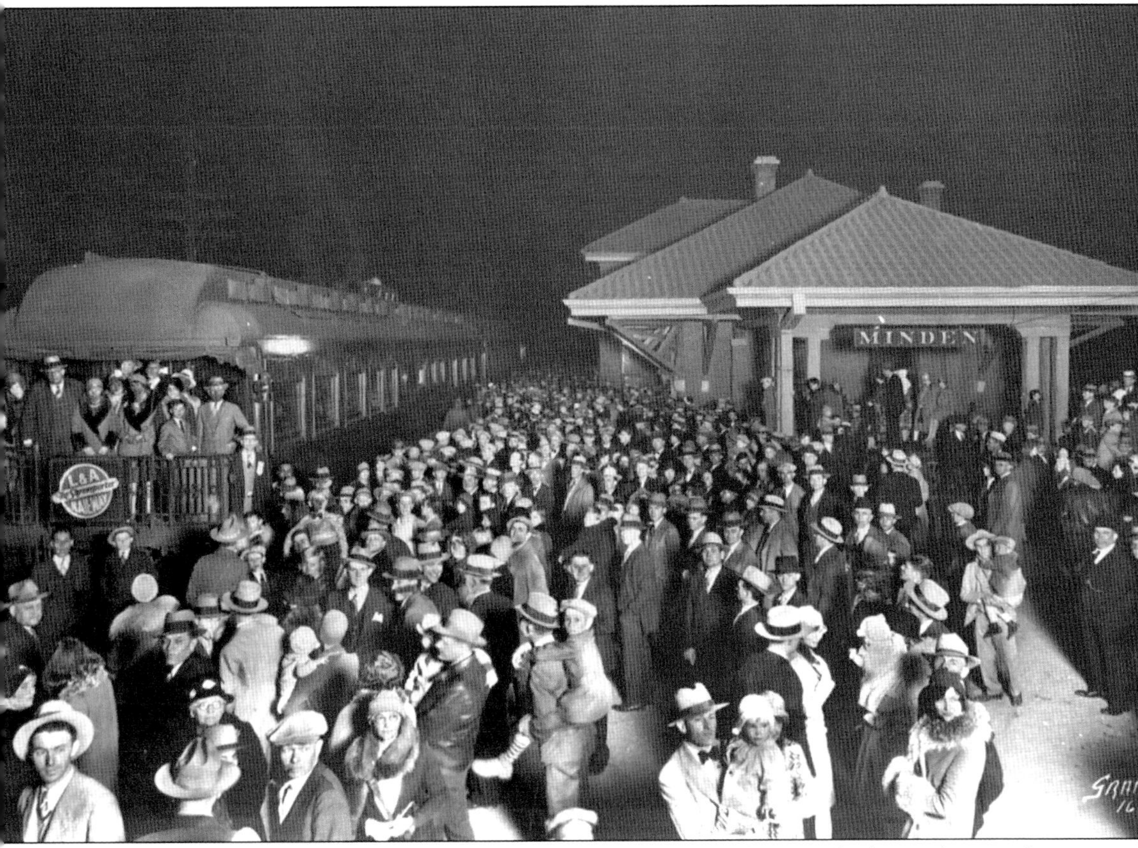

On December 30, 1928, the L&A Railway had the maiden run of its new high-speed train, the Shreveporter. The train arrived at the Minden depot just before midnight and was greeted by this overwhelming crowd, excited by the advent of faster transportation to and from Minden. The number of small children present at such a late hour is surprising. Local rumor has often claimed that this crowd was present to welcome Louisiana's newly elected governor Huey P. Long, but although Long did deliver more than a dozen speeches in Minden over the years, he was not a passenger on the Shreveporter that night. Minden residents were just enthusiastic at more progress in their town, which many had feared would not grow after the mill fire 10 years earlier. The railroad industry had done much to revive Minden, and the town loved the railroads. (Courtesy of LSU-Shreveport Archives and Special Collections, Noel Memorial Library.)

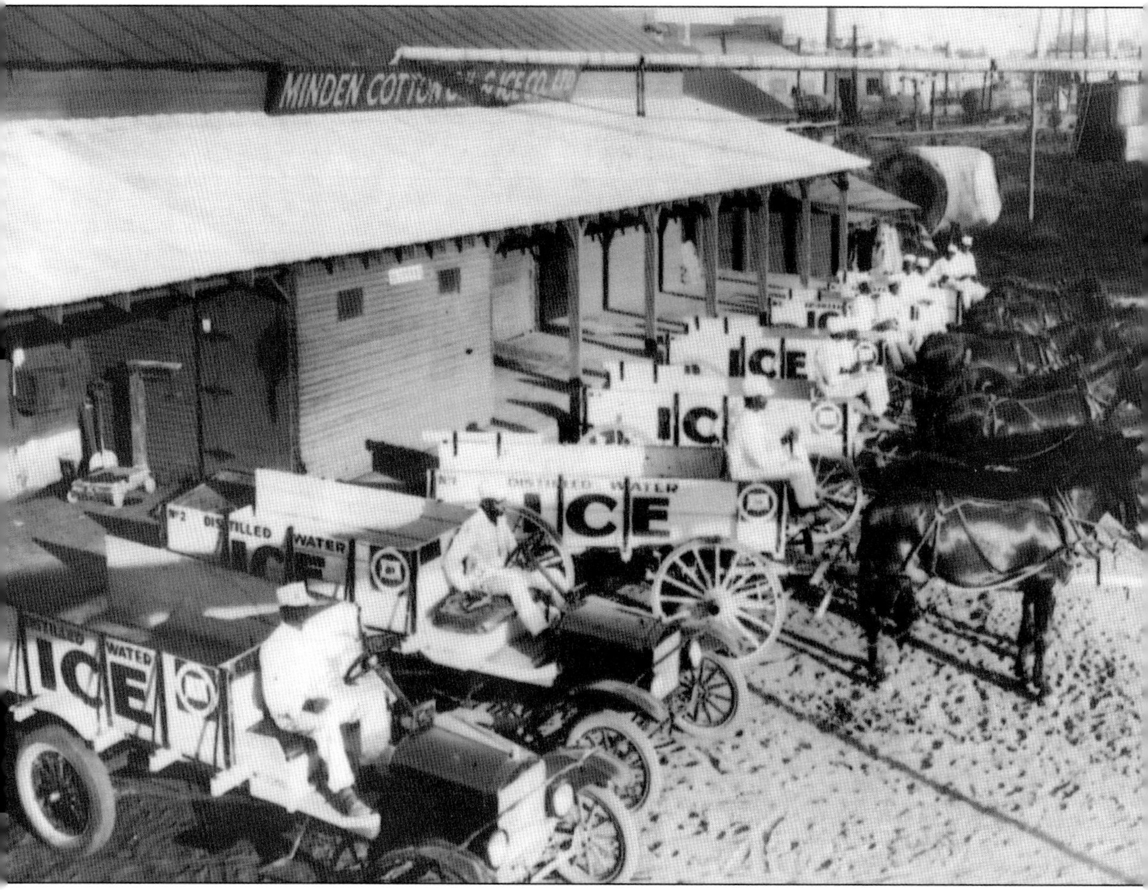

The arrival of north-south rail transportation directly to Minden in 1900 brought new industries of all kinds to the community. Among the businesses that were established in the commercial area along the railroad tracks was Minden Cotton Oil and Ice, founded by local businessmen just after 1900. The mill produced cottonseed oil and fertilizer and provided ice to local residents for many years. The company's brand name for their fertilizer was Black Cat, and its building was adorned with the image of a huge black cat. The building remained in place until the mid-1960s, when the land was purchased by the City of Minden. Today, the city has its main warehouse at the location. This is a transitional picture, as the method of delivery of ice and other products to local customers is shifting from wagons to trucks. (Author's collection.)

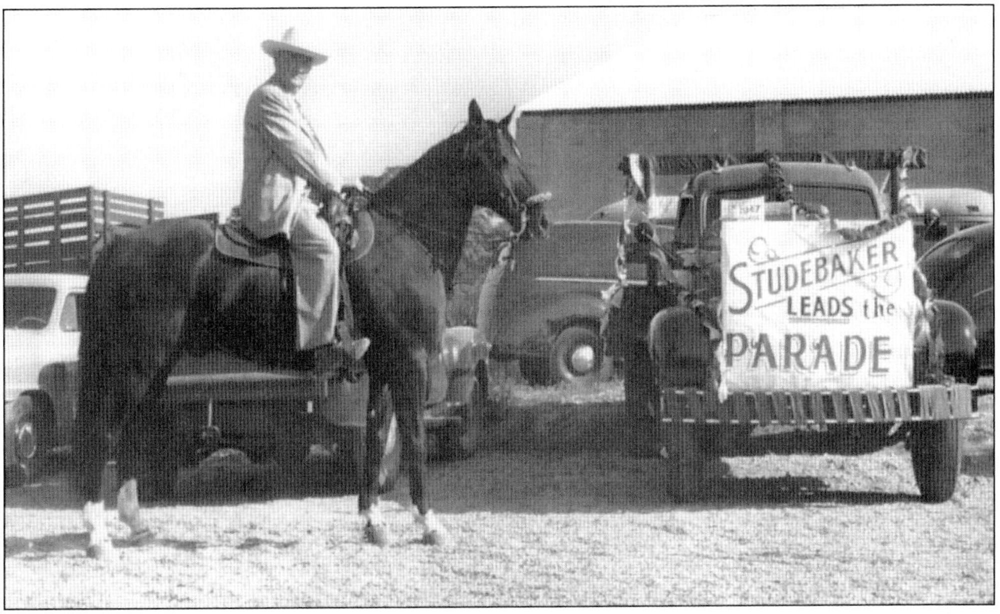

On the edges of downtown Minden were other businesses such as Brackin Motors, the local Studebaker dealer. Here, L.H. Brackin is shown on his horse after leading the Webster Parish Fair Parade in about 1947. (Courtesy of the Webster Parish Library.)

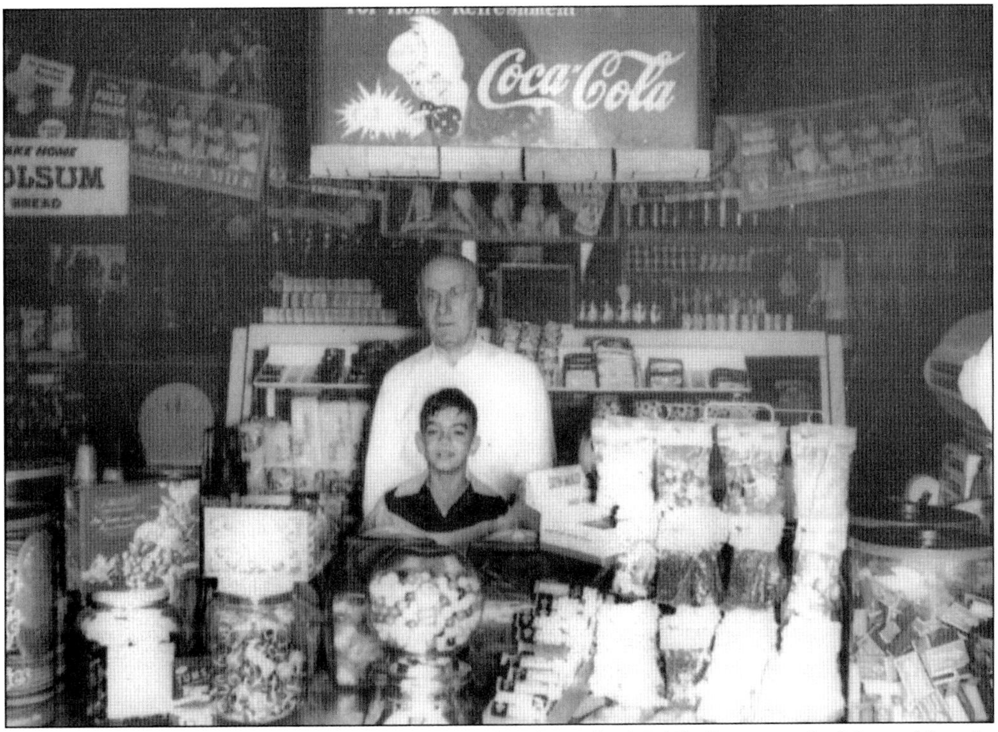

Among the immigrant families coming to Minden from the Middle East was the Mourad family. Here, Isaac Mourad is shown in his store with his younger son, Bobby. The son and grandson of Isaac's elder son, George, have served Minden as firefighters for decades, and his grandson is currently Minden's fire chief. (Courtesy of Bobby Mourad.)

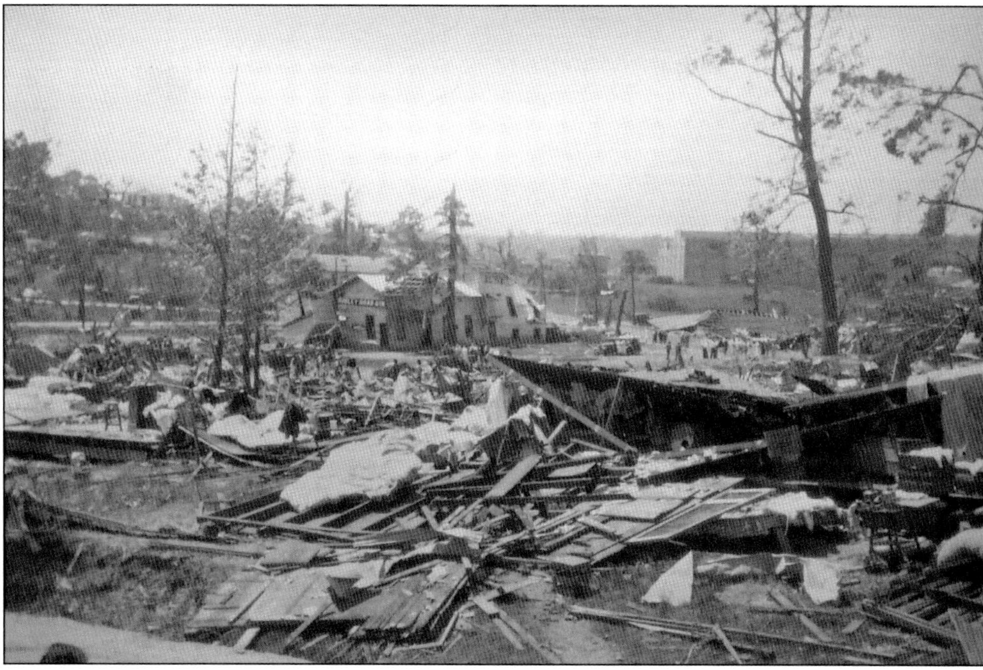

From its earliest days, cotton was a vital part of the local economy. This picture shows the wreckage of the Sibley Road Cotton Gin in the wake of the 1933 tornado. The business was rebuilt and continued to operate through the 1940s and into the early 1950s. (Author's collection.)

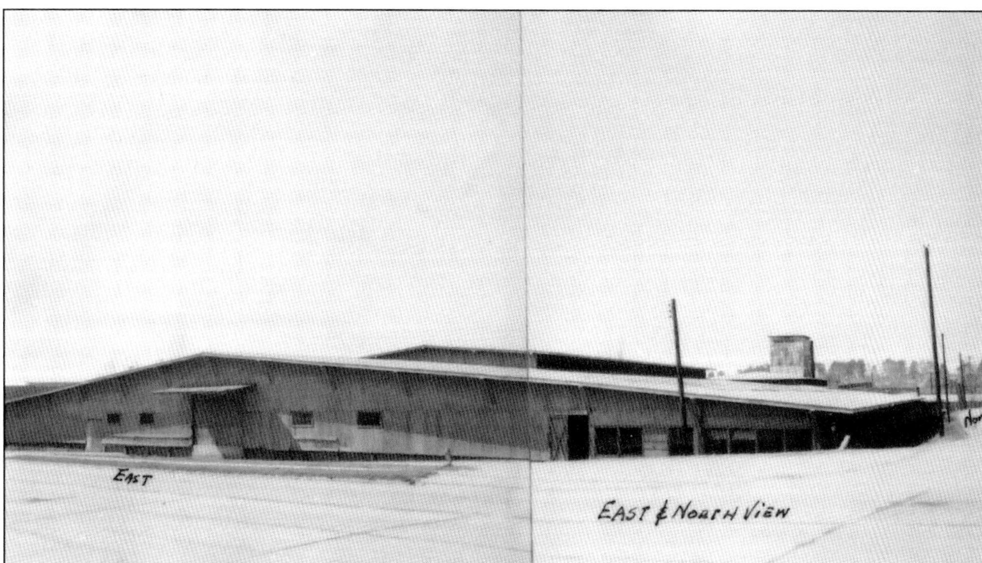

Directly across Sibley Road from the gin was the Minden Cotton Compress, where the ginned cotton was packed into tight bales to facilitate shipping. This massive building stood into the 21st century before being torn down in the past few years. (Courtesy of LSU-Shreveport Archives and Special Collections, Noel Memorial Library.)

Two

SHADOWS OF SPIRES ATHWART THE HEARTHSTONES

RELIGION AND COMMUNITY

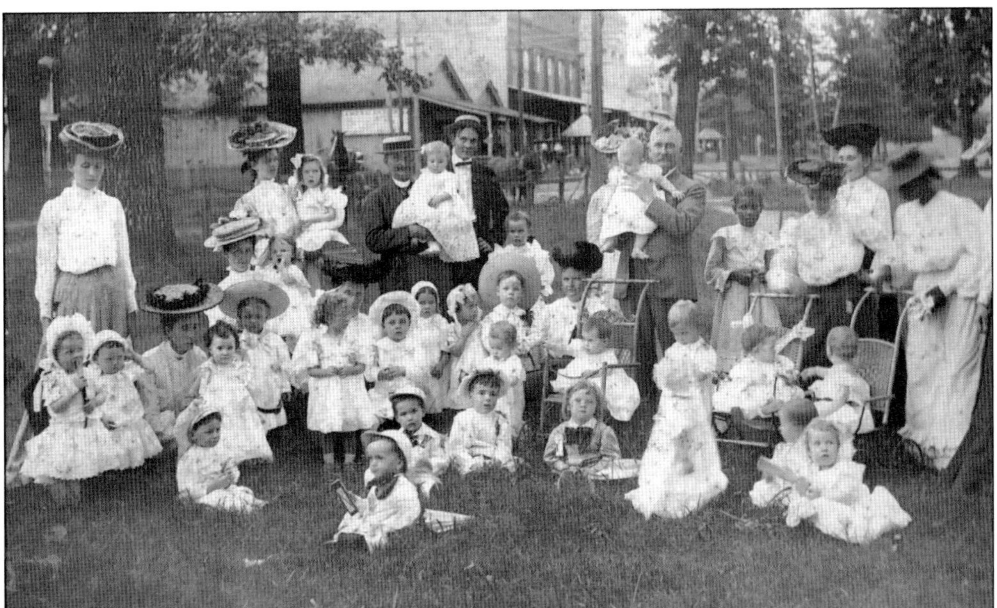

Minden has always been a city of celebrations; this image shows an Easter celebration from around 1900. The hatless gentleman holding the child is Alfred Goodwill, a prominent local businessman whose great-grandson Mike Foster served two terms as Louisiana governor. This portion of downtown would be dedicated a few years later as Civic or Town Park. (Courtesy of Dorcheat Historical Association Museum.)

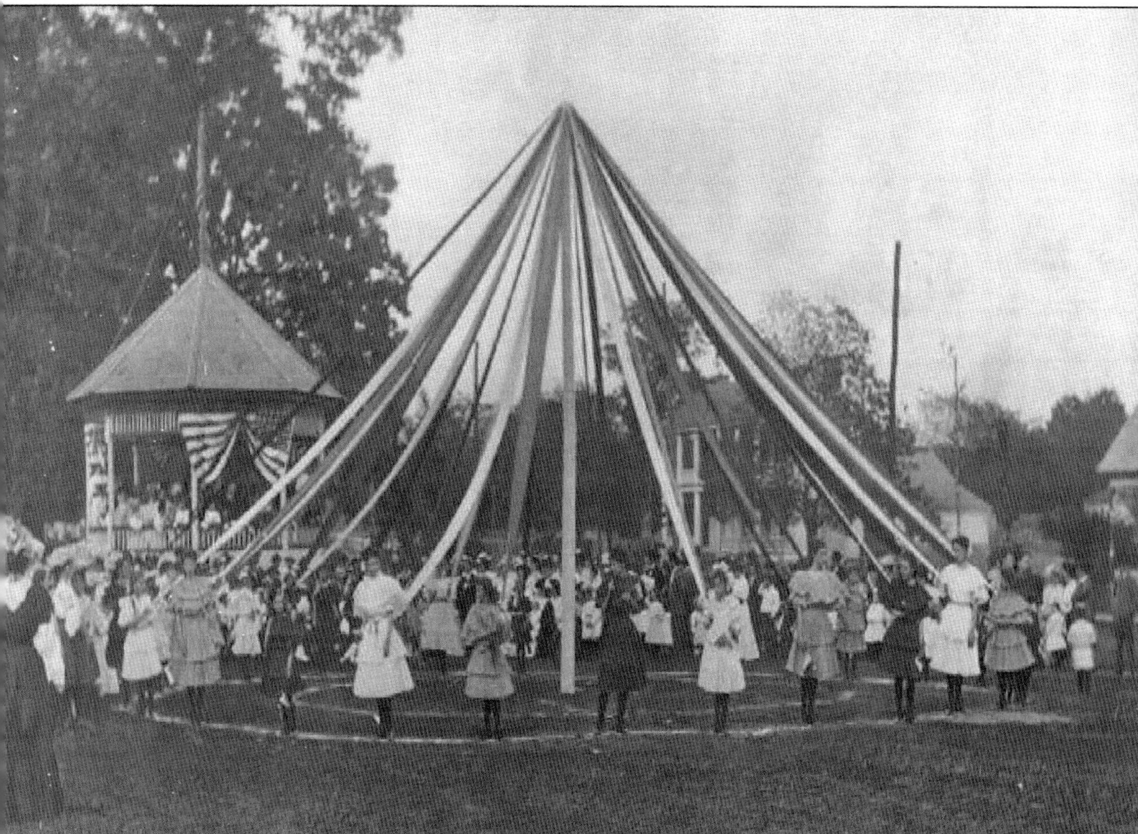

This image, taken on May 1, 1907, shows a May Day celebration in Civic Park complete with a maypole. The park had been created in 1905 through the initiative of the local women's clubs, and the bandstand had been completed for only a few months when this event took place. Over the next 50 years, the bandstand would host speeches from the likes of Huey Long and weekly town band concerts on Friday nights during the summers. Visible in the right background of the picture is the antebellum home constructed for William Hardy in 1855 but best known in Minden as the longtime home of Joe Miller and, later, his daughter Roy Miller Inbanbett. The home is one of a handful of antebellum structures still standing in Minden today and sits behind the 1953 Webster Parish Courthouse. (Courtesy of Richard Carey.)

This group of boys from the 1940s found the bandstand in the park to be the perfect place to hang out on a summer's day in Minden. This is the reconstructed bandstand, after it had been completely destroyed by the killer tornado of May 1, 1933, that devastated Minden. (Author's collection.)

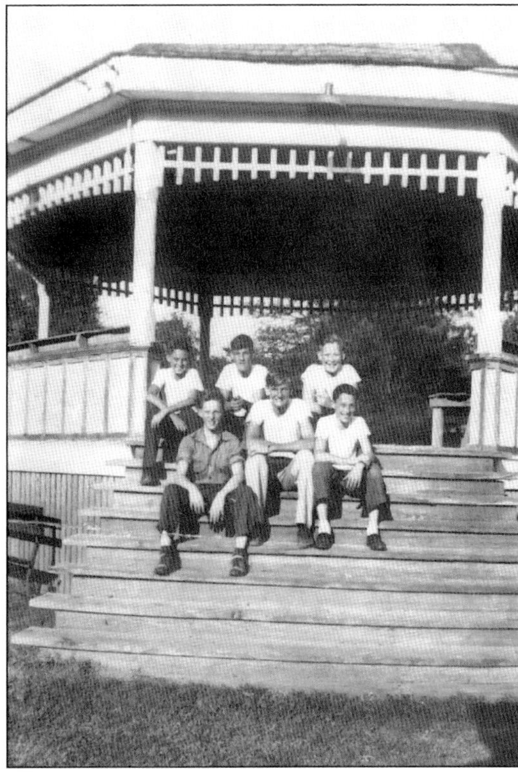

Minden girls are seen on a parade float for Fourth of July celebrations in 1912. Minden began celebrating the Fourth of July again in the mid-1880s, unlike some towns in the old Confederacy that refused to acknowledge Independence Day for decades after the Civil War. (Courtesy of Dorcheat Historical Association Museum.)

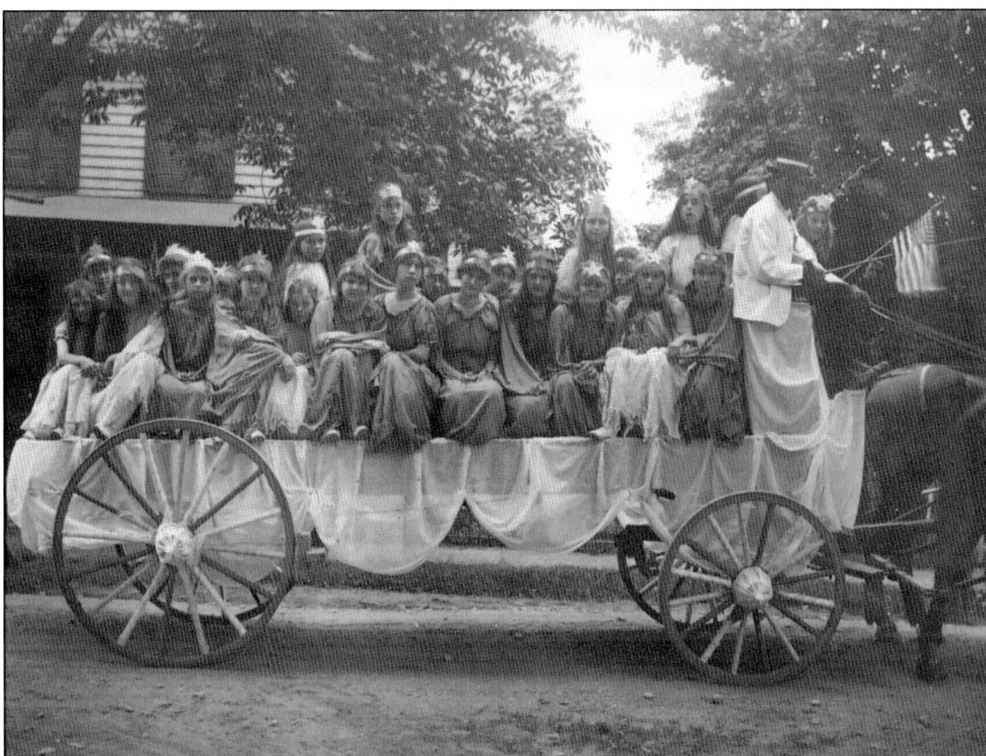

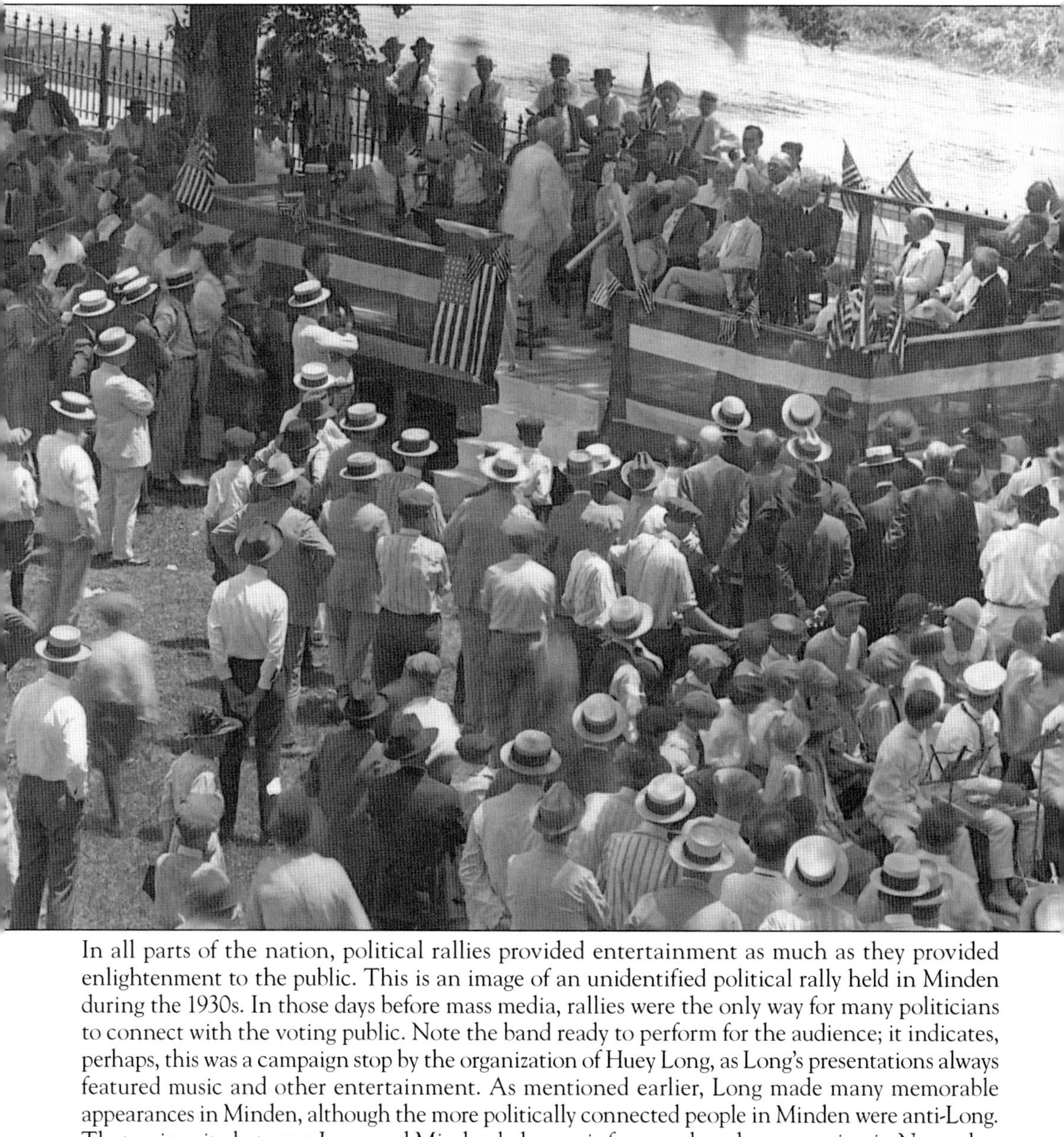

In all parts of the nation, political rallies provided entertainment as much as they provided enlightenment to the public. This is an image of an unidentified political rally held in Minden during the 1930s. In those days before mass media, rallies were the only way for many politicians to connect with the voting public. Note the band ready to perform for the audience; it indicates, perhaps, this was a campaign stop by the organization of Huey Long, as Long's presentations always featured music and other entertainment. As mentioned earlier, Long made many memorable appearances in Minden, although the more politically connected people in Minden were anti-Long. That animosity between Long and Minden led to an infamous showdown meeting in November 1933 when, according to Long biographer T. Harry Williams, a plot was underfoot to kill Long that was foiled by his bodyguards. (Courtesy of Joan Wiley Luck)

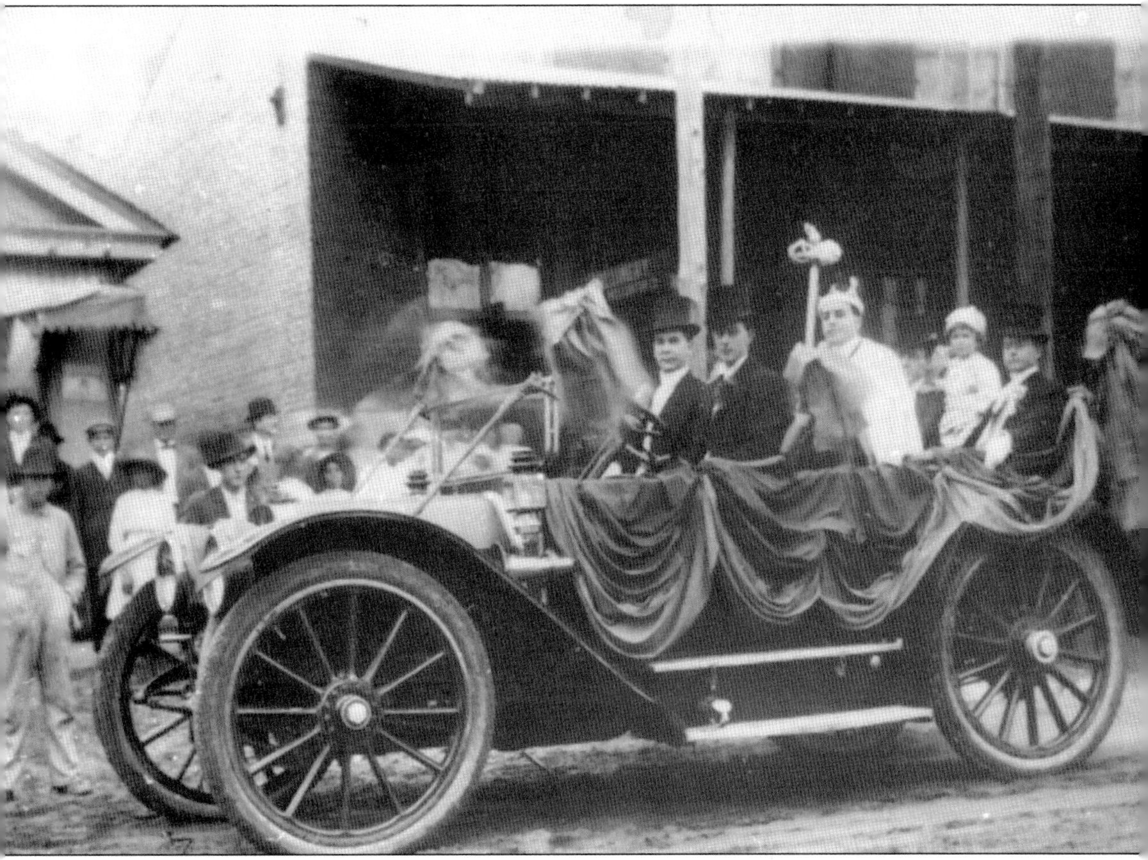

For many years, Mardi Gras was a huge celebration in Minden. Beginning in the 1880s, the festivities grew over time. This image shows an unidentified king and queen of Mardi Gras being driven through town in 1915. Large events were held all day long on Fat Tuesday, and even the town schoolchildren were involved in the celebration. Minden's fascination with carnival faded after a tragic fire at a Mardi Gras pageant in 1923 killed several young girls. Local celebrations began again in the last 30 years, and a local krewe emerged to sponsor parades and other events. The holiday has once again become important in Minden. In the present era, in recognition of the name of the town and its German heritage, the carnival celebrations have been given a German spin, recognizing Minden's roots by celebrating Fasching. (Courtesy of Thad Andress.)

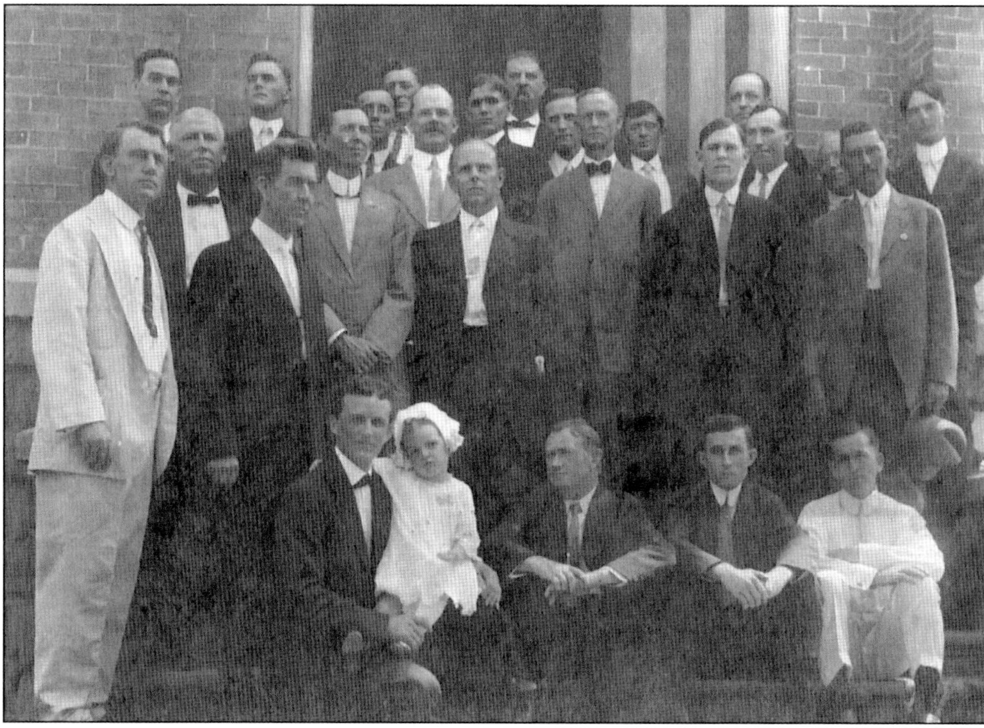

The men of the First Methodist Church of Minden are shown outside the building in about 1908. First Methodist is the oldest church in Minden, having been founded in 1839 by circuit riders in North Louisiana. The building in this picture was constructed in approximately 1905 and was used for nearly three-quarters of a century. (Courtesy of Frank Griffith.)

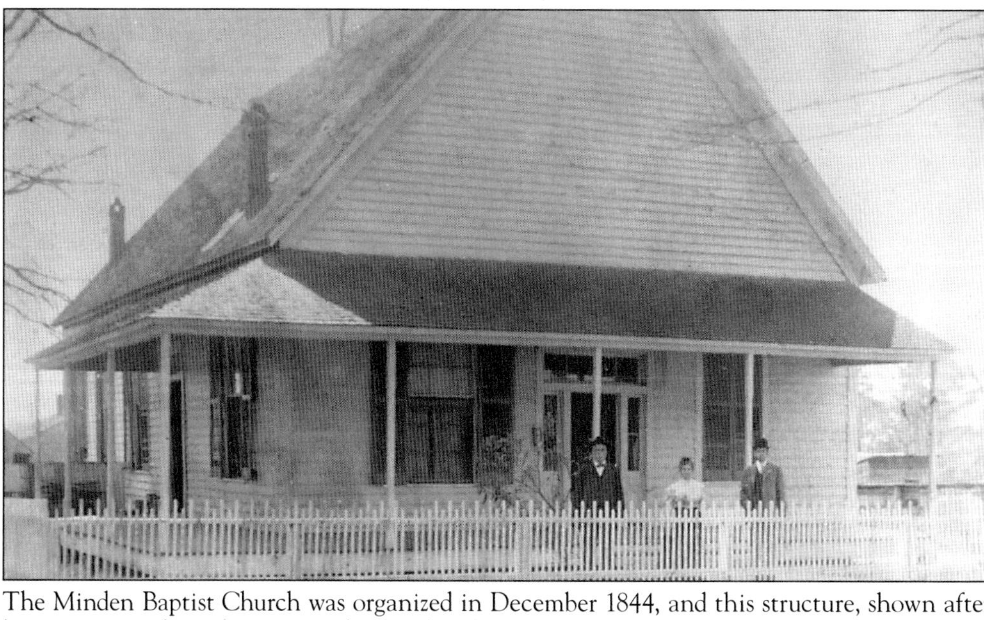

The Minden Baptist Church was organized in December 1844, and this structure, shown after being converted to a home, was the first building erected for the congregation to meet in 1852. The church moved to its second home in 1902, and this structure was destroyed by the tornado of 1933. (Author's collection.)

St. John's Episcopal Church was organized in Minden in the 1850s through the leadership of the Chaffee and Goodwill families. This church building was constructed in 1870 and was used until after World War II, when a newer brick church was built on the edge of downtown Minden. (Courtesy of LSU-Shreveport Archives and Special Collections, Noel Memorial Library.)

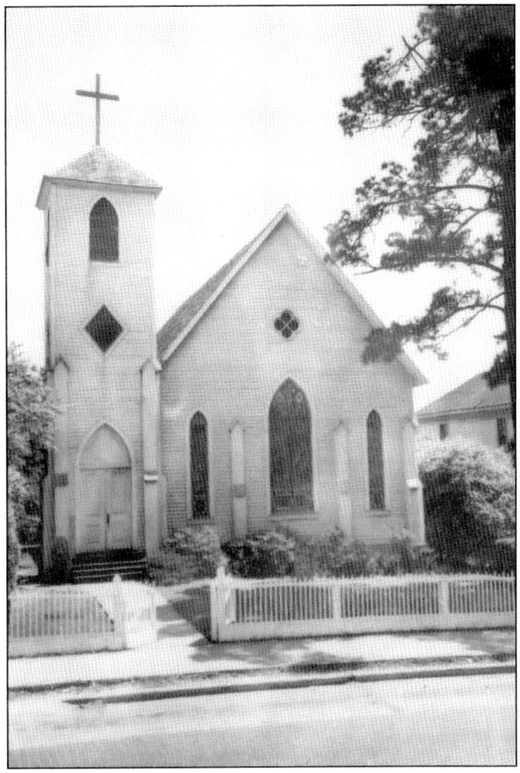

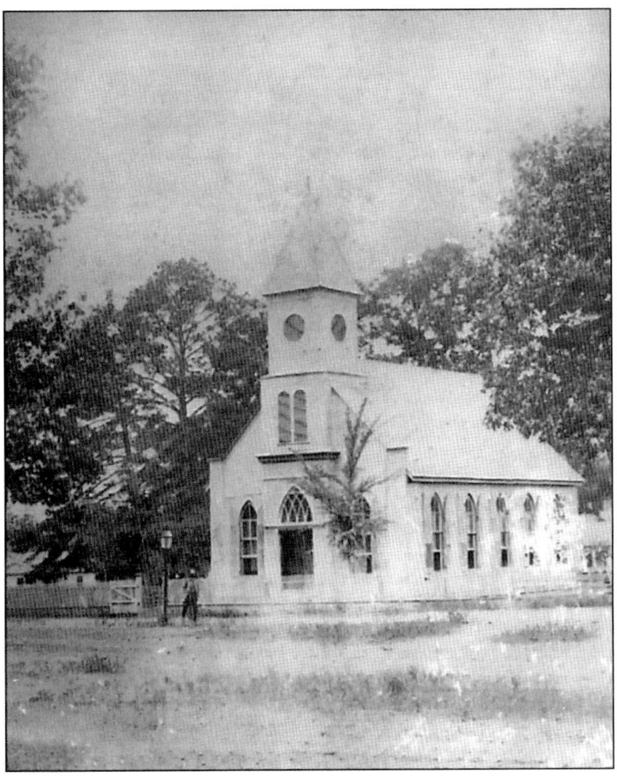

The Minden Presbyterian Church came into being in 1854. This church building was constructed in 1889 and was used until 1924, when the current church building was erected on the same site. (Author's collection.)

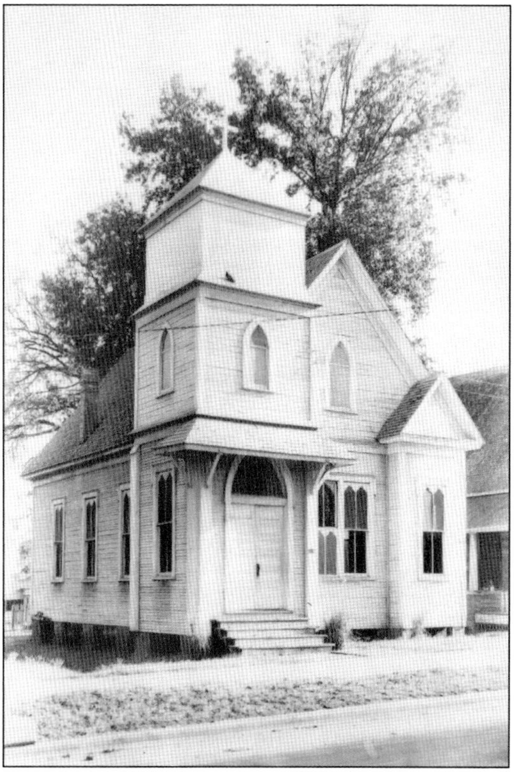

The first Catholic settlers came to Minden from Eastern Europe in the 1850s, and from 1857 to 1867, a visiting priest came to Minden for services. In 1867, a priest was assigned to Minden, and this building was erected as the home for St. Anne's Catholic Church. (Courtesy of LSU-Shreveport Archives and Special Collections, Noel Memorial Library.)

Originally built in the 1850s, this was the home of Drury Murrell, who came to Minden from South Carolina and became a prominent businessman. The residence burned in 1879, and this images shows the reconstructed version. In later years, this structure served as the Green-Kleinnegger Funeral Home. (Courtesy Frank Griffith.)

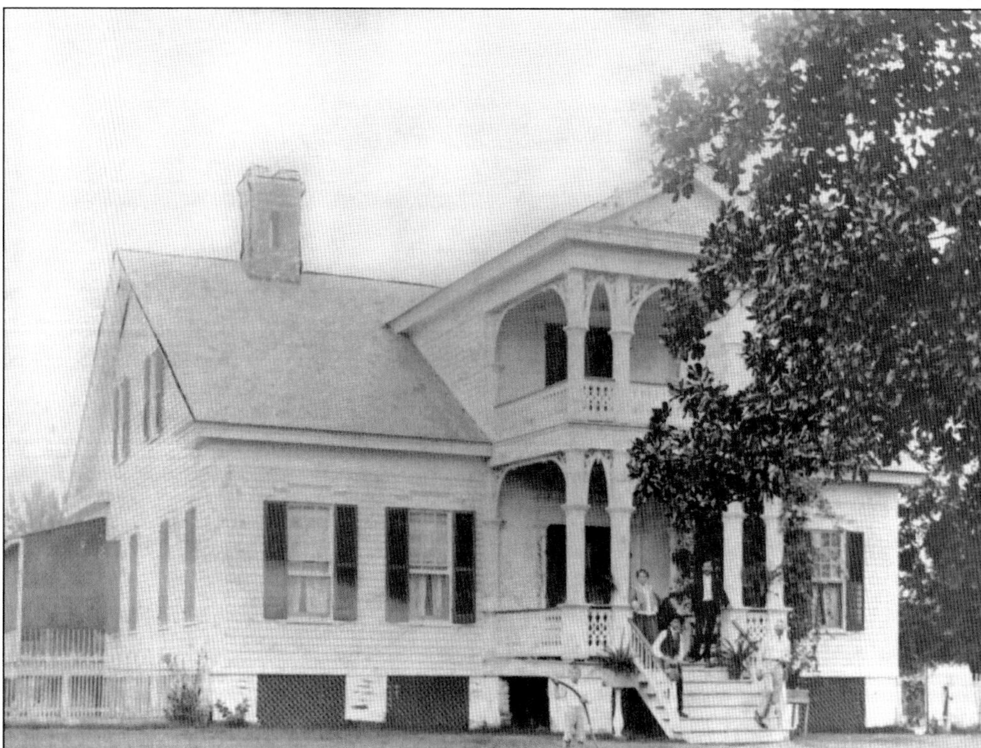

St. John's Episcopal Church was organized in Minden in the 1850s through the leadership of the Chaffee and Goodwill families. This church building was constructed in 1870 and was used until after World War II, when a newer brick church was built on the edge of downtown Minden. (Courtesy of LSU-Shreveport Archives and Special Collections, Noel Memorial Library.)

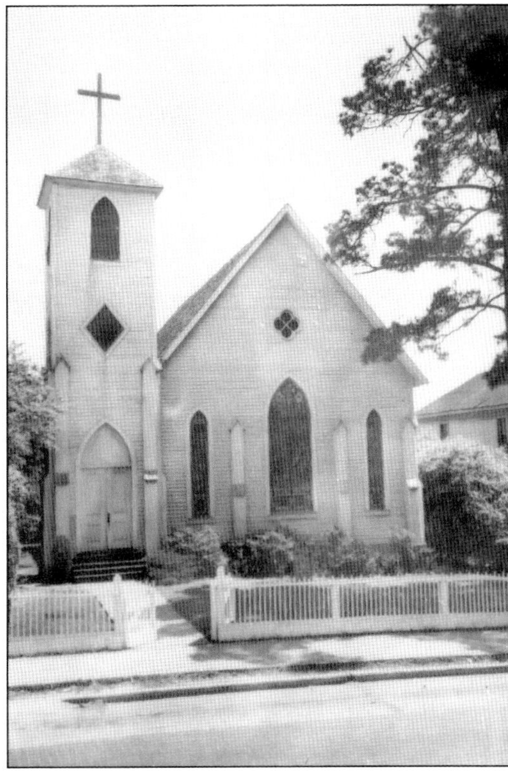

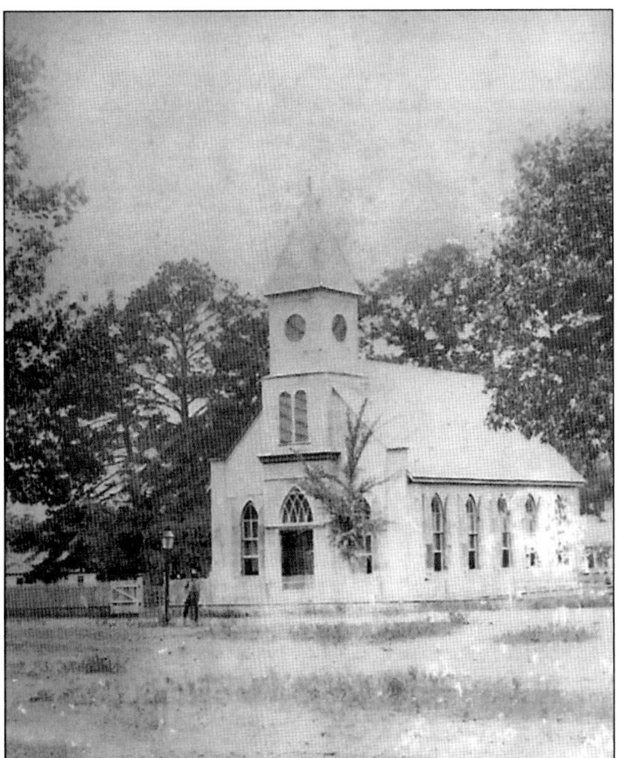

The Minden Presbyterian Church came into being in 1854. This church building was constructed in 1889 and was used until 1924, when the current church building was erected on the same site. (Author's collection.)

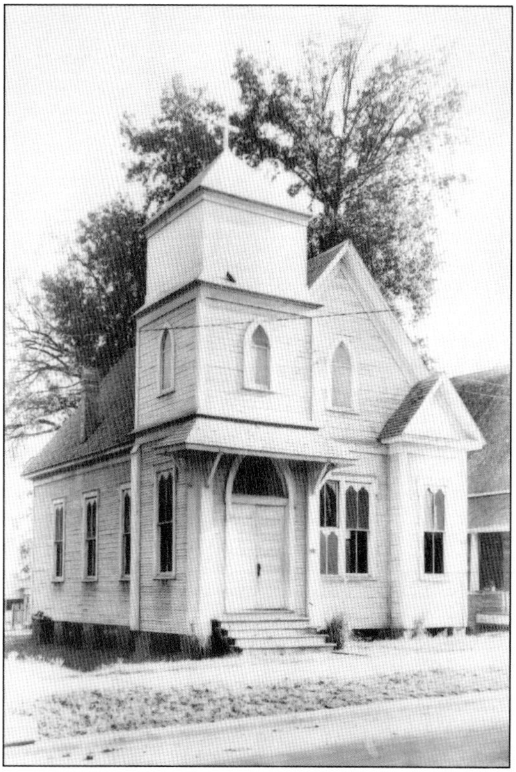

The first Catholic settlers came to Minden from Eastern Europe in the 1850s, and from 1857 to 1867, a visiting priest came to Minden for services. In 1867, a priest was assigned to Minden, and this building was erected as the home for St. Anne's Catholic Church. (Courtesy of LSU-Shreveport Archives and Special Collections, Noel Memorial Library.)

Originally built in the 1850s, this was the home of Drury Murrell, who came to Minden from South Carolina and became a prominent businessman. The residence burned in 1879, and this images shows the reconstructed version. In later years, this structure served as the Green-Kleinnegger Funeral Home. (Courtesy Frank Griffith.)

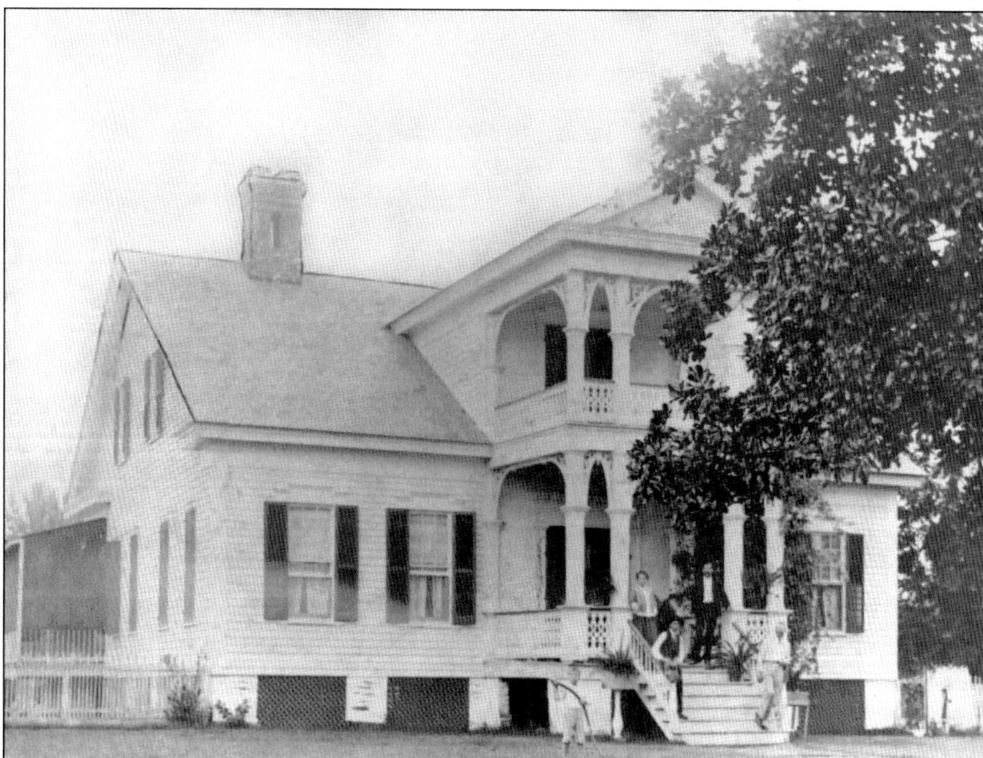

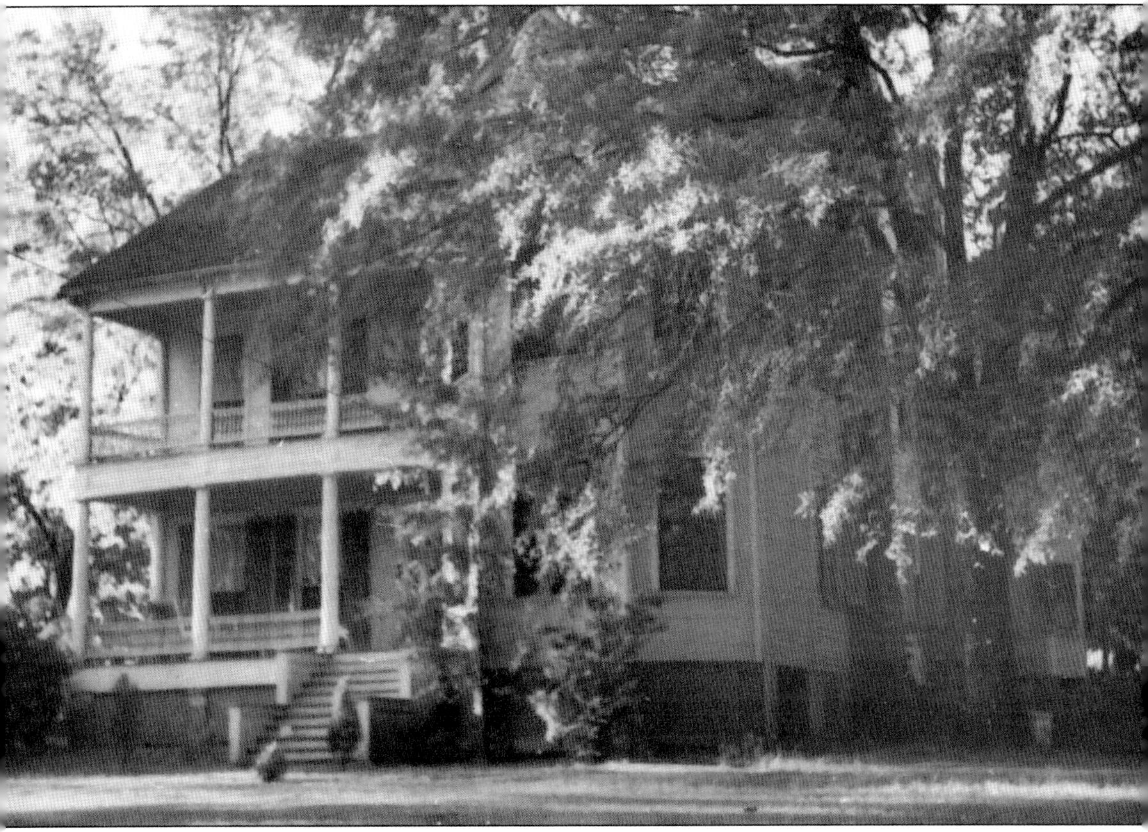

John D. Watkins came to Minden in 1848 to teach at the Minden Academy and rose to become the president of the Minden Male Academy, which replaced the old Minden Academy. He later became an attorney, prosecuting attorney, and district judge, as did his son John Thomas Watkins, who built this home on College Street in Minden. John T. was also a noted religious leader, serving as president of the Louisiana Baptist Convention. He capped his political career by serving eight terms in the US House of Representatives between 1905 and 1921. Fellow Minden resident John N. Sandlin defeated him in a bitter campaign in the fall of 1920. In the aftermath of that race, Watkins lived out his life in Washington, DC, not returning to live in this home. He died in 1925 and is buried in the Minden Cemetery. (Courtesy of LSU-Shreveport Archives and Special Collections, Noel Memorial Library.)

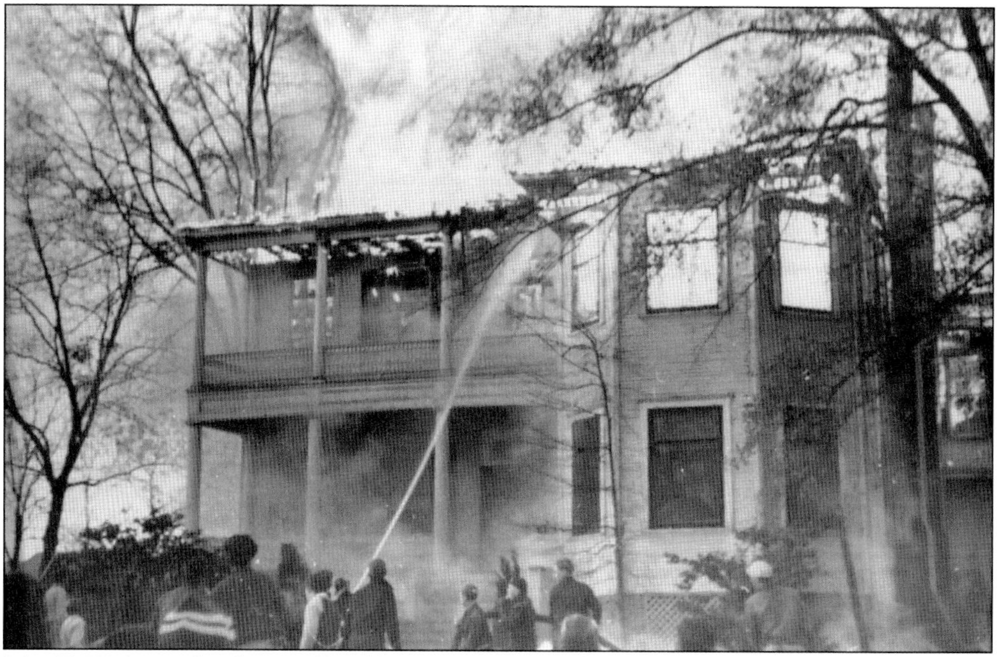

John T. Watkins's daughter Mell and her husband, attorney Clifford Hays, lived in the home after the death of the congressman. On the morning of January 8, 1942, a fire sparked by the explosion of a hot water heater broke out at the home, as seen in this image. (Courtesy of LSU-Shreveport Archives and Special Collections, Noel Memorial Library.)

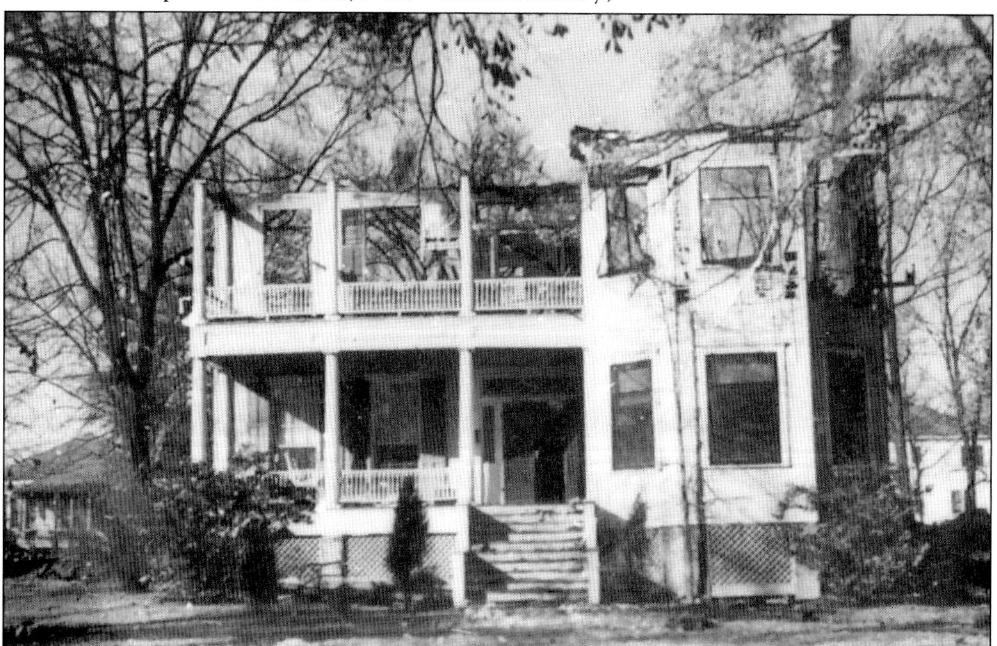

The Minden Fire Department was unable to put out the fire in time to save the home, and when the blaze was finally extinguished, this was all that was left of the house. Today, the Minden Church of Christ occupies that spot on College Street. (Courtesy of LSU-Shreveport Archives and Special Collections, Noel Memorial Library.)

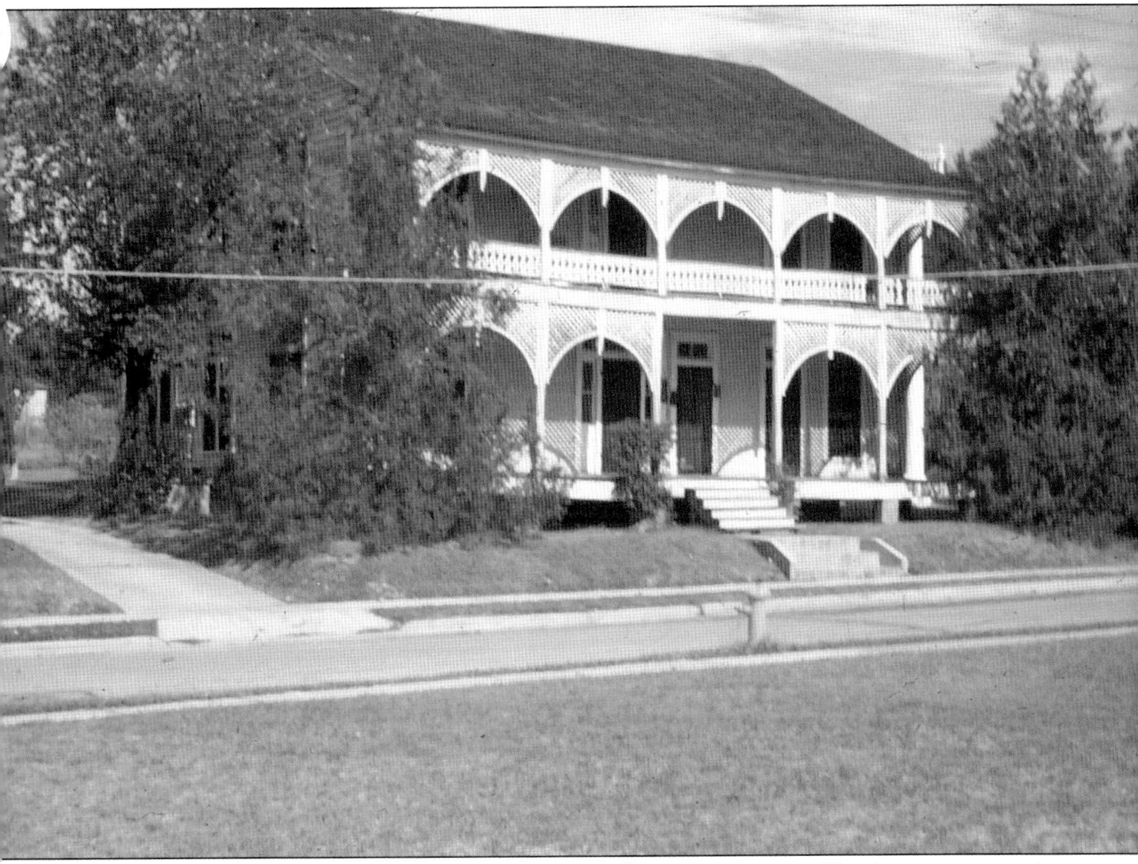

After the fire, the Hayses moved to this property on Sullivan Street, owned by the congressman's estate, one block north of the destroyed home. After the death of Clifford Hays, Mell Hays would remain in this house for years, finally moving to a much smaller house next door in the last years of her life in the 1970s. This Sullivan Street residence had once been the main building of the Minden Male Academy before that institution closed around 1900. At the time of the closing, John Watkins purchased the campus building for a total of $50, contingent on him removing the buildings from the campus so it could be converted to what is today Academy Park. It was an amazingly low price for a house that would remain in use for nearly 60 years after the purchase. It was truly a wise investment choice. (Courtesy of LSU-Shreveport Archives and Special Collections, Noel Memorial Library.)

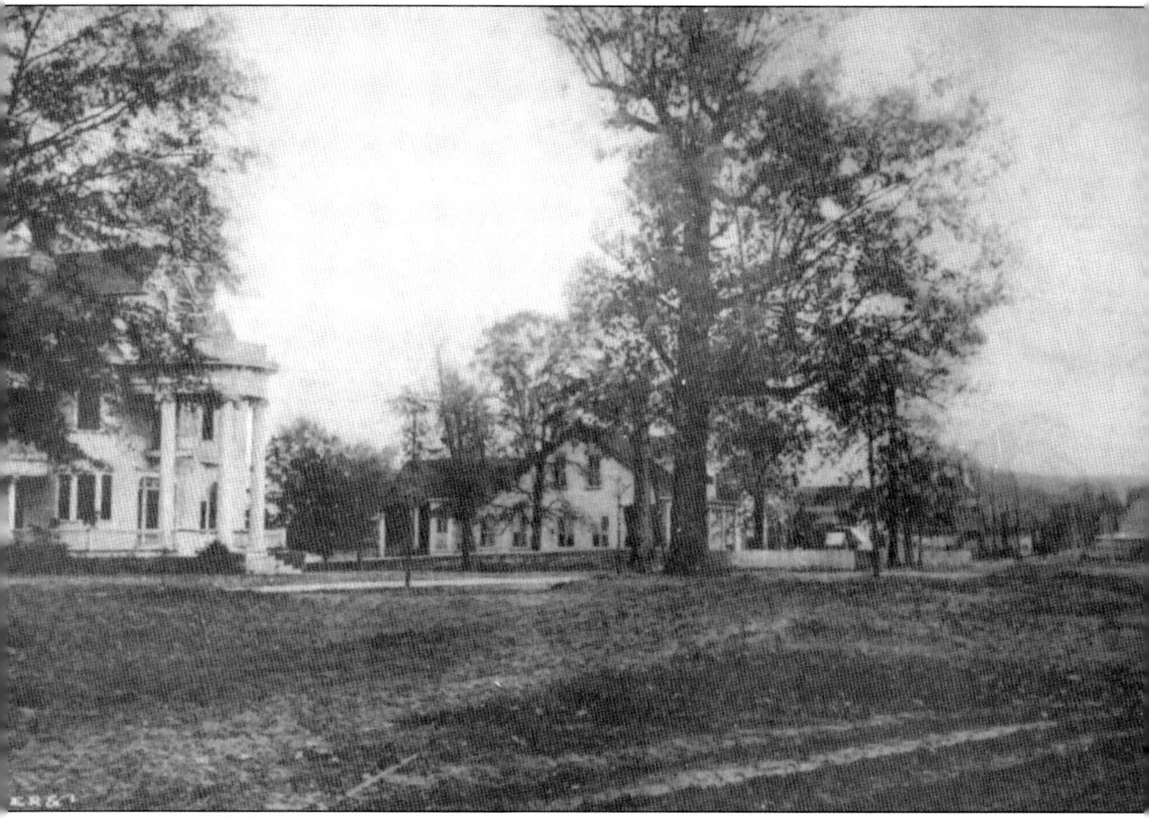

This postcard shows a residential section of Broadway in Minden during the first decade of the 20th century in a view looking west toward downtown. The house to the left is the Jack Crichton home, which became to be known as the Sandlin home to most Minden folks. Crichton died, and his widow, Emma Palmer Crichton, married Judge John N. Sandlin in 1913. The Sandlins lived in this house together until Emma died in the mid-1950s. Judge (later Congressman) Sandlin lived on at this residence until his death on Christmas Eve 1957. The home just to the right, or west, is the English home, which was torn down in 1925. The First Baptist Church of Minden bought the English home, and it would erect its third church building on that site in 1925. (Author's collection.)

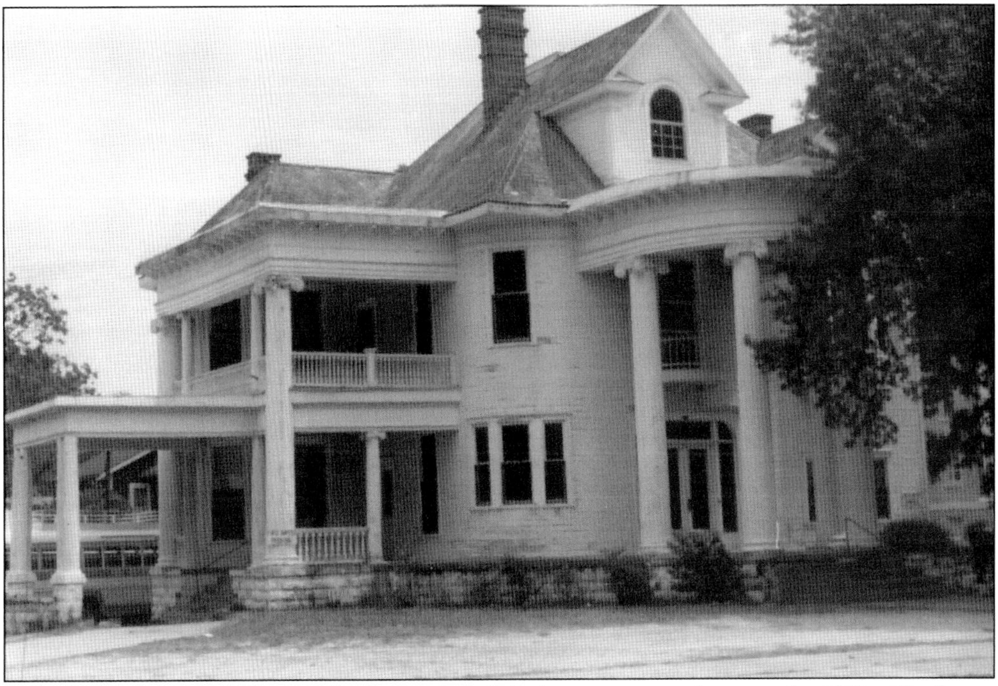

Here is a later image of the Sandlin home shortly before it was torn down in the 1970s. The home had been acquired by the First Baptist Church of Minden and was used for church activities until it was removed for parking spaces. Sandlin served in the US House of Representatives from 1921 to 1937. (Author's collection.)

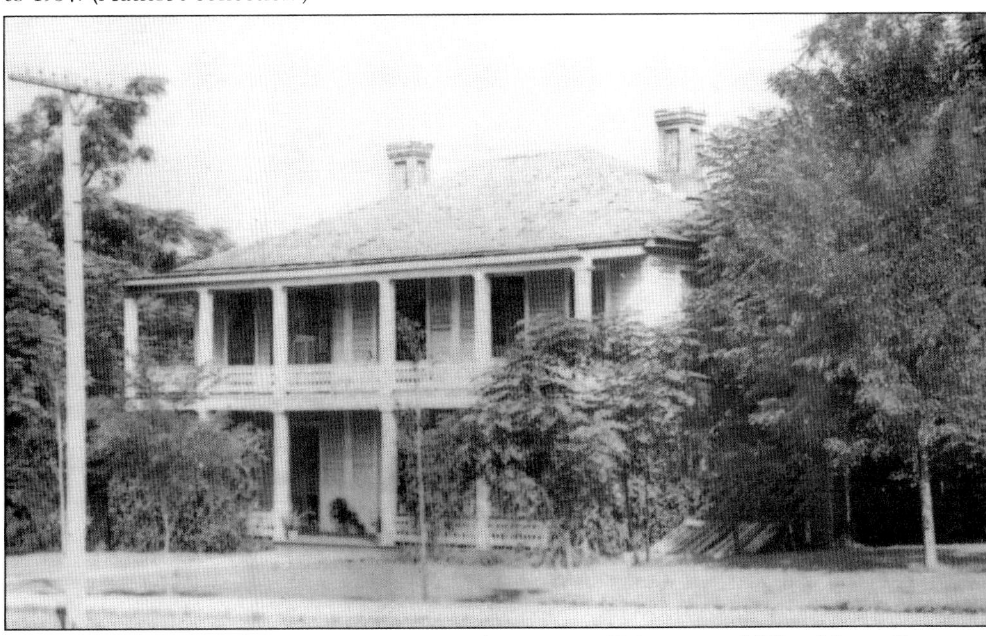

The Grigsby home stood for many years on the corner of Monroe and West Union Streets in Minden. It was torn down to provide a new location for the local telephone company and was yet another of the grand residences of the 1800s that did not survive the 20th century. (Courtesy of LSU-Shreveport Archives and Special Collections, Noel Memorial Library.)

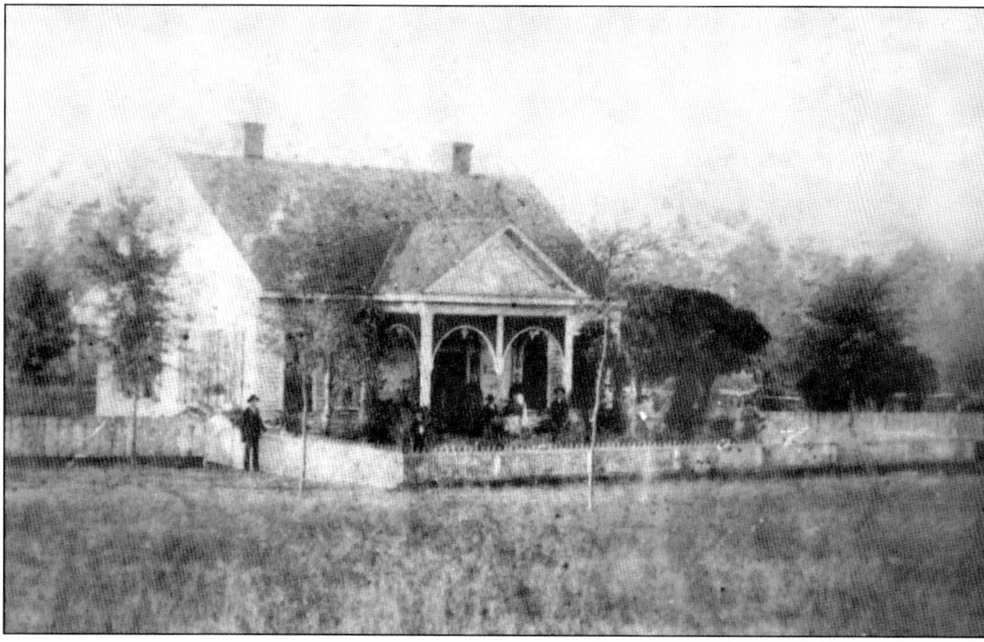

Originally built by Edward E. Bright of the Minden Female College, this residence was home to John Sidney Killen and his family from 1886 through his death in 1903. Killen was a civic, government, and religious leader in the community and a major landholder who immigrated to Louisiana on a wagon train in the 1840s. (Courtesy of LSU-Shreveport Archives and Special Collections, Noel Memorial Library.)

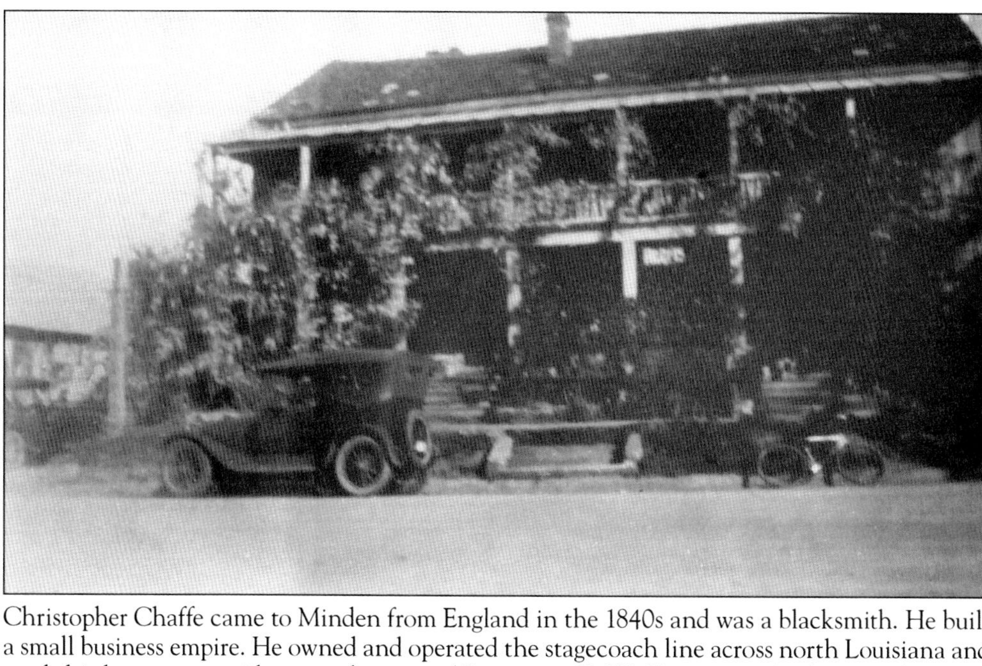

Christopher Chaffe came to Minden from England in the 1840s and was a blacksmith. He built a small business empire. He owned and operated the stagecoach line across north Louisiana and used this home as a residence and an inn. (Courtesy of LSU-Shreveport Archives and Special Collections, Noel Memorial Library.)

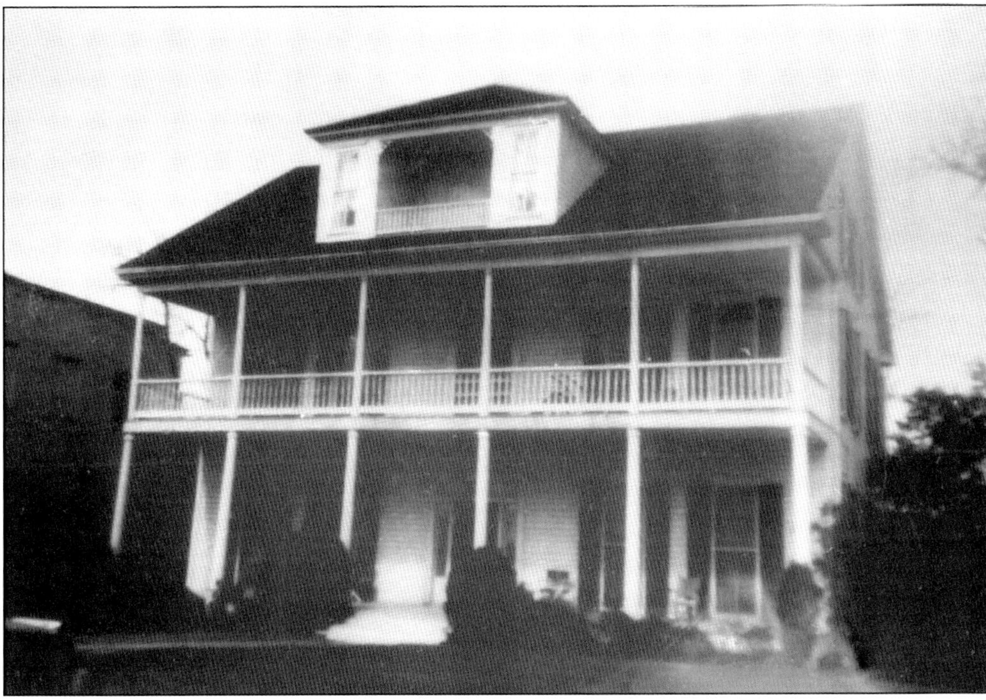

This Chaffe family home, located across Main Street from the inn, was the home of his daughter Treeby, who became the wife of R.H. Miller, a prominent Minden businessman and leader in civic and educational affairs. (Courtesy of LSU-Shreveport Archives and Special Collections, Noel Memorial Library.)

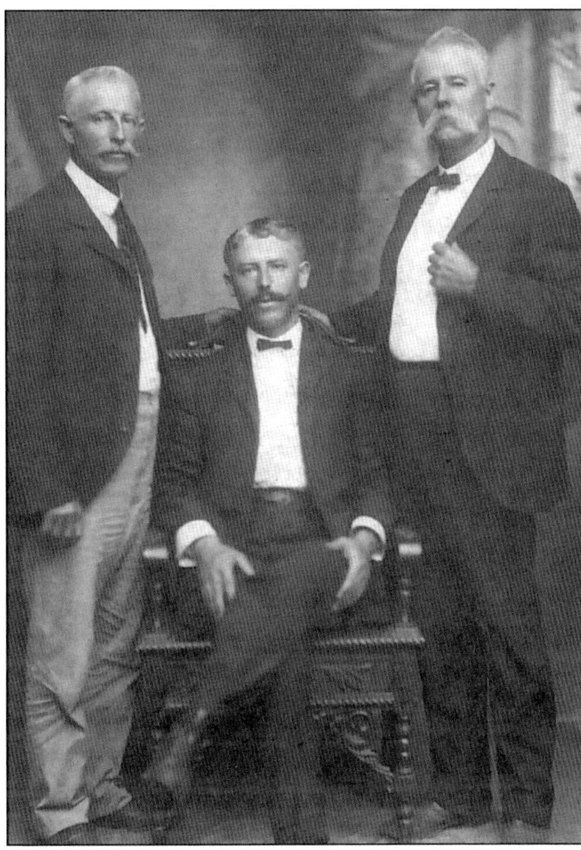

Seated is business and civic leader B.F. Griffith Minden, flanked on each side by his brothers. Griffith served as Webster Parish sheriff from 1900 to 1908 and was founder of the Webster Parish Fair. Today, the town baseball park, Griffith Stadium, bears his name. (Courtesy of Frank Griffith.)

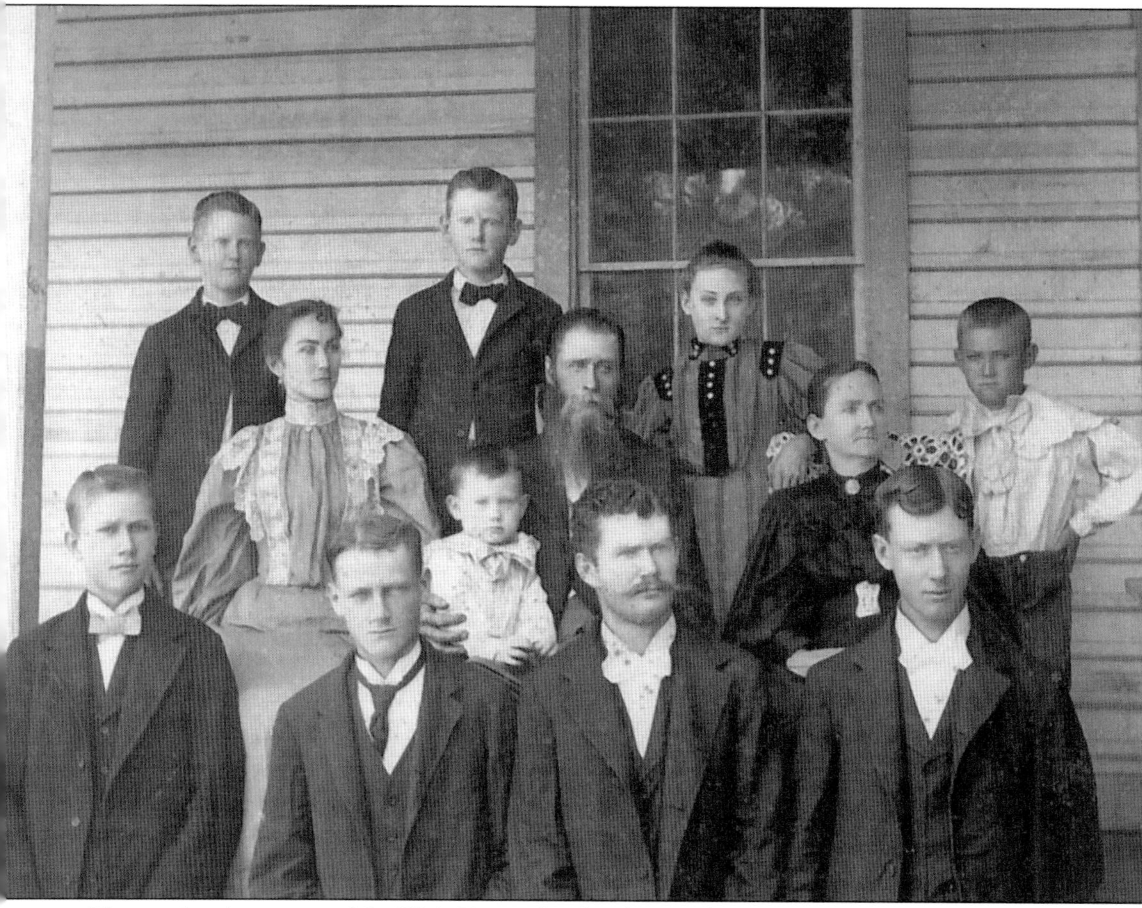

This is a family portrait of the W.A. Turner family taken in the 1890s; Turner married a daughter of John Sidney Killen, whose home is pictured on page 58. Family members are, from left to right, (first row) Elva Turner, Penn Turner, June Turner, and Blackshire Turner; (second row) Lola Turner, W.A. Turner, Phares Turner (on knee), Emma Killen Turner, and John Turner; (third row) Sidney Turner, Bobby Turner, and Effie Turner. The Turner family served the local community in many ways, as the family's timber-related businesses touched many in Minden. The family also provided the land where today's E.S. Richardson Elementary School is located. They were also leaders in religion and teachers and administrators in the schools. The Turner descendants are still active today in Minden, particularly in the field of education. (Courtesy of George Turner.)

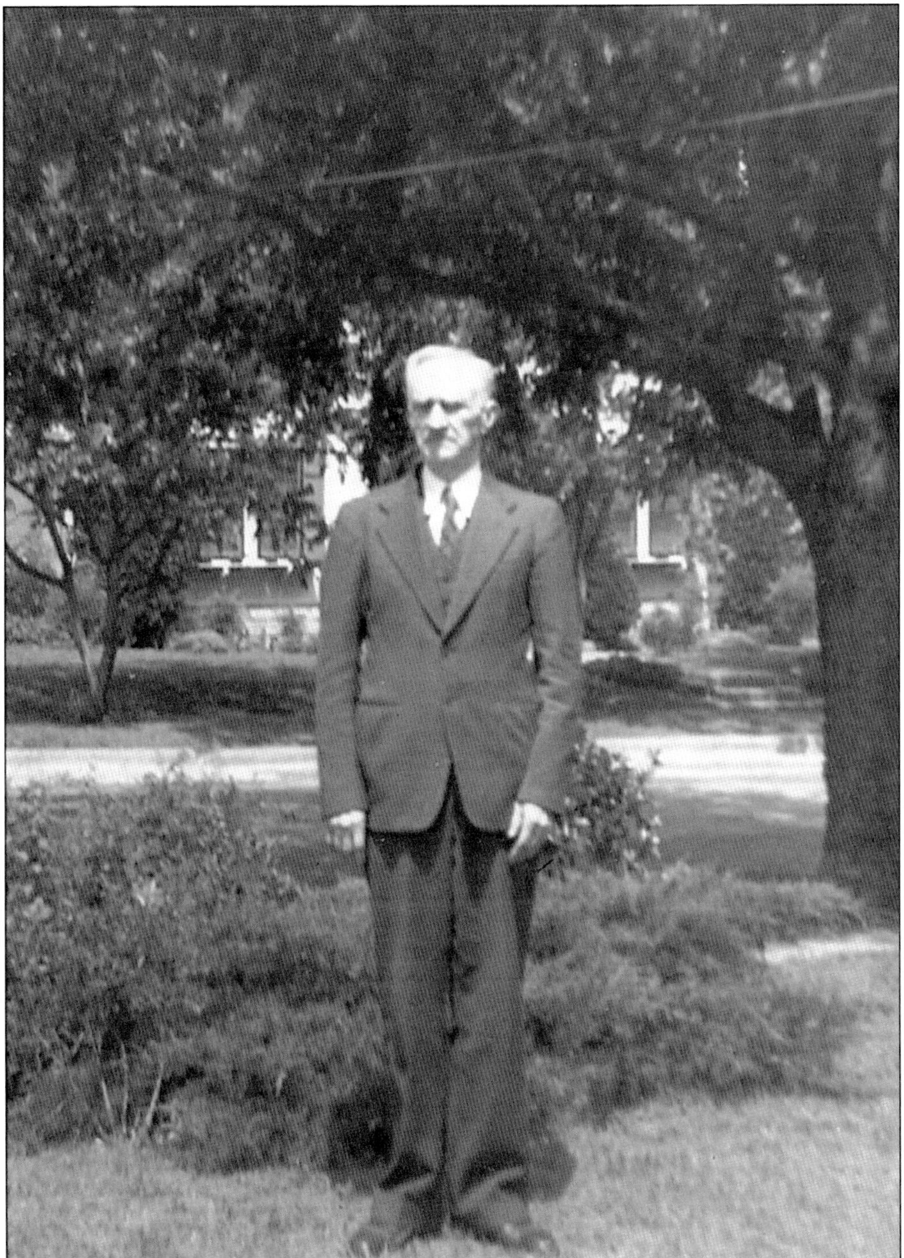

This book is titled *Lost Minden*, and much has been lost. However, without the work of two individuals, so much more of the town's legacy would have been gone. The first is Dr. Luther Longino, who was born in the 1850s and on the local scene for nearly 100 years. His earliest published writing was an account of a stagecoach journey across North Louisiana during the 1870s. Beyond his work as a physician, he served as parish health officer and a cotton investor. After the town of Minden banned wooden structures in downtown in 1902, he erected several brick commercial buildings that are still in use today. He wrote newspaper columns and books and left a lasting record of both the life he lived and the stories he was told. At 92, shortly before his death, he launched a campaign to bring a museum to Minden. (Author's collection.)

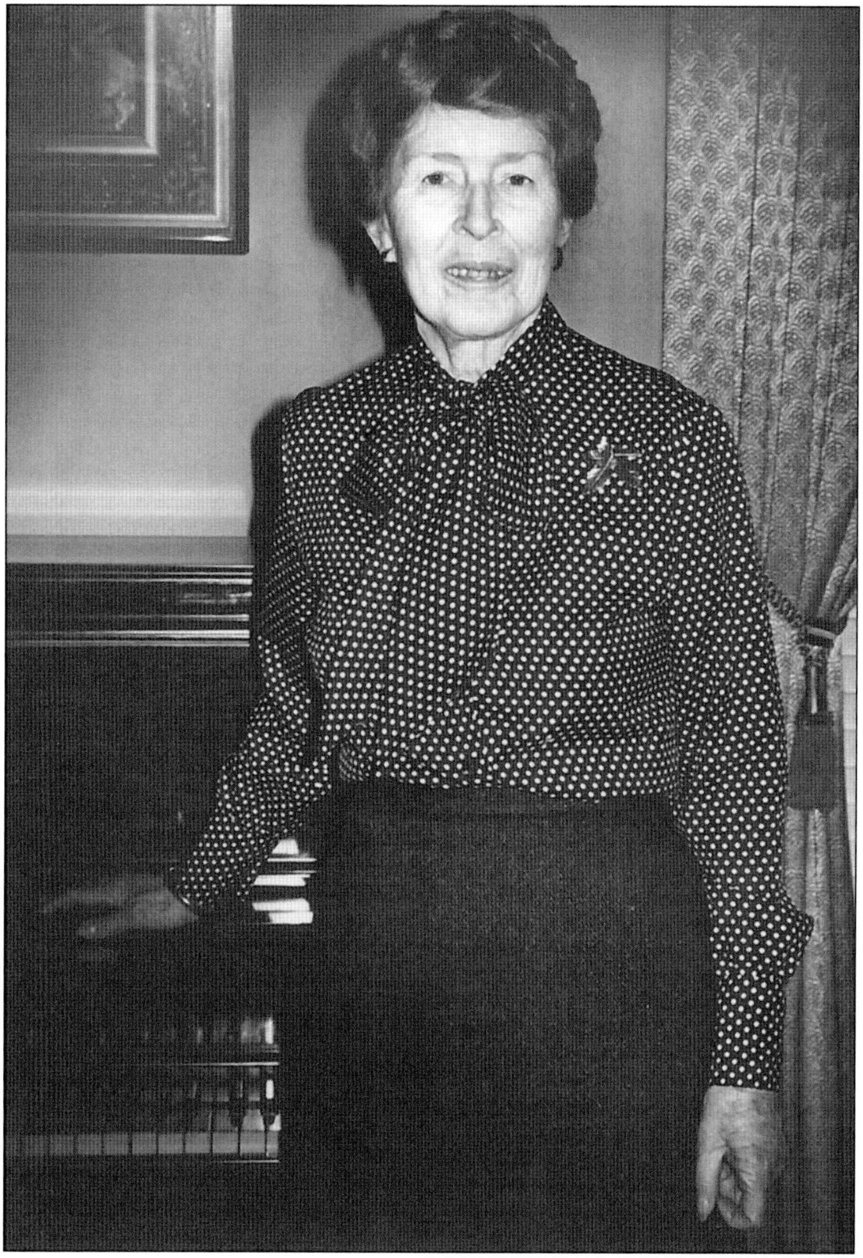

The second preservationist is Thomas Lorraine Campbell. A native of Missouri, she came to Minden around 1940 with her husband, Dr. Paul Campbell, and adopted Minden as her home, while the community adopted her as its record keeper. She chronicled so many stories of Minden, and through her many newspaper articles and journal publications, she saved the town's heritage. She was able to talk with and record the memories of students at the Minden Female College; of those who worked with the great industries that came to Minden, the Minden Lumber Mill, the L&A Railway, and the Louisiana Ordnance Plant; and of others who lived the history almost from the beginning. The recollections of those early settlers and pioneer families are a precious, priceless source of heritage for Minden. The Webster Parish Police Jury named her the first official parish historian. (Author's collection.)

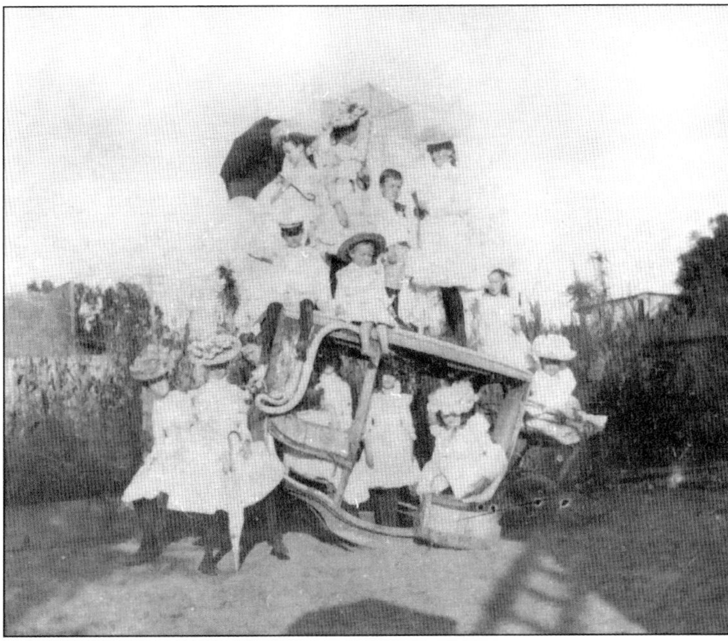

Recreation of all sorts was also a tradition in Minden. Here is a group of children gathered on one of Christopher Chaffe's stagecoaches. Clearly, the stagecoach had seen its better days and was no longer in use, except as a prop for pictures. This image dates from the 1880s. (Courtesy of LSU-Shreveport Archives and Special Collections, Noel Memorial Library.)

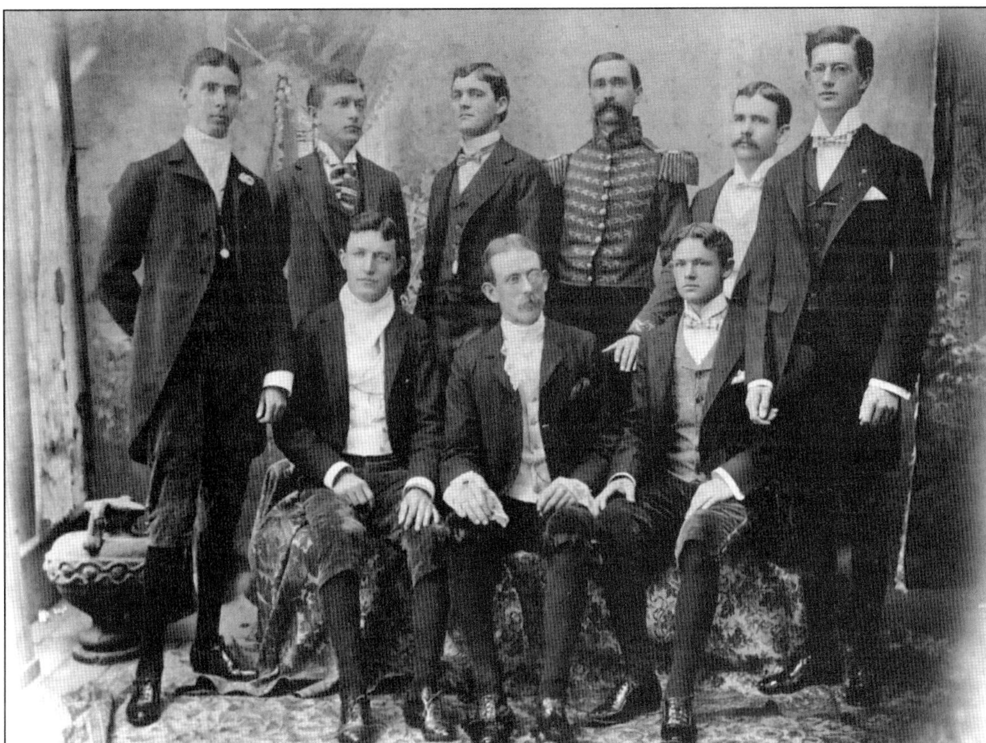

In the 1890s, a dance club called the German Club became the rage at colleges across the South. Minden's young men formed a local club. They loved to dress the part. The young man in the military coat with the impressive mustache is Connell Fort, who later served several terms as Minden's mayor. (Courtesy of LSU-Shreveport Archives and Special Collections, Noel Memorial Library.)

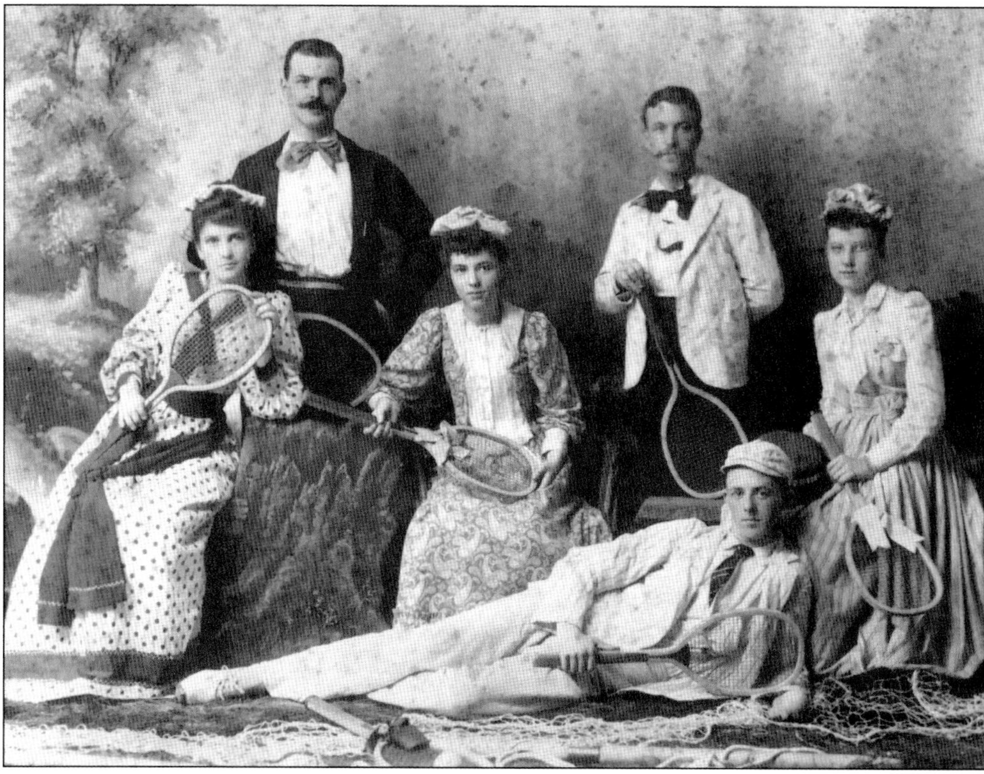

A group of young Minden folks is posing in a Dallas photograph studio as the Minden Tennis Club. While tennis was played in Minden at that time and these teens may have well played, the equipment simply consists of props provided by the photographer. (Courtesy of Thad Andress.)

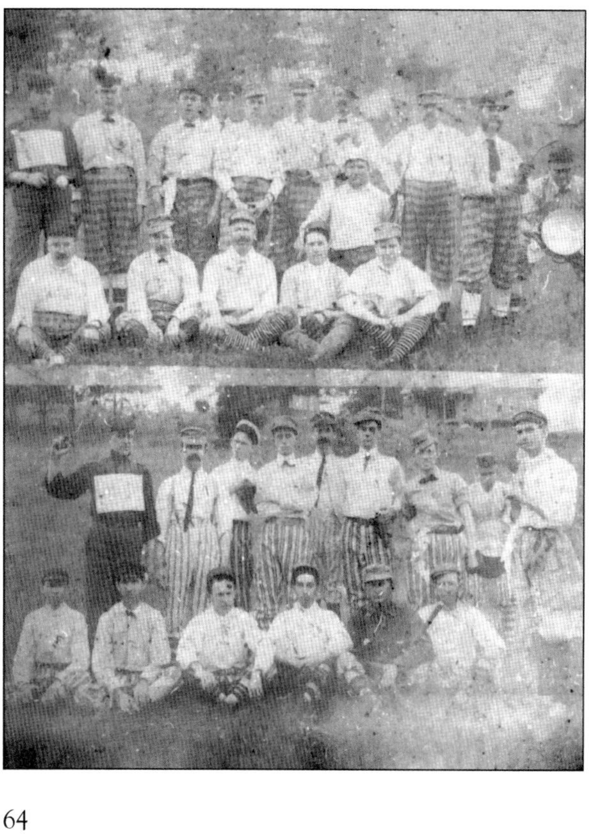

A summer tradition in Minden became the "Fats and Leans" baseball game. The men of the community would self-identify with one of the two teams, and they would meet at a town picnic with the proceeds used for civic improvements. (Courtesy of LSU-Shreveport Archives and Special Collections, Noel Memorial Library.)

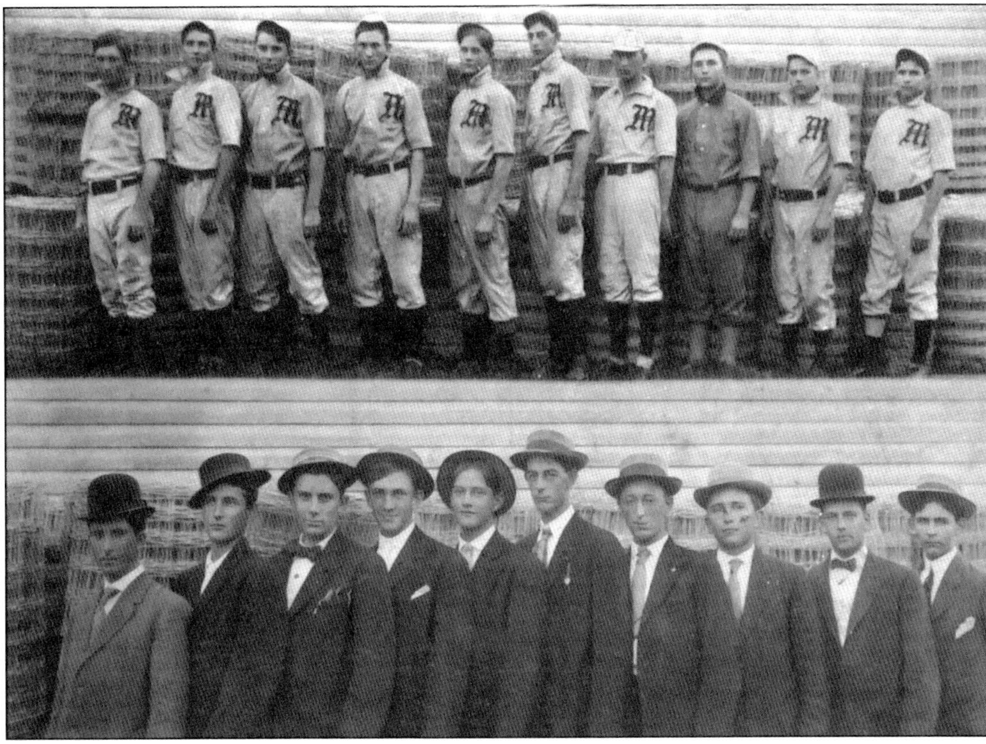

Baseball became a town passion, and town teams were formed at all age levels to compete with teams from nearby towns such as Homer. This is the Minden team from about 1904 shown in uniform and in "travelling clothes." (Courtesy of LSU-Shreveport Archives and Special Collections, Noel Memorial Library.)

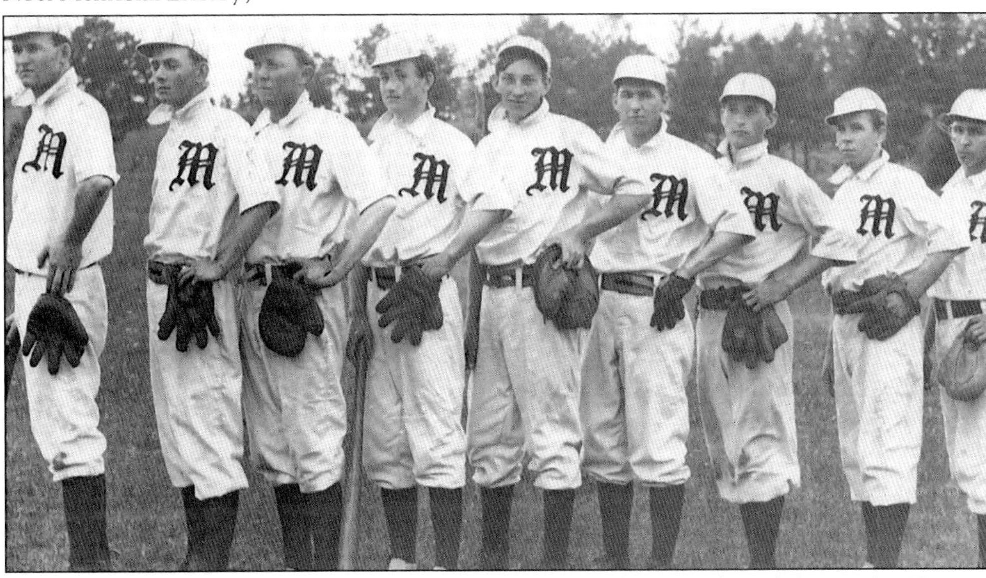

This image is the 1908 Minden town baseball team. Members are, from left to right, Harmon Drew, manager and second base; Alden Rathbun, shortstop; Tabor, first base; Caldwell Drew, outfield; Jack Hardeman, catcher; Norman McCrary, pitcher; Valmey Crichton, outfield; Watson Griffin, outfield; and Douglas Maddry, third base. (Author's collection.)

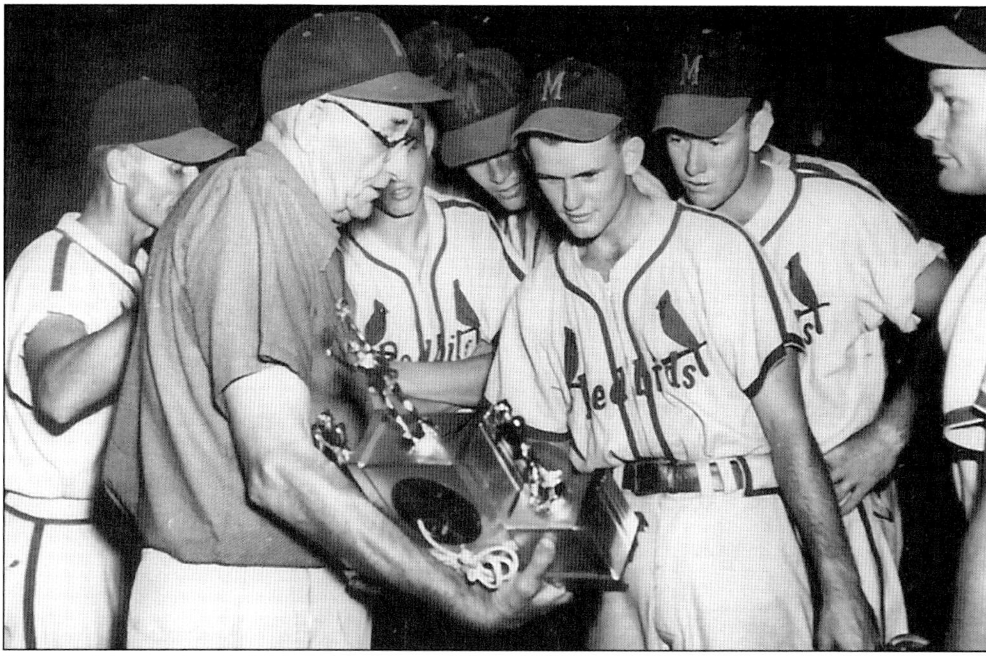

Semiprofessional baseball garnered a huge following in the Minden area in the years after World War II. The local team, the Minden Redbirds, was a traditional power in what was called the Big Eight League. Here is team manager T.C. Bloxom Sr. showing the championship trophy to players. (Courtesy of Ben Hunter.)

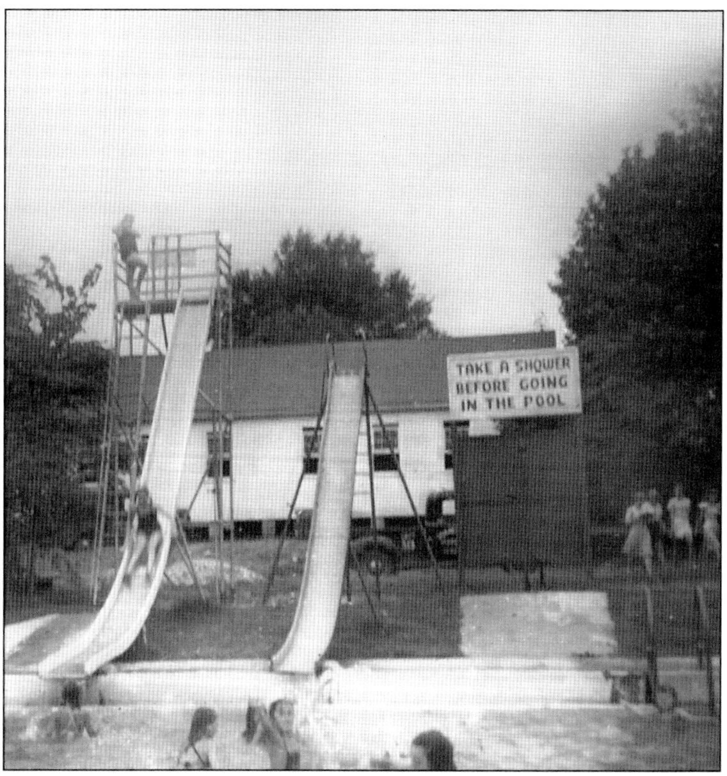

Beyond baseball, the sport of swimming moved from the banks of ponds and bayous into modern swimming facilities. Minden had a town natatorium as early as 1920, but this is an image of the pool at Hunter's playground, which was opened to children in Minden by the Hunter family. (Courtesy of LSU-Shreveport Archives and Special Collections, Noel Memorial Library.)

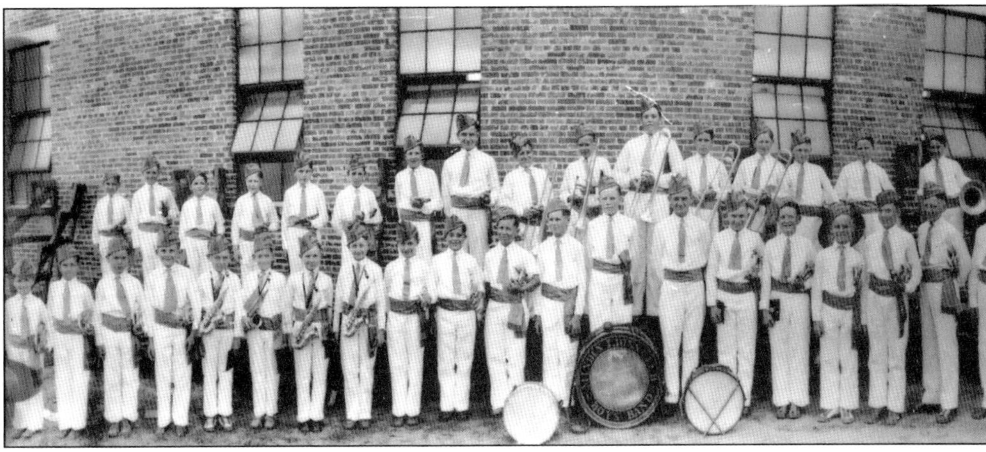

Minden traditionally had a town band for many years, but in the 1920s, the newly formed Minden Lions Club established the "Lions Boys Band." This group lasted for nearly two decades and provided a musical foundation for local youth. (Courtesy of LSU-Shreveport Archives and Special Collections, Noel Memorial Library.)

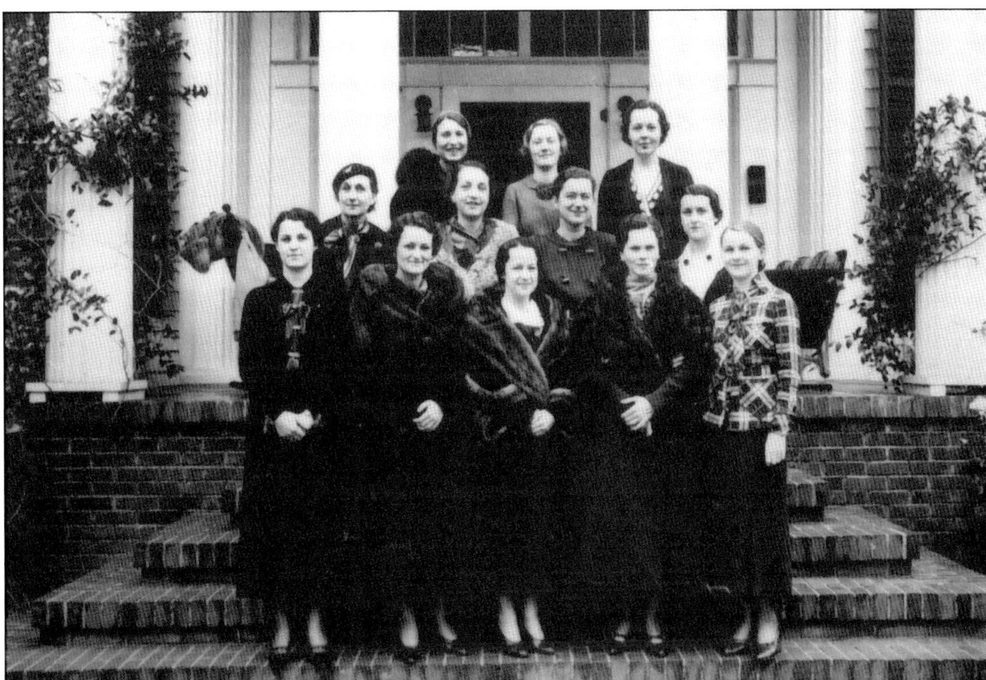

These ladies are the members of the Junior Service League of Minden during the mid-1930s. The club has a long history of contributions to the local community and, more than 80 years after it was first organized, is still benefitting Minden. (Courtesy of LSU-Shreveport Archives and Special Collections, Noel Memorial Library.)

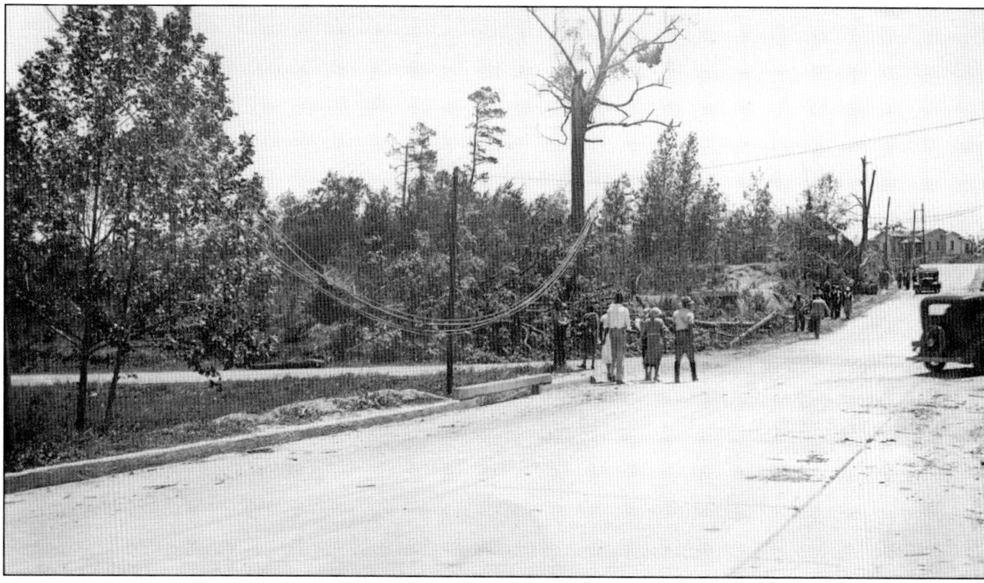

At about 4:00 p.m. on Monday, May 1, 1933, Minden was struck by a tornado estimated to be one of the most powerful in Louisiana history. At least 27 lives were lost, and the next few pictures will show some of the damage from the storm. (Courtesy of Craig Farley.)

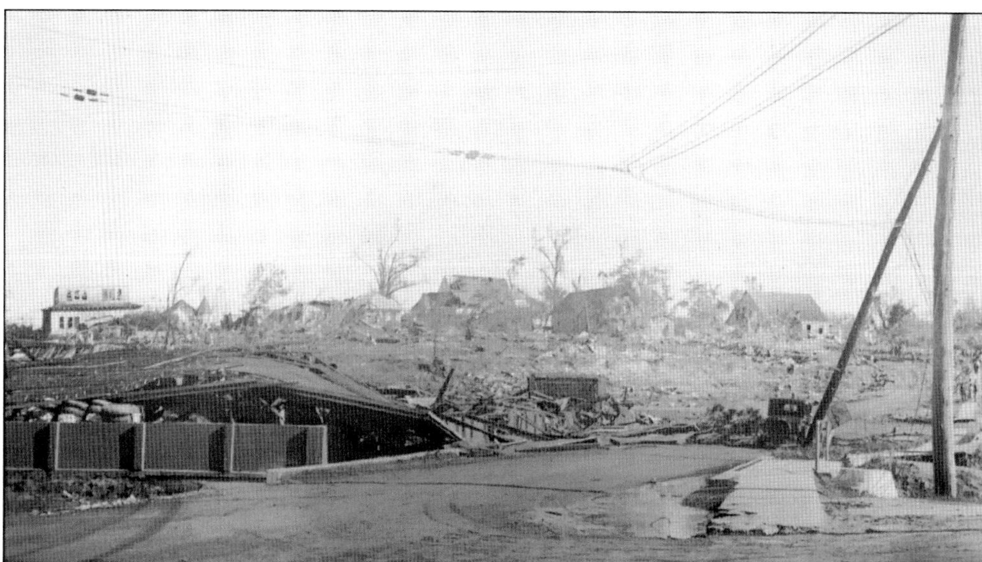

This was the view from the Sibley Road looking north toward Depot Hill after the 1933 tornado. The scope of damage is clear, as every structure has suffered severe trauma from the storm. (Courtesy of Craig Farley.)

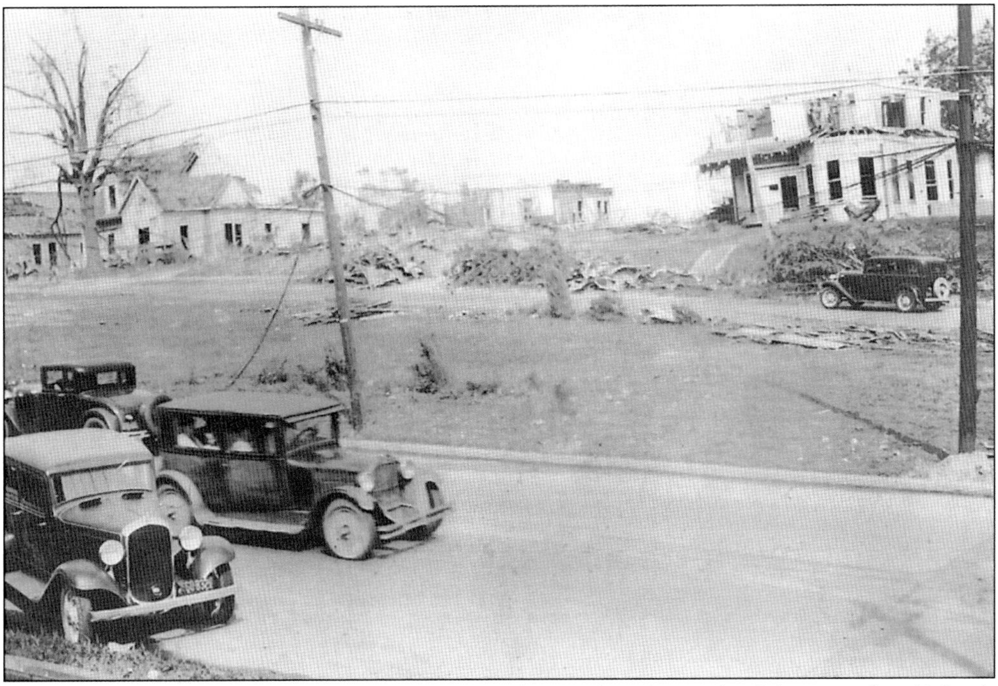

This is a panoramic image of Depot Hill in Minden in the aftermath of the tornado of May 1, 1933. Homes on this slope sustained severe damage along with the almost complete destruction of the headquarters of the L&A Railway. Some of the first fatalities from the storm were young girls attending a birthday party at a home on the hill. (Author's collection.)

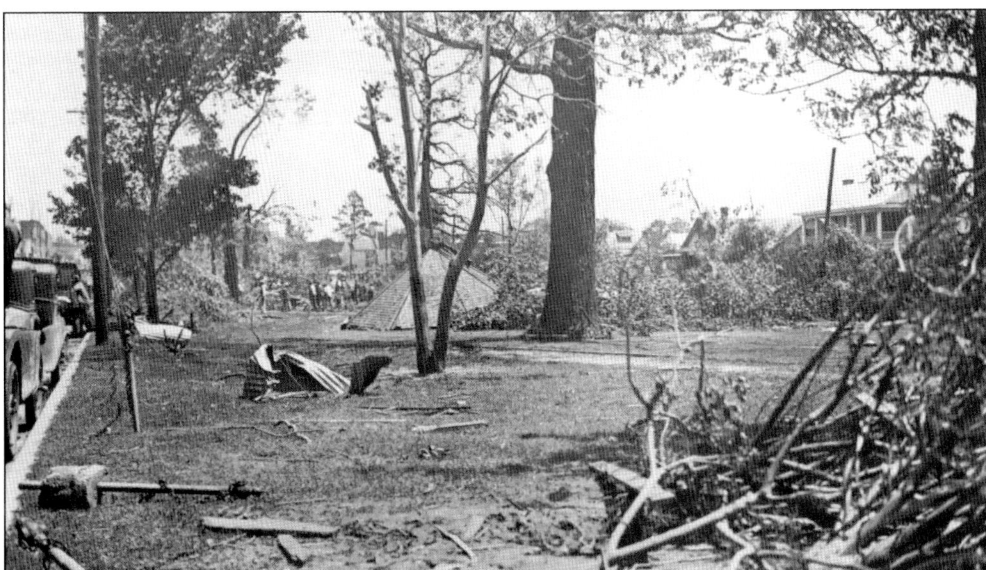

This is the wreckage of the bandstand/gazebo in Town Park in Minden after the tornado of May 1, 1933. The bandstand was a vital part of the community for many years and was rebuilt after the tornado. It was finally destroyed when the Town Park was traded to Webster Parish as the site for a new Webster Parish Courthouse. (Author's collection.)

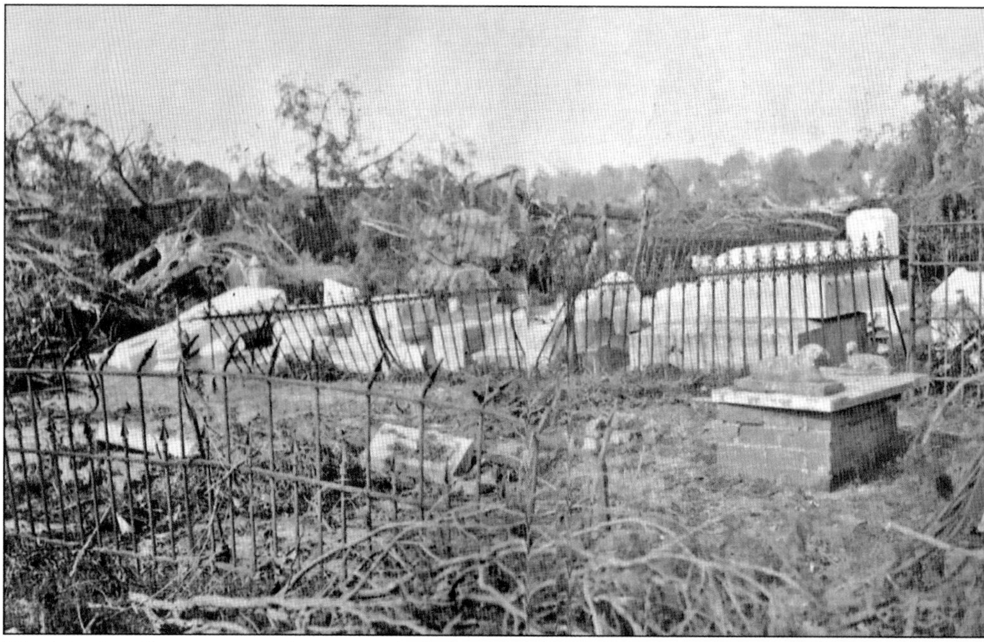

The Minden Cemetery was hit particularly hard by the May 1, 1933, tornado. This picture shows some of the wrecked family plots and destroyed trees in the cemetery. Many old, tall headstones were toppled, and even today, many graves remain unmarked after their markers were carried away in the storm. (Courtesy of Henry Hobbs.)

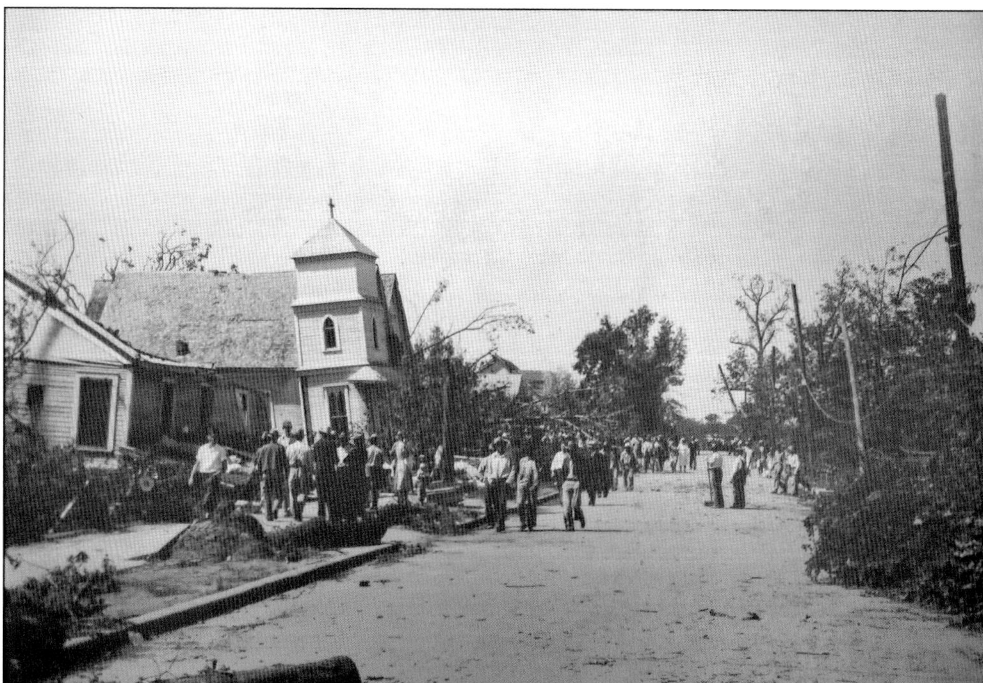

This view is looking west on Broadway (Back Street) after the 1933 tornado, with the wrecked St. Anne's Catholic Church visible on the left. Just to the right of this image was the Civic Park with its bandstand demolished and many trees toppled. (Author's collection.)

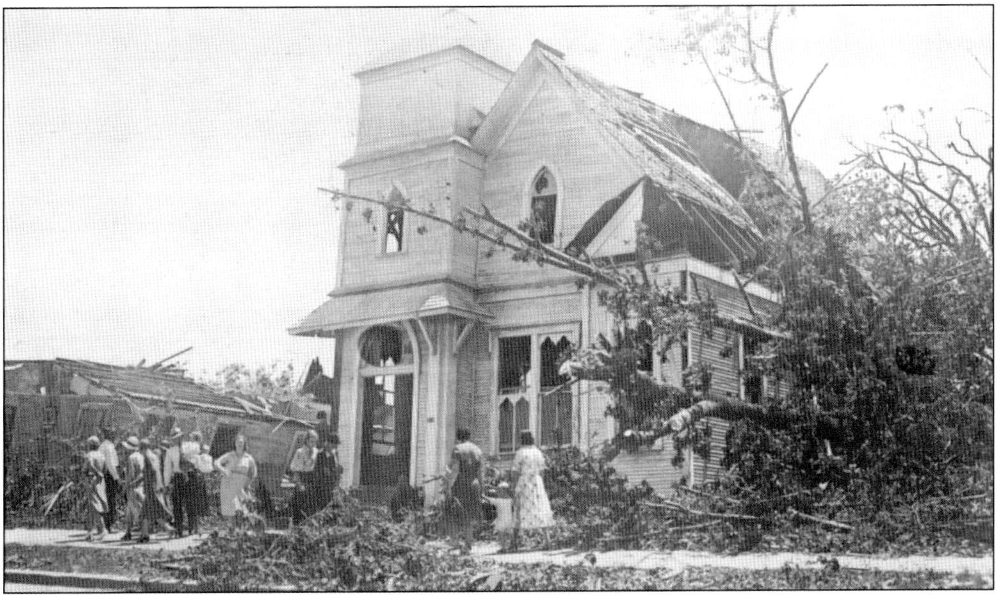

Among the amazing stories emerging from the storm was the statuary located inside St. Anne's Church. Despite the severe damage shown in these images, there were several delicate porcelain statues in the church that were left untouched by the storm. (Author's collection.)

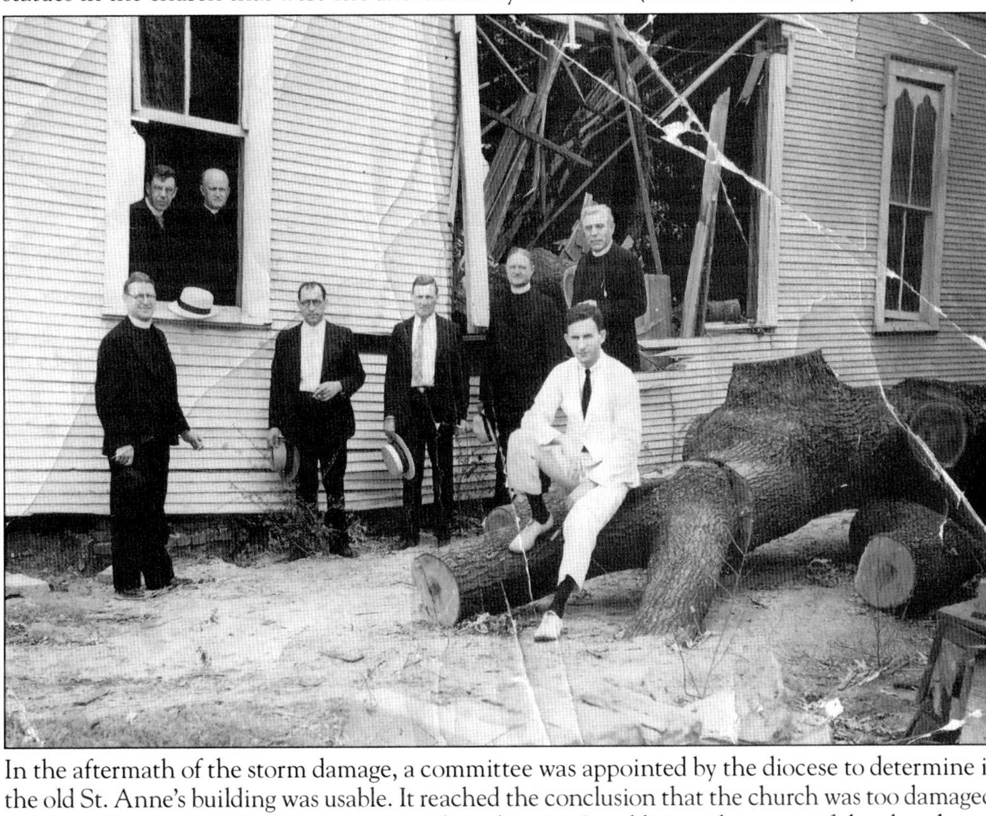

In the aftermath of the storm damage, a committee was appointed by the diocese to determine if the old St. Anne's building was usable. It reached the conclusion that the church was too damaged to use, and a new building was constructed on this site. In addition, the name of the church was changed from St. Anne's to St. Paul's. (Author's collection.)

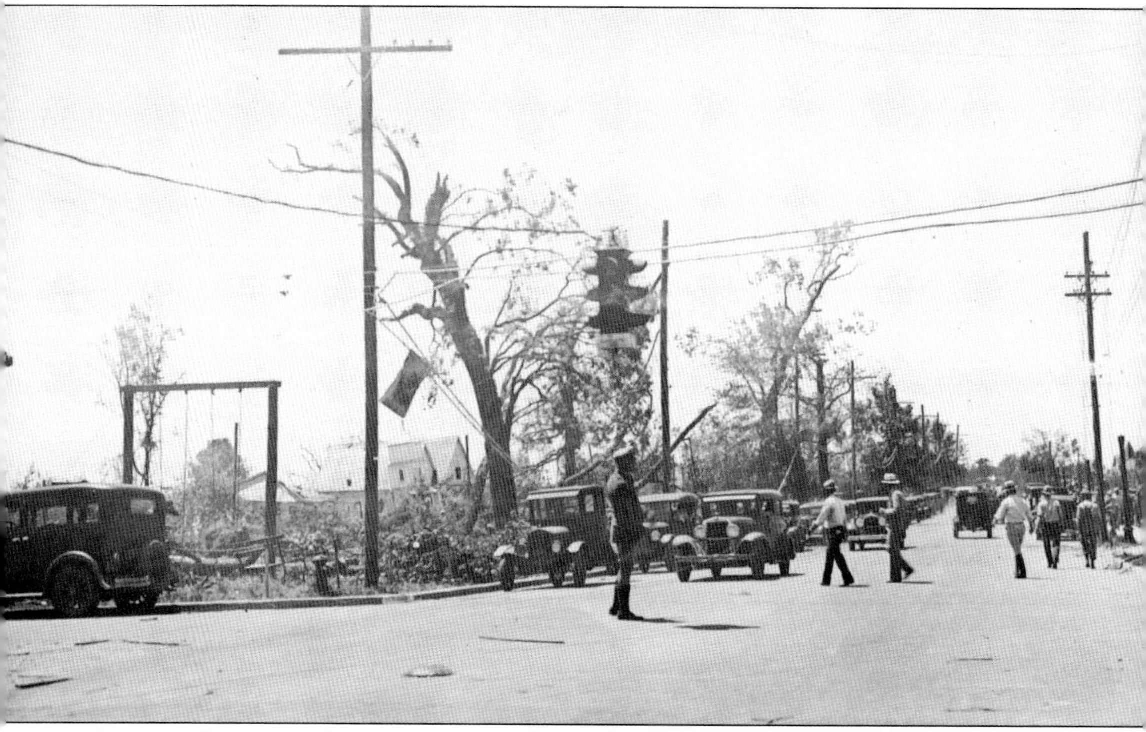

A state policeman is shown directing traffic at the intersection of Pine and Main Streets in Minden in the days after the 1933 tornado. The search for survivors took several days, and the local public safety officials were so overwhelmed that outside help, such as the National Guard and state police, was needed to keep order. Hit particularly hard by the storm were the black areas of Minden; because many of those homes were not well built, the area was largely flattened. The sheer amount of damage in those areas has led to speculation that the death count was actually much higher than the official estimate of 27. When bodies were found days after the storm, it often did not make sense to families to take them to the makeshift morgue to be counted. They simply buried their own dead. (Courtesy of Craig Farley.)

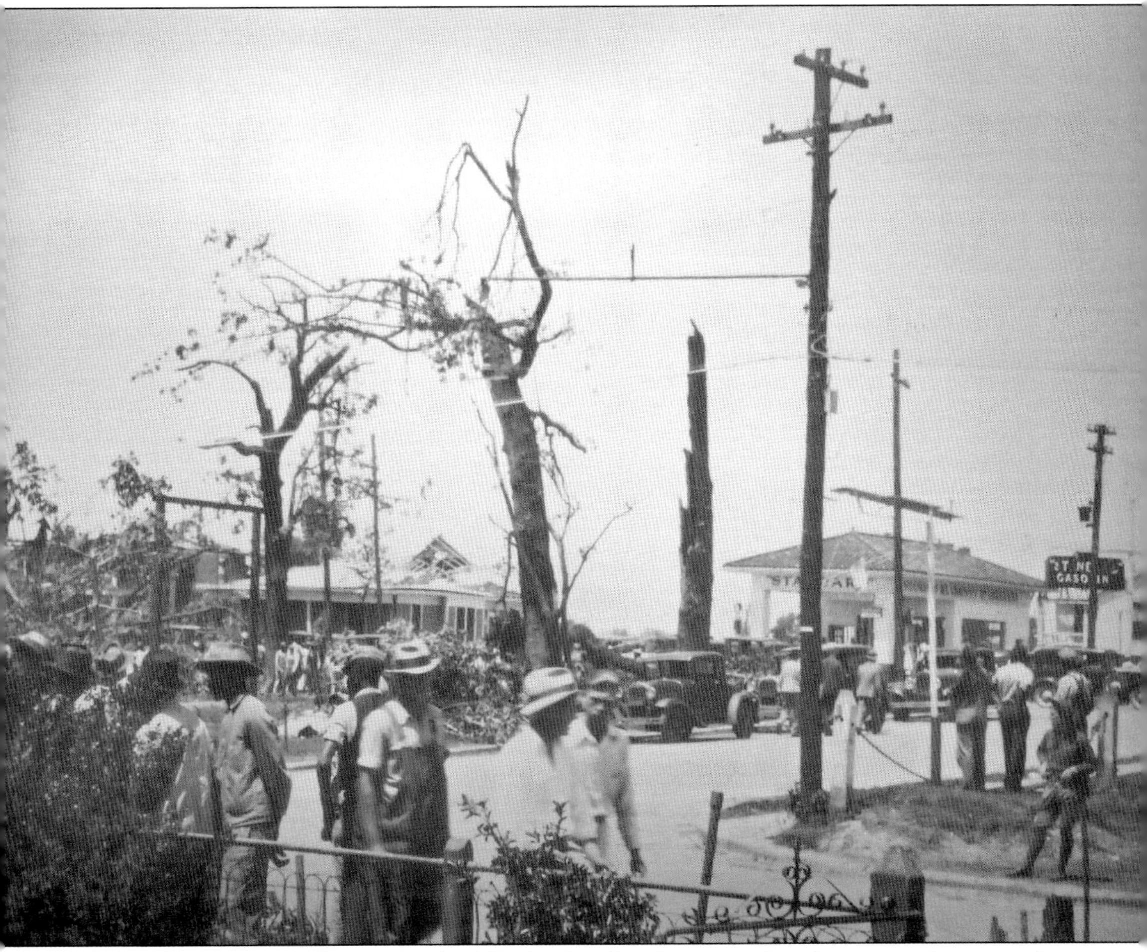

Taken in downtown Minden on May 2, 1933, the day after the storm, this photograph shows people surveying the damage to Town Park, in a view looking east toward the Standard Oil gasoline station on the corner of Main and Pine Streets. This was about the eastern edge of the damage in downtown Minden. Though the destruction to the community by the tornado was severe, a shift of the storm two blocks to the east would have caused it to hit the downtown business district on a workday afternoon. Without a doubt, the amount of property damage would have been greater, and more lives would likely have been lost. The winds did damage to the already compromised dome of the Webster Parish Courthouse, which had been scheduled for repairs that summer, forcing a replacement of that damaged structure instead of a simple renovation. (Author's collection.)

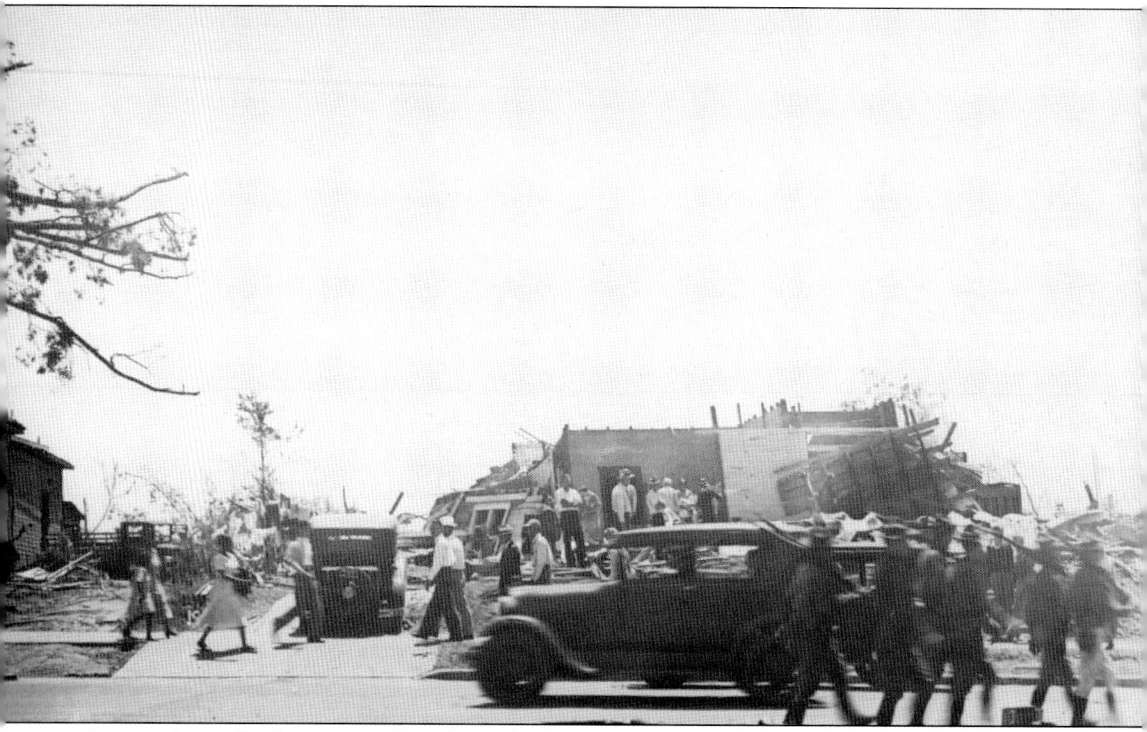

Troops from the Louisiana Guard are shown marching in Minden in the aftermath of the tornado of May 1, 1933. Because of the damage and the influx of sightseers coming to the town, the troops remained in town serving police functions for several days after the storm. Local Boy Scout troops and private citizens combed the wreckage for bodies, and the schools were closed for the remainder of the school year. Property damage totaled more than $1 million, and though only 27 bodies were brought to the official morgue, the estimated death total has been suggested to approach 80. Coming after a major fire and a bank failure earlier in the year and followed by a rain that destroyed the year's cotton crop, the tornado of 1933 is remembered as the worst event of the most tragic year in Minden's history. (Courtesy of Craig Farley.)

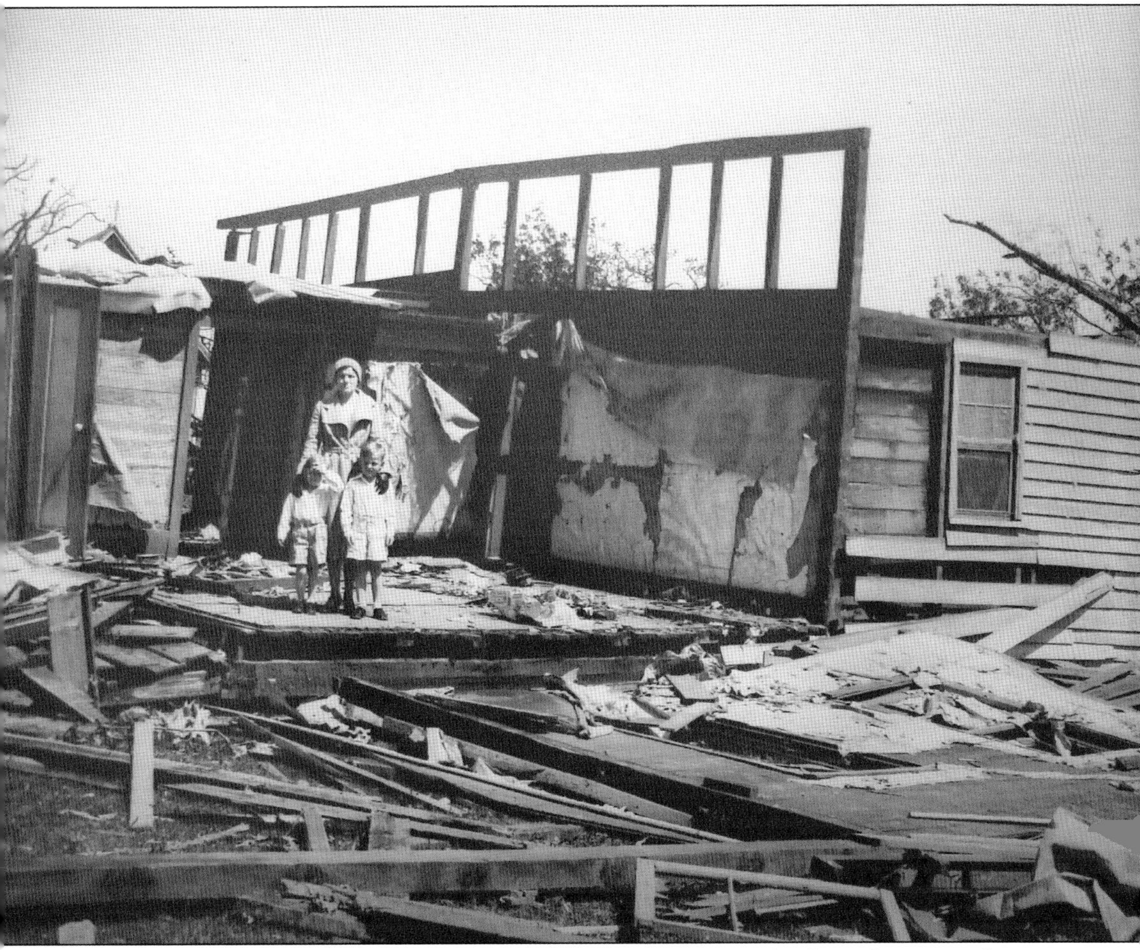

Maggie (Mrs. John) McCowen, with her two sons, John Jr. (right) and Billy, is shown standing in the wreckage of her home destroyed by the May 1, 1933, tornado. John McCowen Jr. would grow up to be a local merchant and serve many years on the Minden City Council during the 1950s and 1960s, while Billy McCowen would also grow up to be a local businessman. The McCowen family lived in a residential area close to the L&A Railway shops along the Sibley Road going south out of downtown Minden. While the damage to the McCowen home was more severe than most, many tales of strange, less tragic, happenings during the storm emerged from this neighborhood. These included accounts of cows being carried through the air and homes being turned to face in a different direction on their foundations. (Courtesy of Meg McCowen.)

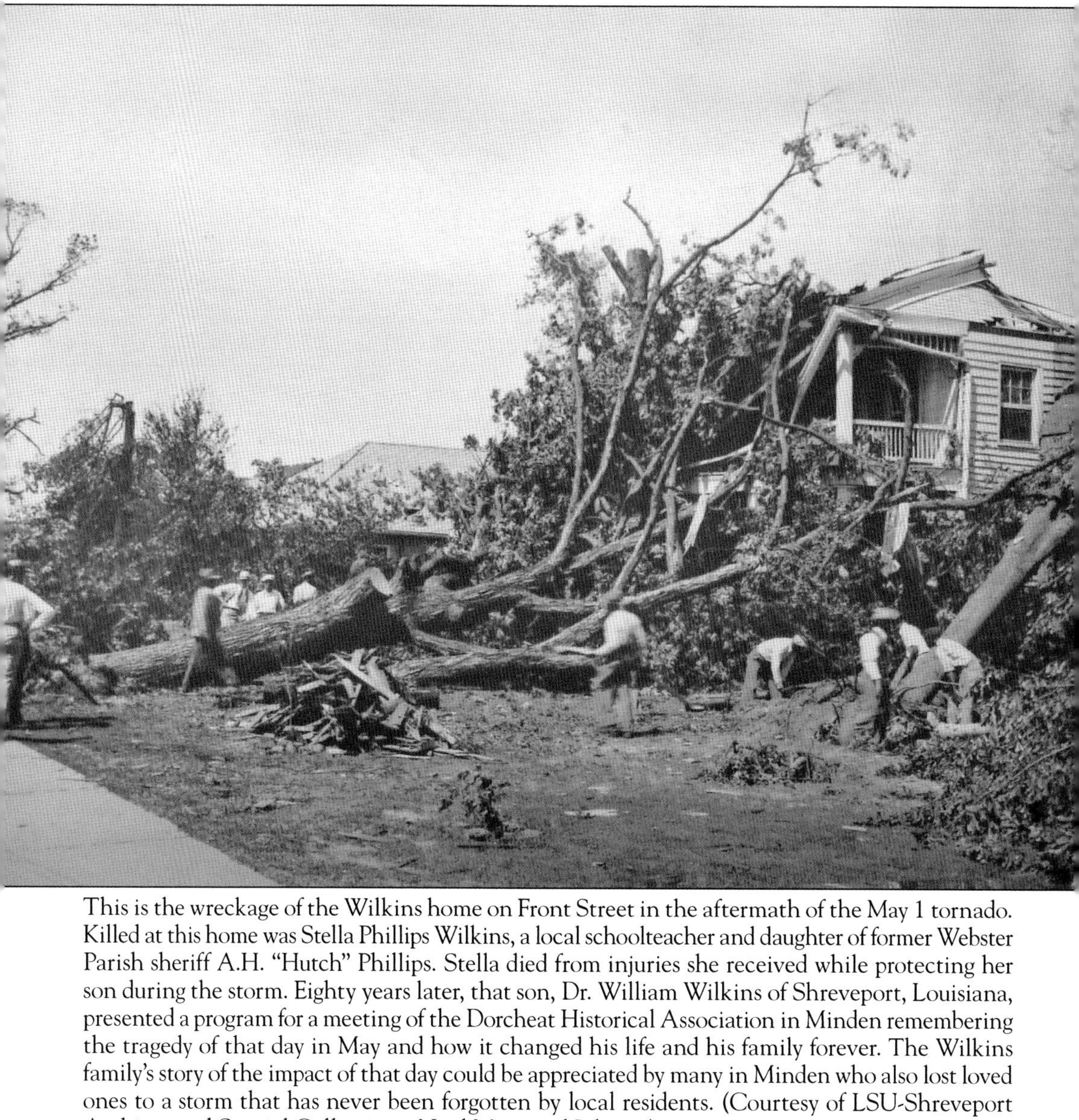

This is the wreckage of the Wilkins home on Front Street in the aftermath of the May 1 tornado. Killed at this home was Stella Phillips Wilkins, a local schoolteacher and daughter of former Webster Parish sheriff A.H. "Hutch" Phillips. Stella died from injuries she received while protecting her son during the storm. Eighty years later, that son, Dr. William Wilkins of Shreveport, Louisiana, presented a program for a meeting of the Dorcheat Historical Association in Minden remembering the tragedy of that day in May and how it changed his life and his family forever. The Wilkins family's story of the impact of that day could be appreciated by many in Minden who also lost loved ones to a storm that has never been forgotten by local residents. (Courtesy of LSU-Shreveport Archives and Special Collections, Noel Memorial Library.)

Three

Erecting a Building for Academic Purposes

Education and Government

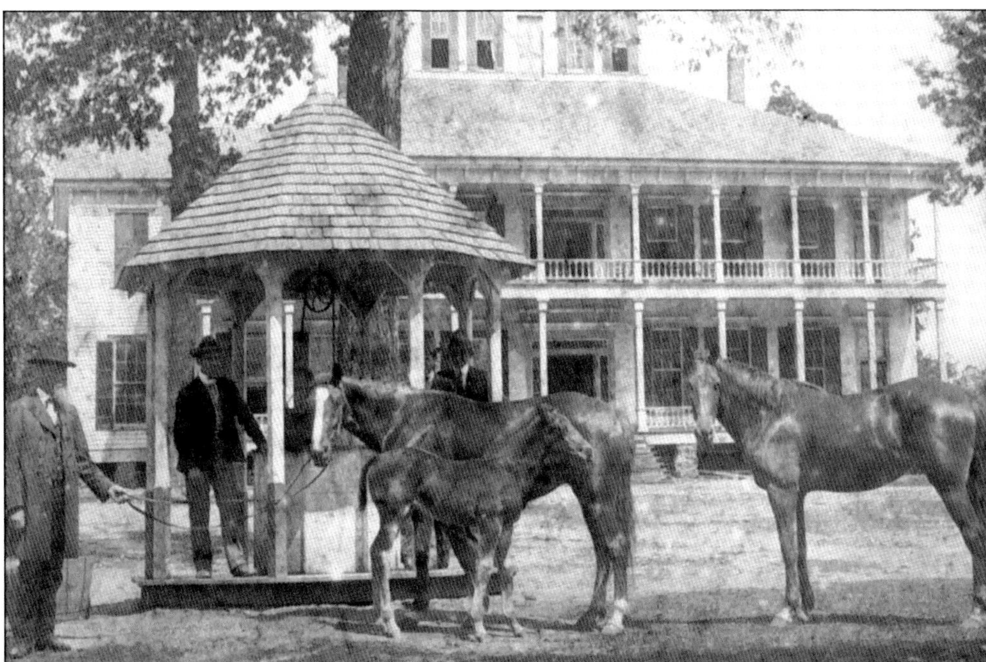

Opened in 1850 as a successor to the Minden Academy on property donated by W.A. Drake, the Minden Male Academy operated for more than 50 years before closing in 1901. The buildings were sold to the city, and the site became the present-day Academy Park. (Author's collection.)

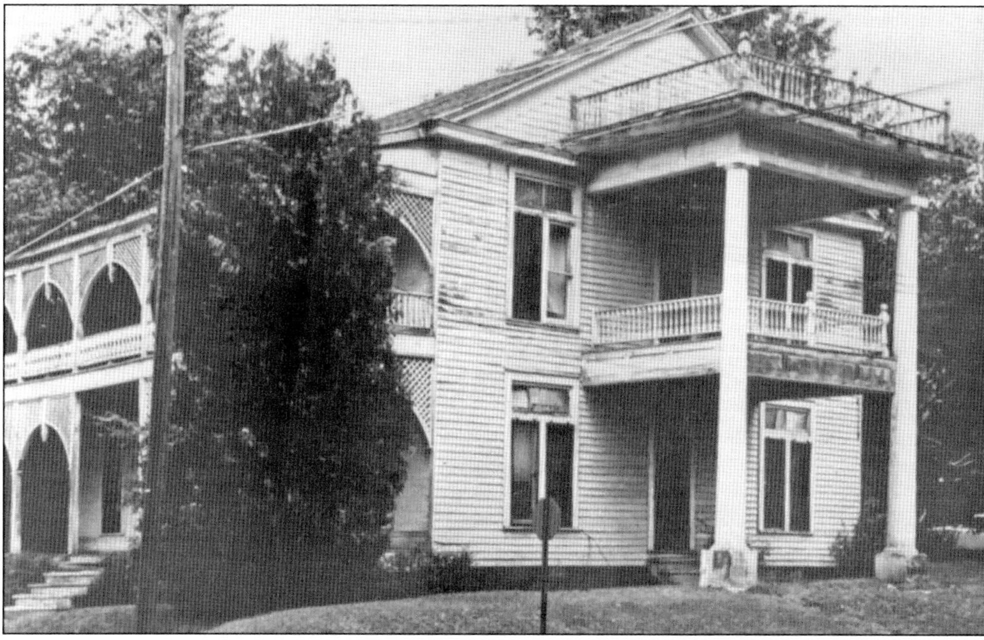

After the Minden Male Academy closed, Congressman John T. Watkins, whose father had been president of the school, purchased the main building from the city. The congressman moved the building about one block to this location where it lived out its life as a home and later apartment building. (Author's collection.)

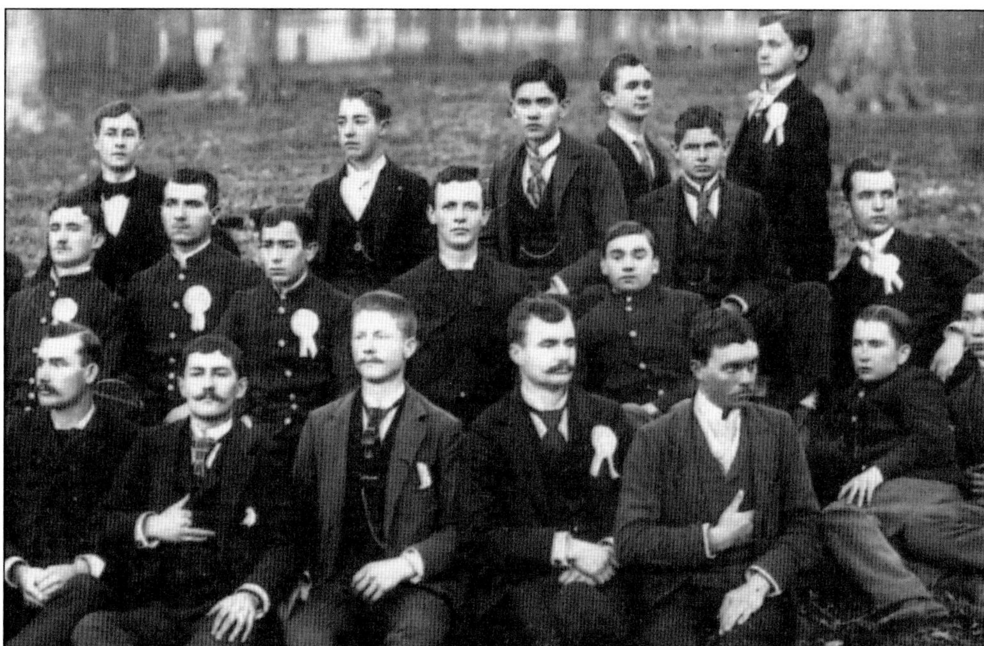

Here are the students of the Male Academy in an image taken in the 1880s. Most of the local community leaders of those years were graduates of the school. Included among them were Congressman Watkins and his brother Lynn K. Watkins, who served on the Louisiana State Court of Appeals. (Author's collection.)

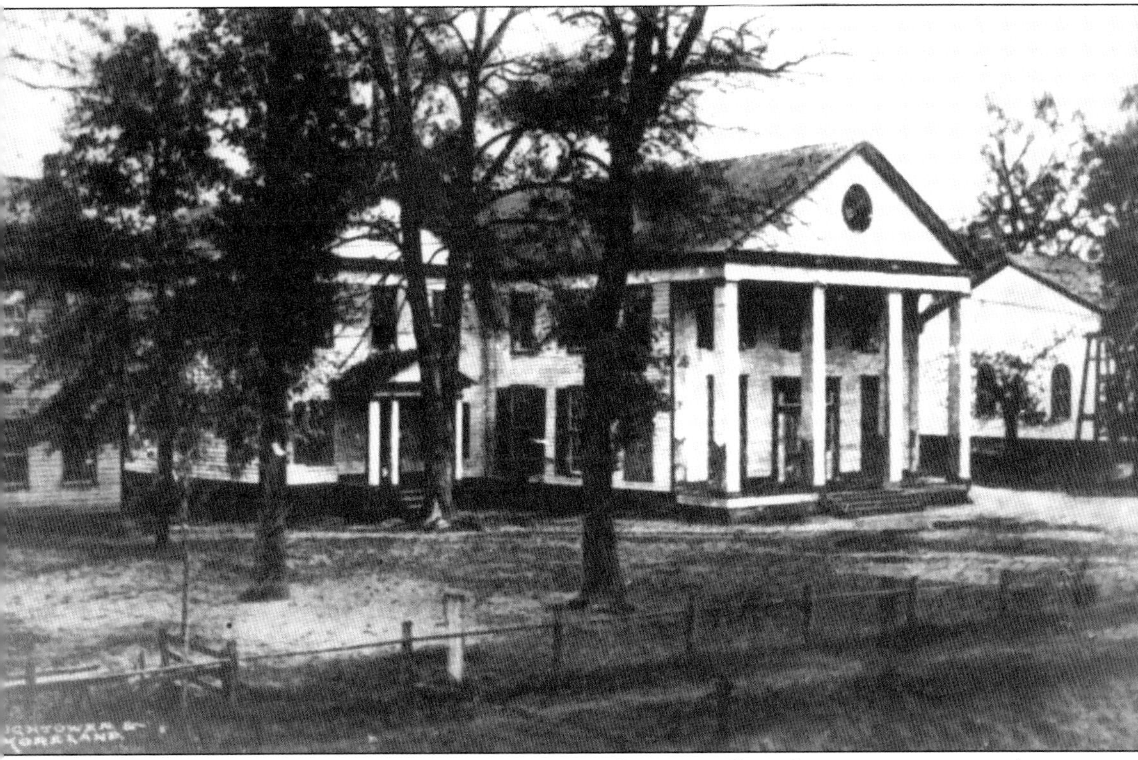

At the same time the Minden Male Academy opened, a new college for women was created in Minden in cooperation with the Presbyterian Church. The Minden Female College would offer a high-quality education in the arts and sciences to students from all across the Mid-South for more than four decades. The school managed to survive the trauma of the Civil War and remained a successful enterprise until the economic downturn of the mid-1890s. The college buildings were used for most important civic meetings and some statewide events. After the college closed, the facilities were used as the home of Minden's new public school when it was opened in 1900. The old college served that purpose for a decade until most of the buildings were destroyed in 1910 after the new high school was completed. (Courtesy of LSU-Shreveport Archives and Special Collections, Noel Memorial Library.)

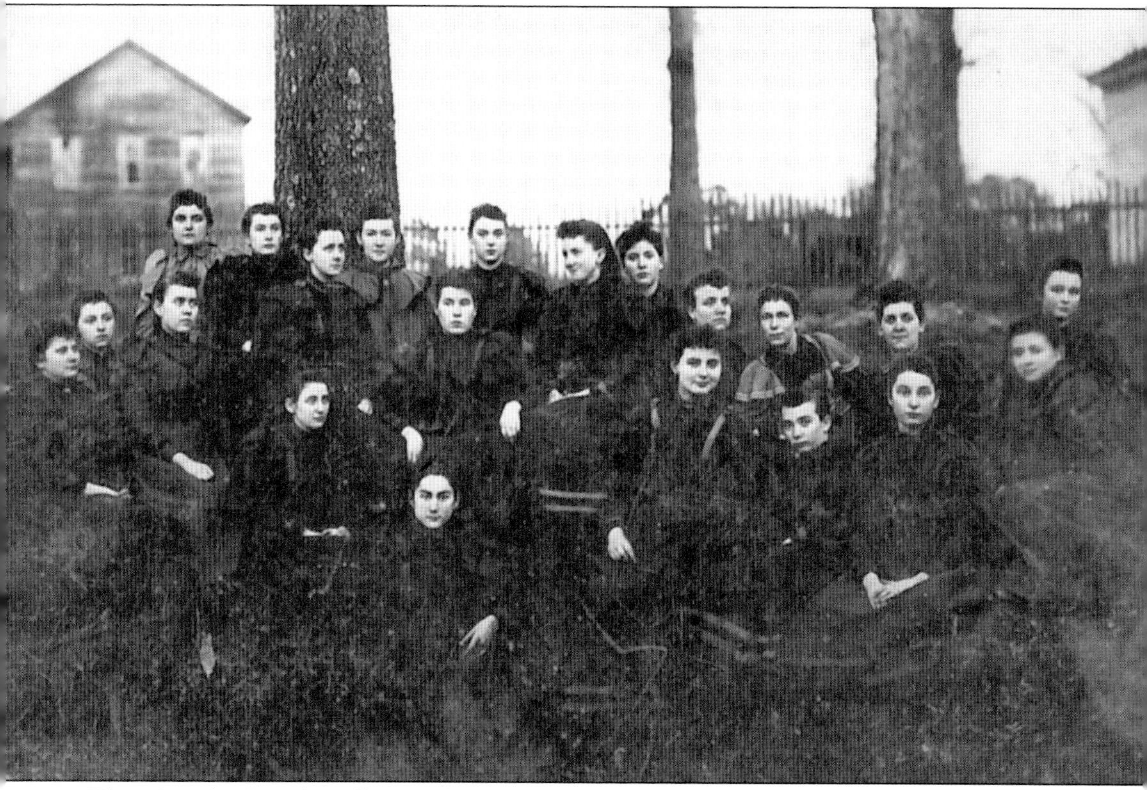

These Minden Female College students were photographed at the same time as the earlier image of the Minden Male Academy students. The two schools were not affiliated in any way, and the campuses were about a half mile apart, so it seems likely a visiting photographer stopped at both schools while in town and posed the respective students bodies at a location of his choice. The presence of two schools has often led to confusion in Minden, as the original site of the Minden Academy became the Female College and, even today, that property is the location of Minden High School. The Minden Male Academy was founded to the east of the Minden Female College, but many local residents do not realize the schools were separate entities under different boards. The Minden Female College ceased operation in the mid-1890s, while the Minden Male Academy lasted until 1900. (Author's collection.)

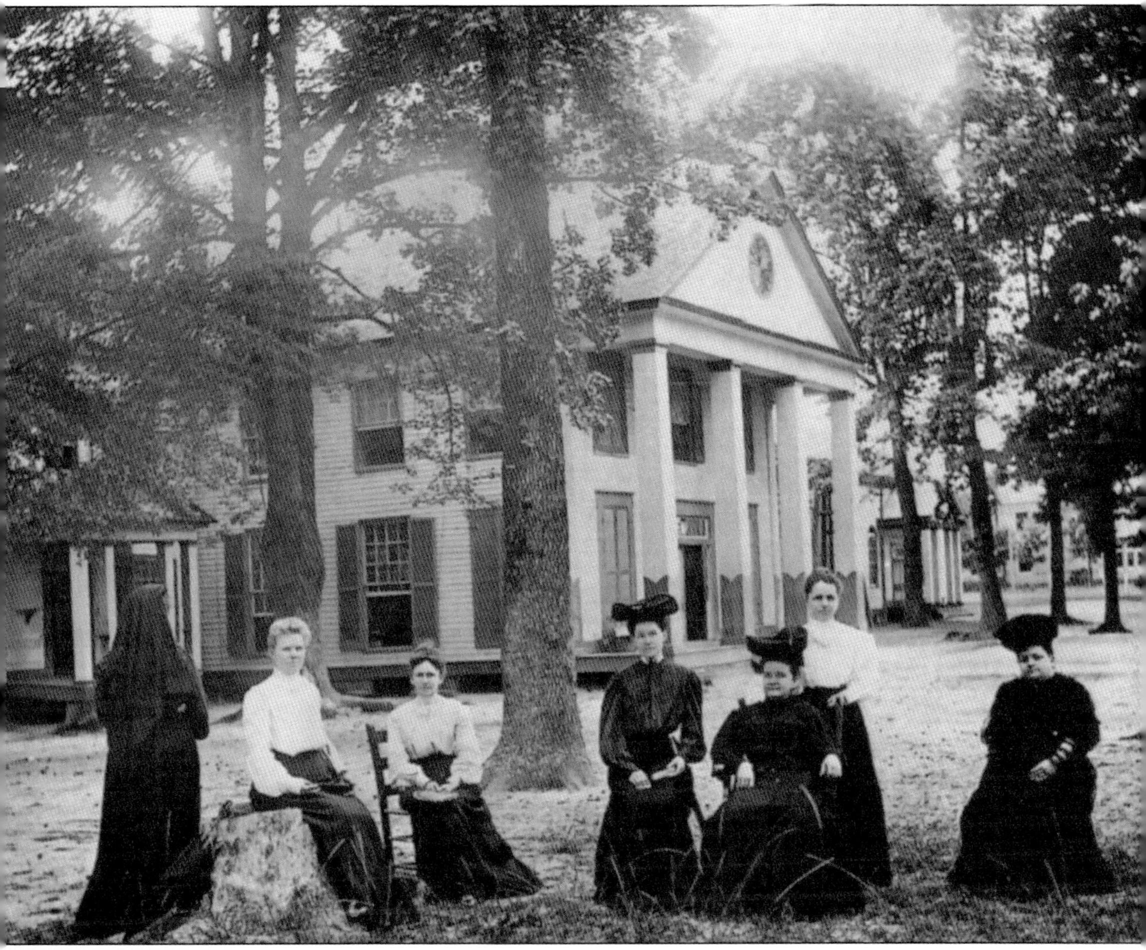

Pictured in the mid-1890s is a gathering of some Minden Female College alumnae. It is thought that these women are the graduates of the class of 1875 meeting on the 20th anniversary of their graduation. The lady at the far left, with her back to the camera, is Elizabeth Chaffe. Periodically, graduates would get together and remember their times on "College Hill," as the campus was known. The local newspapers would usually interview some of these ladies and give a glimpse back at a very different time in Minden and in this nation. The quality of education provided for women at the Minden Female College was somewhat amazing considering the status of women's education in most of the South. (Author's collection.)

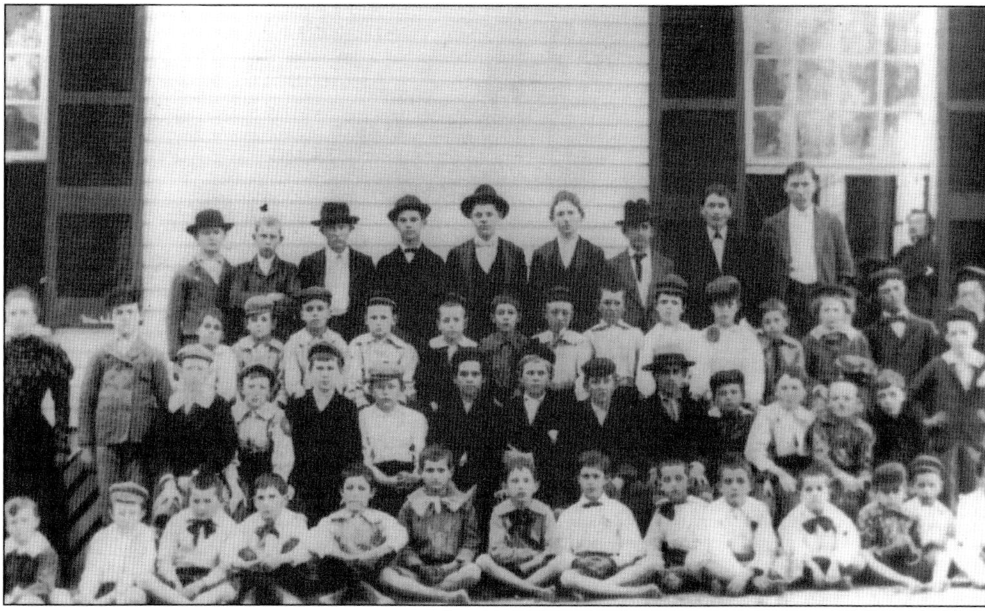

This is one of the last classes of the Minden Male Academy. The school closed after the passage of the Louisiana Constitution of 1898 that set up a funding mechanism for public schools and public schools in Webster Parish were opened. (Courtesy of Lillian Life Willis.)

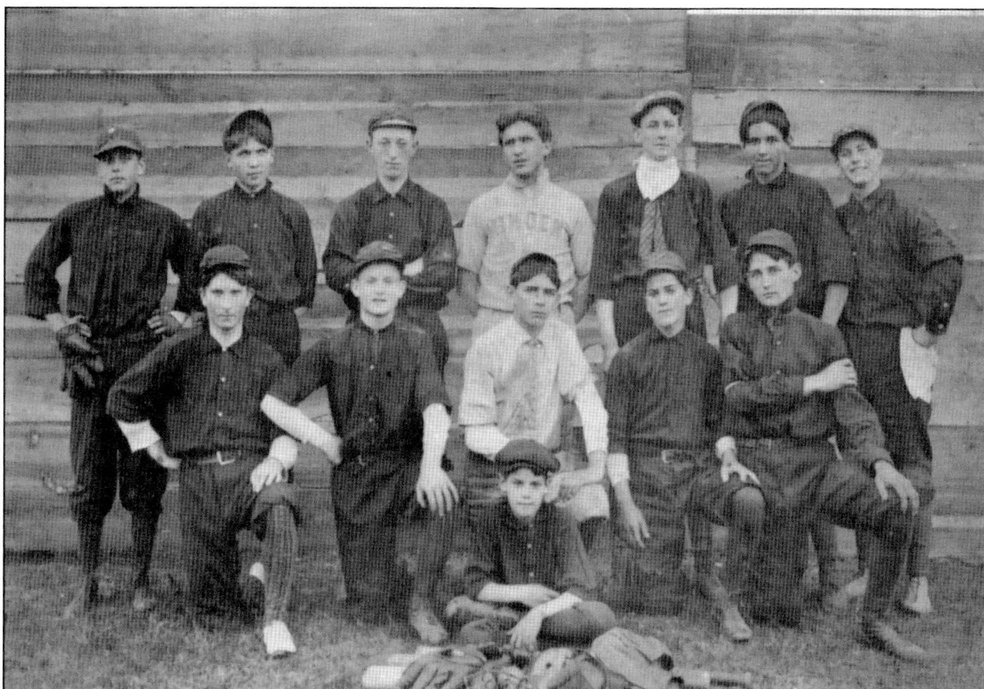

From the start, athletics played a big role in Minden schools. This is one of the first Minden High School baseball teams, from the period of 1902 to 1904. Records do not indicate if the school sponsored any other sports in those years. (Courtesy of LSU-Shreveport Archives and Special Collections, Noel Memorial Library.)

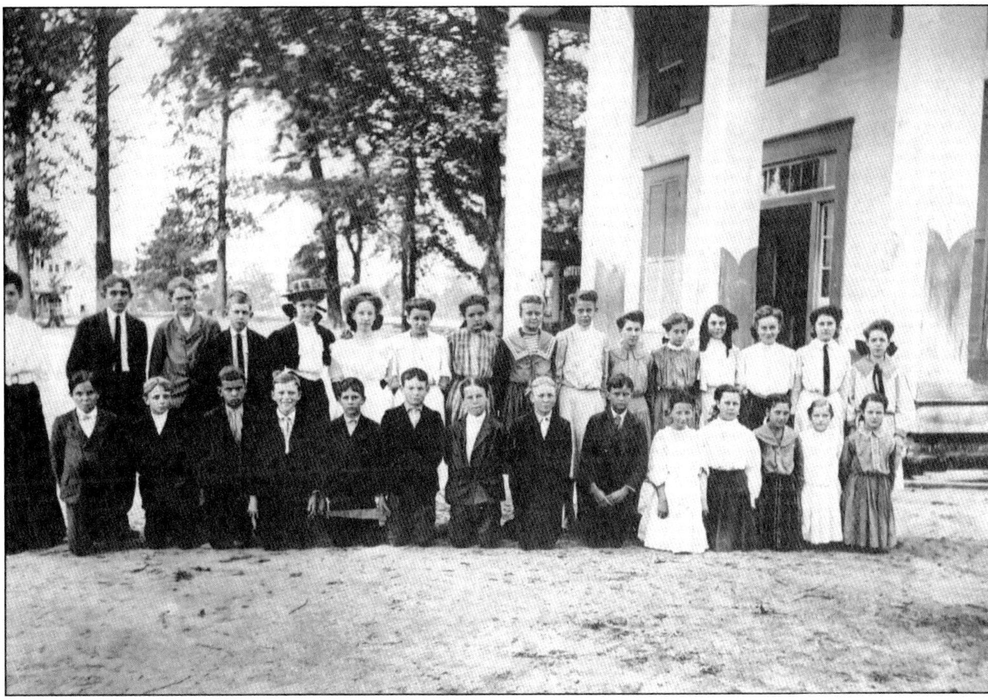

After using the Minden Female College buildings for 10 years, Minden voters approved the construction of a new modern high school. The next four images are of the students at the Minden High School in the 1909–1910 school year, the final school year before the new school building. The new high school building was the first erected for public education in Minden. (Both, courtesy Webster Parish Library.)

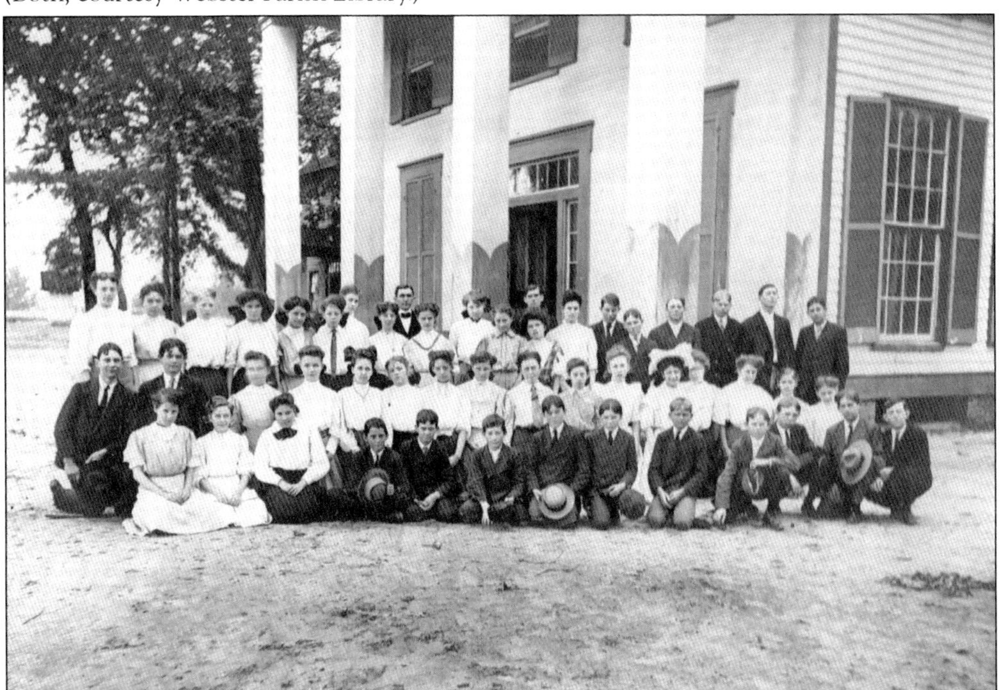

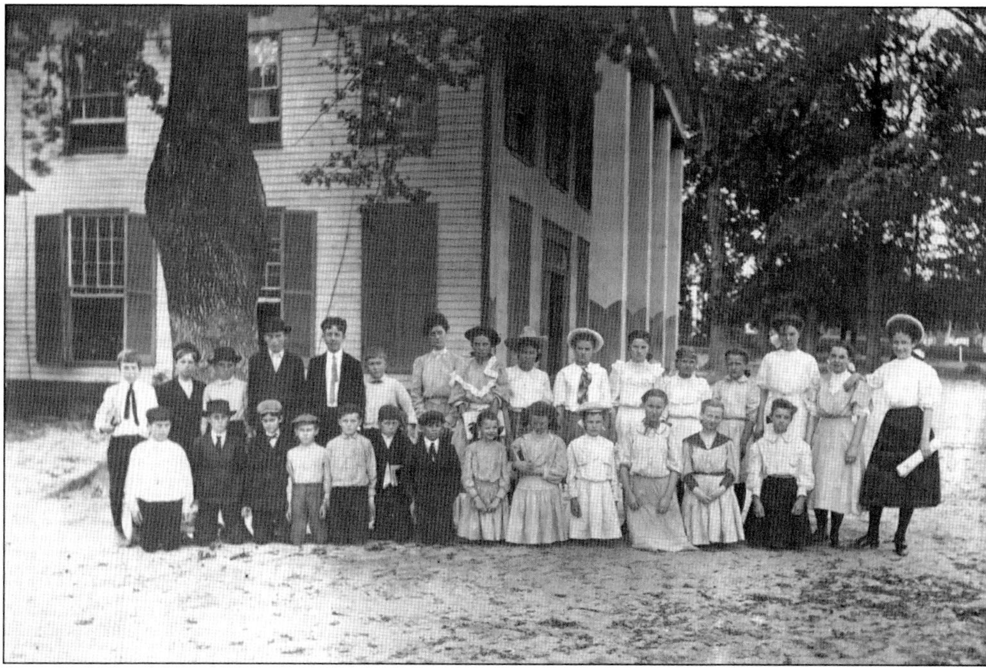

The new Minden High School was intended to serve Minden and the surrounding area for years to come. Ironically, because of population growth, the school that was considered too large by some in the community was filled to capacity in little more than a decade. (Both, courtesy Webster Parish Library.)

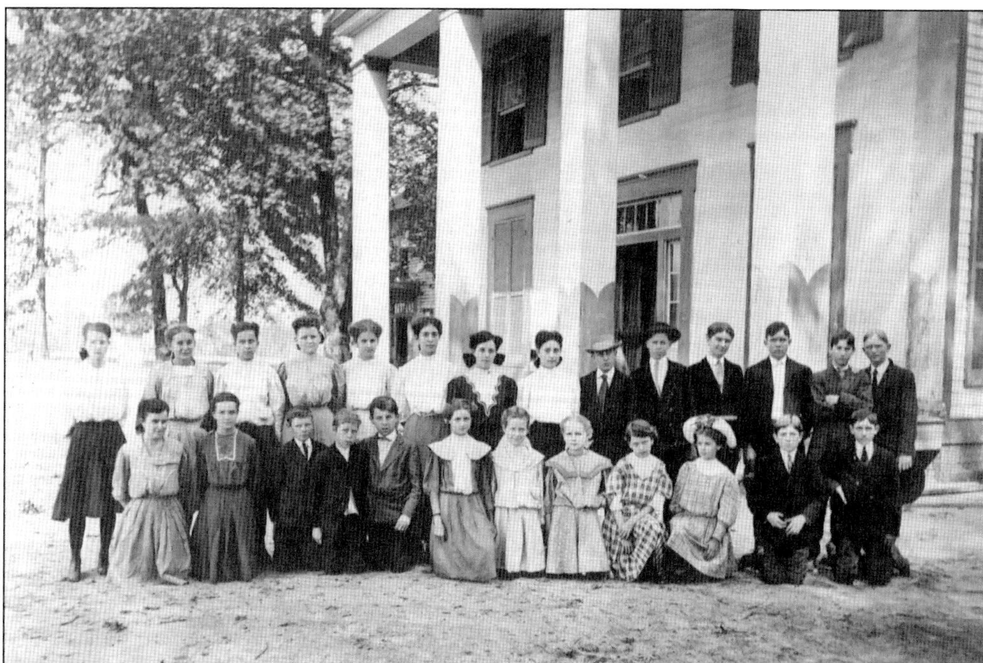

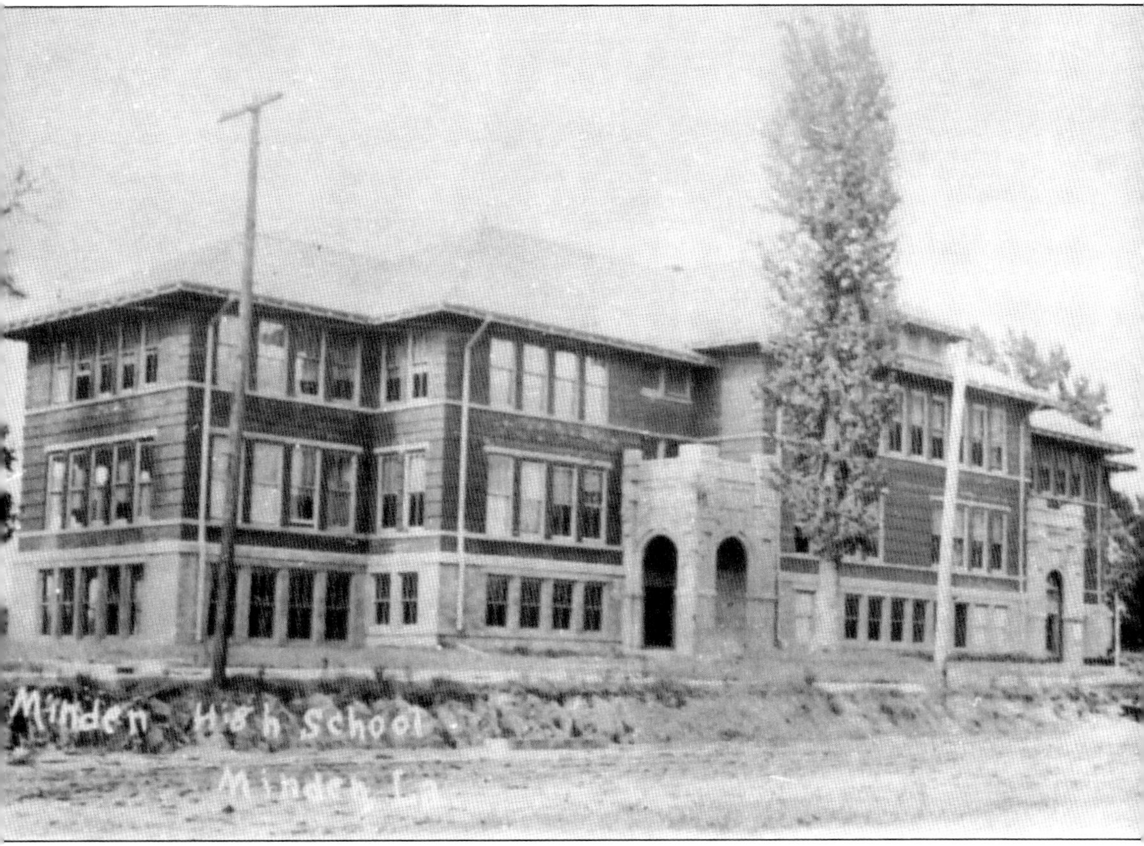

The new three-story brick building was one of the educational showplaces of North Louisiana when it was finished for the 1910–1911 school session. The principal of Minden High School at that time was C.A. Ives, later to be the longtime head of the College of Education at Louisiana State University. Ives sparked the drive for a modern building. According to Ives's memoirs, when he was hired in Minden, he was asked what he thought of the facilities in use, the old Female College buildings, and in his memoirs Ives replies, "They should be burned down." The board, which included several alumnae of the Minden Female College, was stunned, but hired him anyway. Here is an image of the 1910 high school building after completion but prior to being landscaped and occupied. (Courtesy of LSU-Shreveport Archives and Special Collections, Noel Memorial Library.)

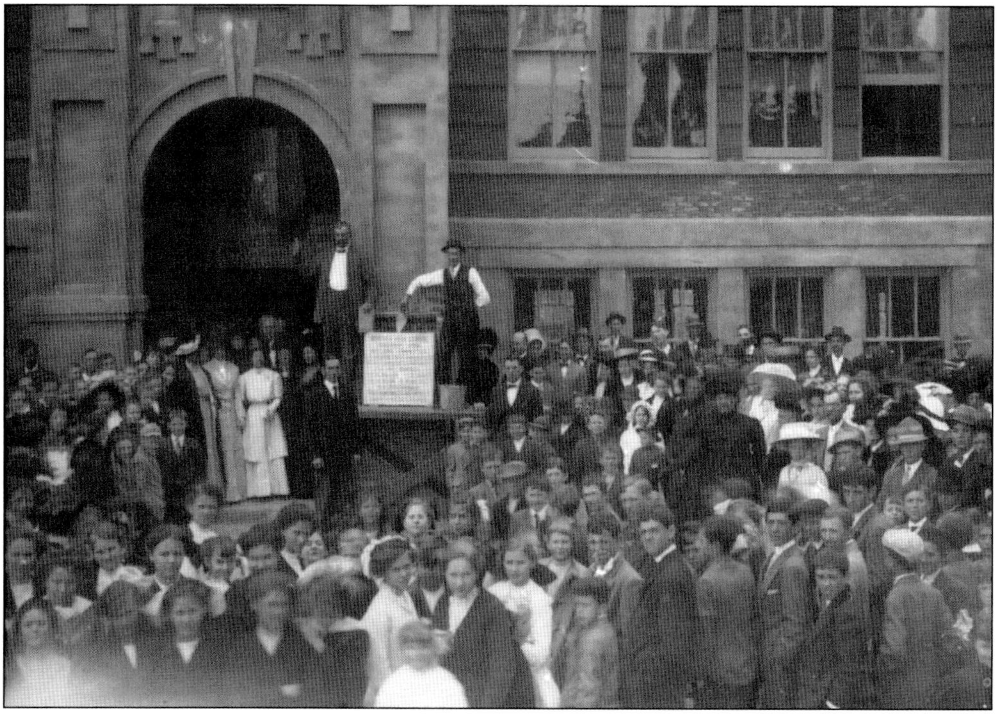

Here is a scene from the laying of the cornerstone of the new Minden High School in 1910. The ceremonies featured an address by the state superintendent of education James Aswell and dignitaries from across the South. (Courtesy of LSU-Shreveport Archives and Special Collections, Noel Memorial Library.)

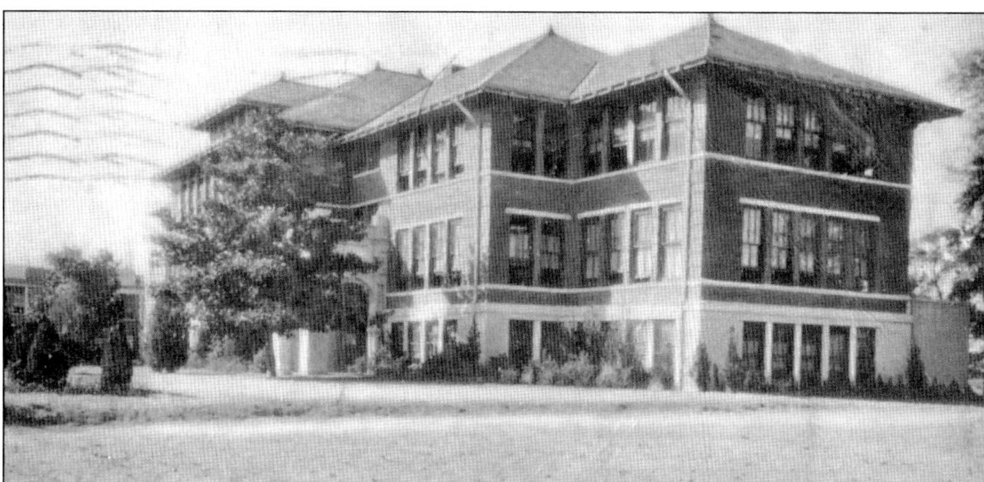

This is a postcard showing the high school from the east after landscaping had been completed and the school was in use. For rural students coming from one-room schools held in homes or churches, the site of this modern structure was an impressive introduction to education. (Courtesy of LSU-Shreveport Archives and Special Collections, Noel Memorial Library.)

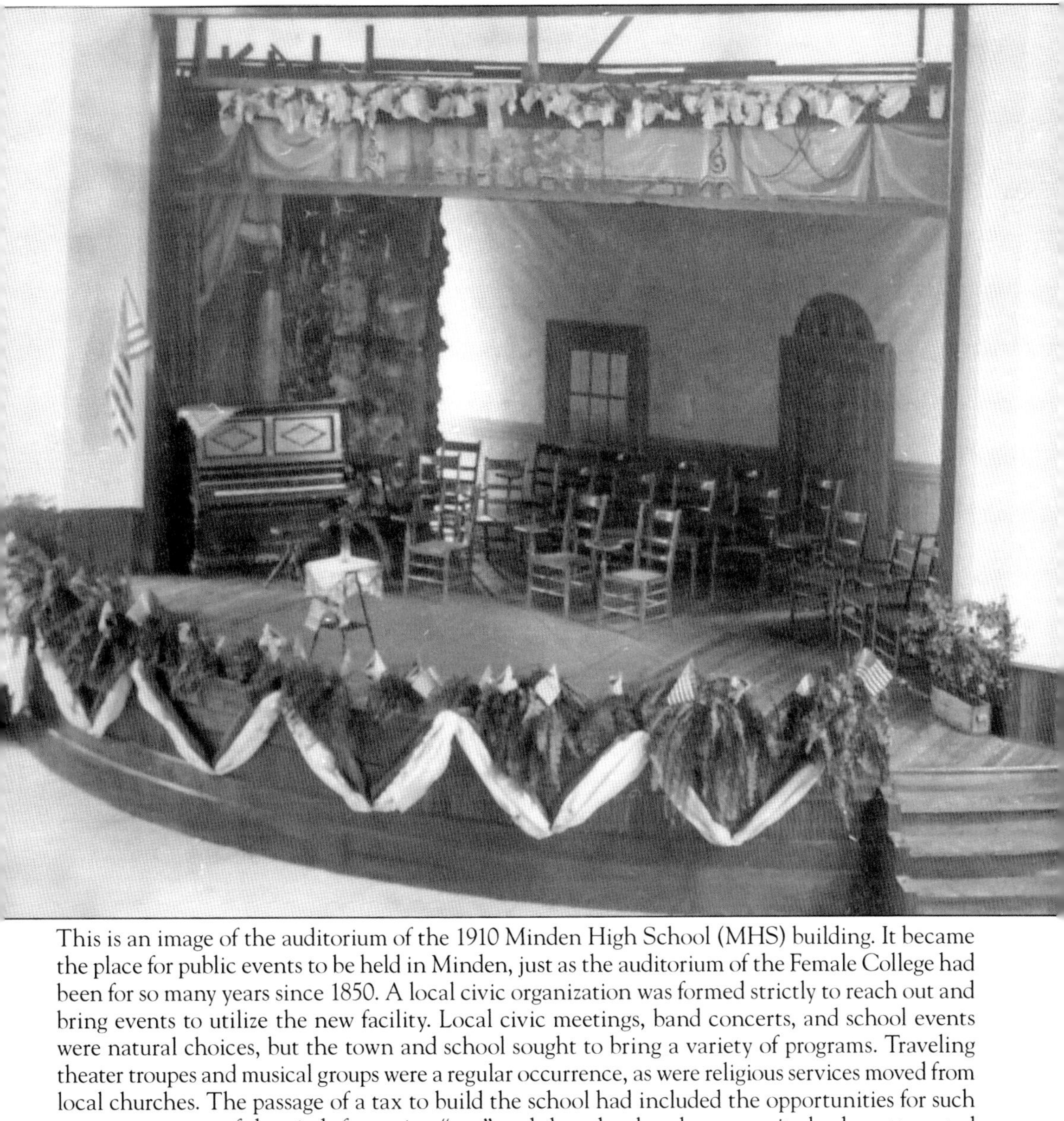

This is an image of the auditorium of the 1910 Minden High School (MHS) building. It became the place for public events to be held in Minden, just as the auditorium of the Female College had been for so many years since 1850. A local civic organization was formed strictly to reach out and bring events to utilize the new facility. Local civic meetings, band concerts, and school events were natural choices, but the town and school sought to bring a variety of programs. Traveling theater troupes and musical groups were a regular occurrence, as were religious services moved from local churches. The passage of a tax to build the school had included the opportunities for such programs as part of the pitch for voting "yes," and the school and community leaders attempted to live up to that promise. (Courtesy of LSU-Shreveport Archives and Special Collections, Noel Memorial Library.)

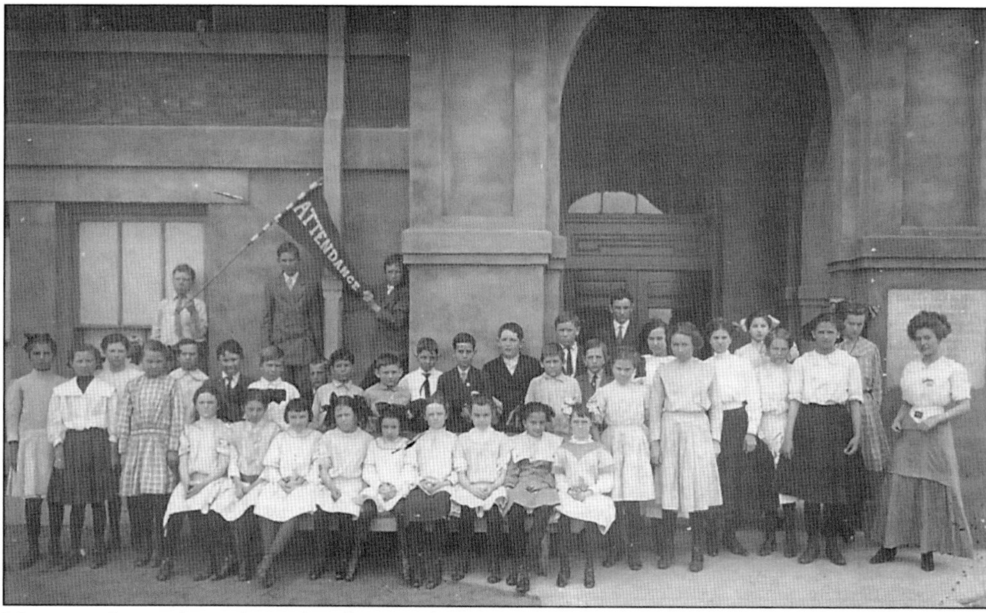

Here are the students from the class at the Minden High School that received the banner for highest attendance during the school year. Although it was an accredited high school, all students in grades one through eleven attended the same campus. (Author's collection.)

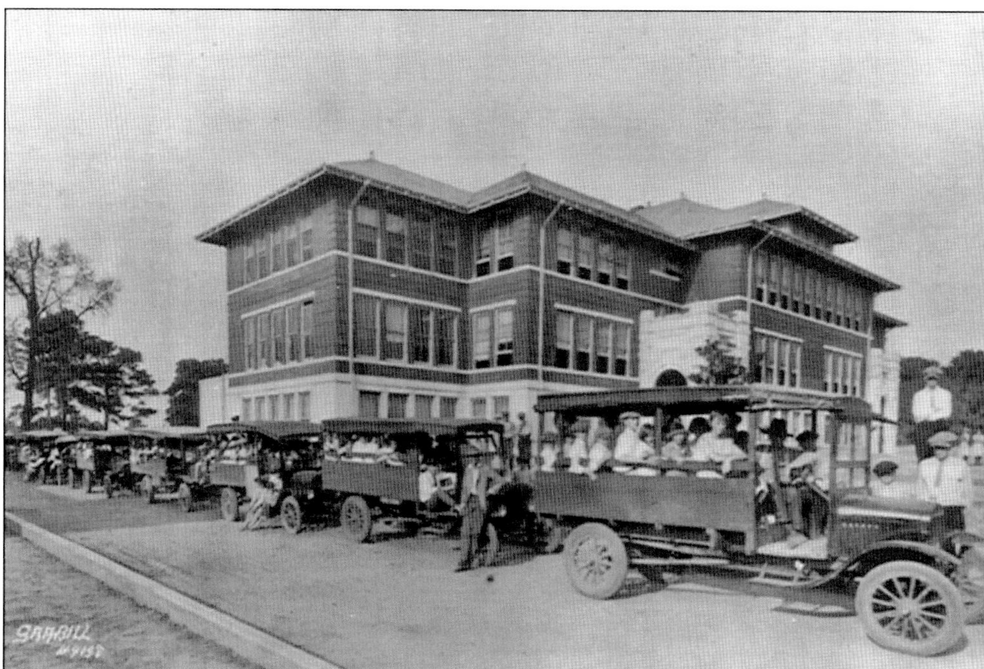

In 1920, Webster Parish hired a new parish superintendent of schools, E.S. Richardson. Richardson instituted a program of consolidation and parish-wide transportation that required this fleet of busses. (Courtesy of LSU-Shreveport Archives and Special Collections, Noel Memorial Library.)

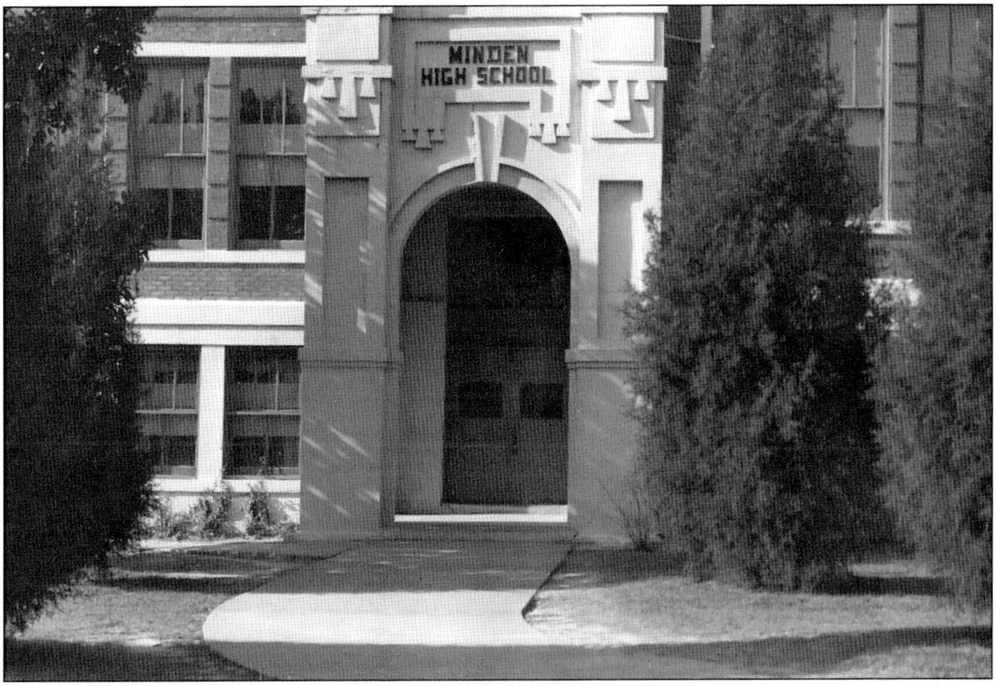

This image gives a close-up view of one of the entrances of the 1910 Minden High School building. Although its use as the main high school only lasted for 15 years, the building was part of the school system for over 40 years. (Author's collection.)

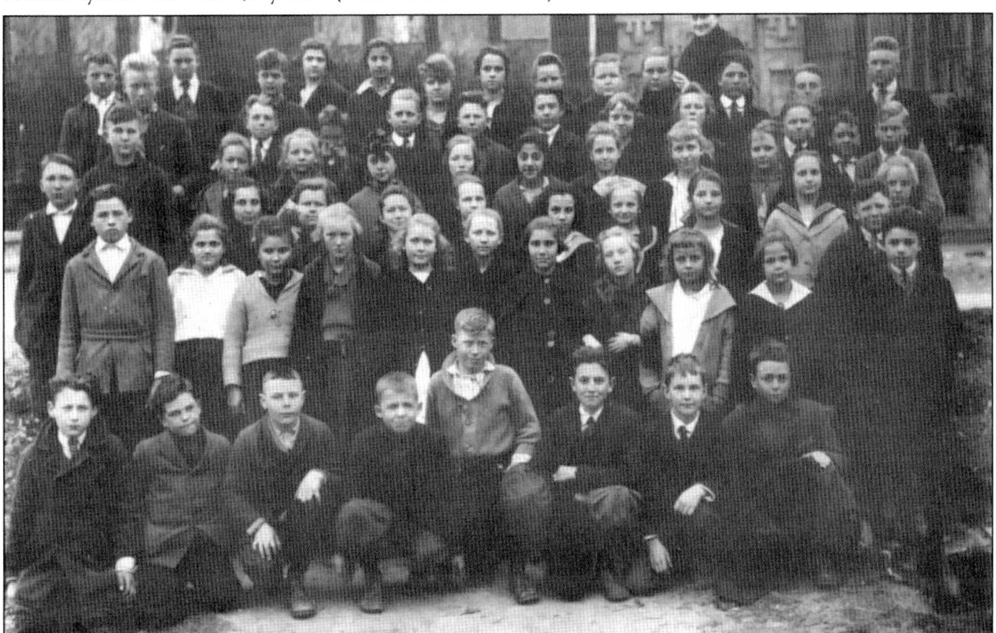

The students of what today would be considered middle school enrolled at the Minden High School in 1920. In those years, there were only two divisions, grammar school and high school, and these are the oldest students from the grammar school division. (Courtesy of LSU-Shreveport Archives and Special Collections, Noel Memorial Library.)

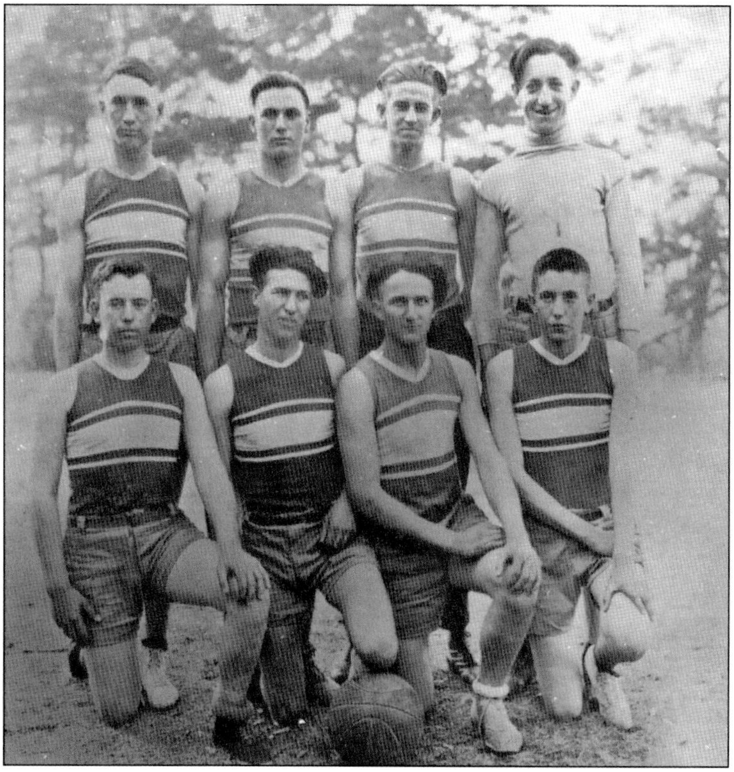

By 1921, Minden High School was sponsoring athletic teams in several sports, which were proving to be very competitive in their efforts. These two images show the girls' and boys' basketball teams for the 1921–1922 school year. While these teams existed, basketball did not grab the local fans' attention nearly as much as football and baseball until the 1950s. (Both, courtesy of LSU-Shreveport Archives and Special Collections, Noel Memorial Library.)

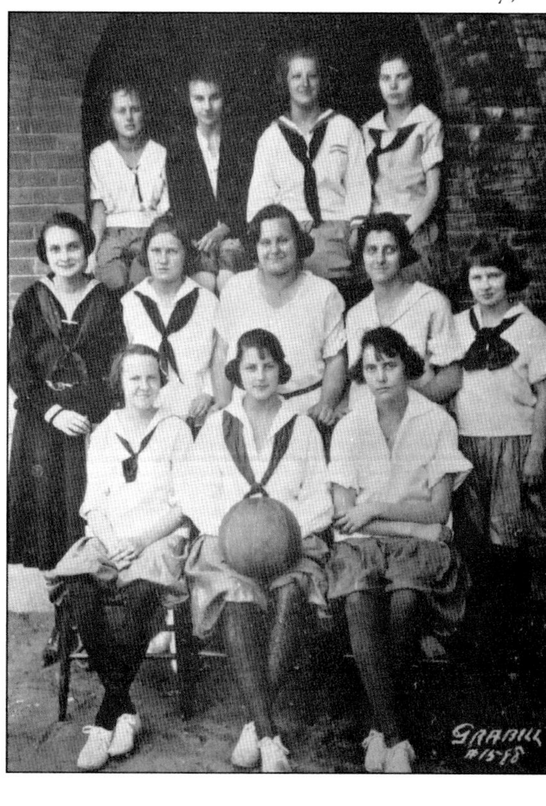

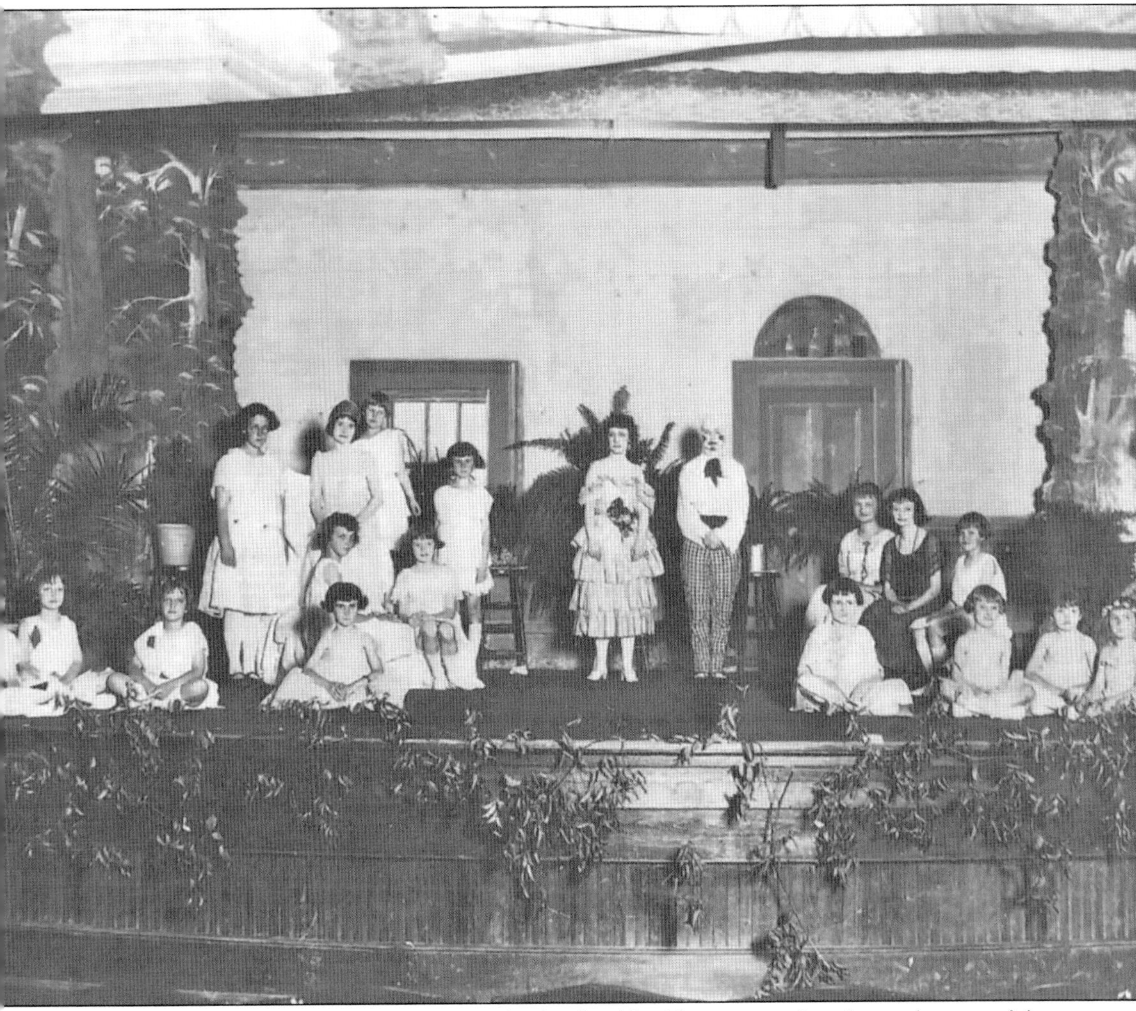

One of the last events held before the 1910 high school building was replaced was also one of the most tragic. On Tuesday night, February 13, 1923, the Minden High School auditorium was the site of the annual Mardi Gras Pageant. During the performance, sparklers being held by some of the participants in the show ignited the dresses worn by a group of young girls dressed as angels. Sadly, four of the girls died from their injuries, and others suffered severe burns. Minden would not fully celebrate Mardi Gras again for more than a half-century. This photograph shows the cast of the pageant at rehearsal the afternoon before the fire. (Courtesy Cynthia Garrison Payne.)

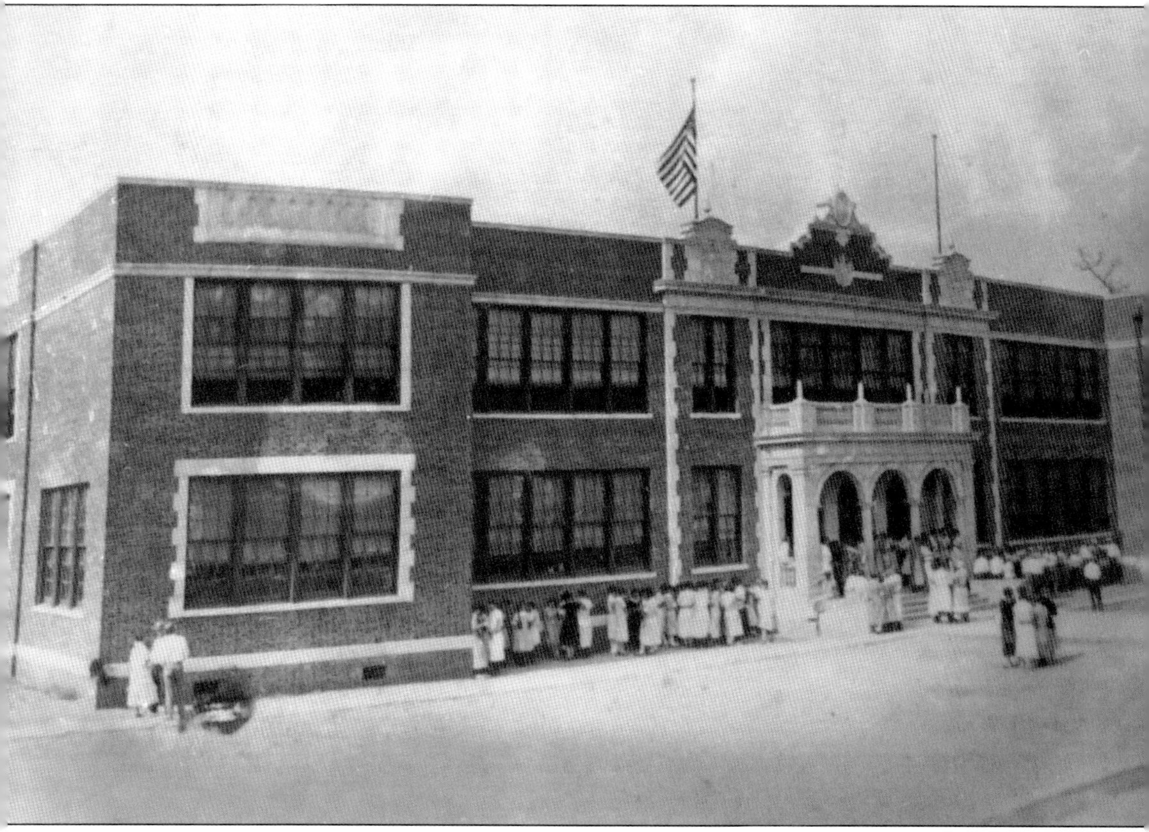

In 1923, the L&A Railway had relocated much of its operation to Minden, and the influx of population required the local voters to approve funding to construct this modern high school. A bond issue was passed in 1922, and it was expected the building would be occupied by the start of 1923. However, a nationwide shortage of bricks delayed completion of both the high school and the shops for the L&A. The school was first used in the 1923–1924 school year and housed only the high school students. The 1910 building kept the grammar school pupils, and this arrangement would remain in place until the late 1940s, when new elementary schools were erected. Like elsewhere in the South, though, black students were not included in the student population at this school. They were educated across town in what was called a "training school." (Courtesy of LSU-Shreveport Archives and Special Collections, Noel Memorial Library.)

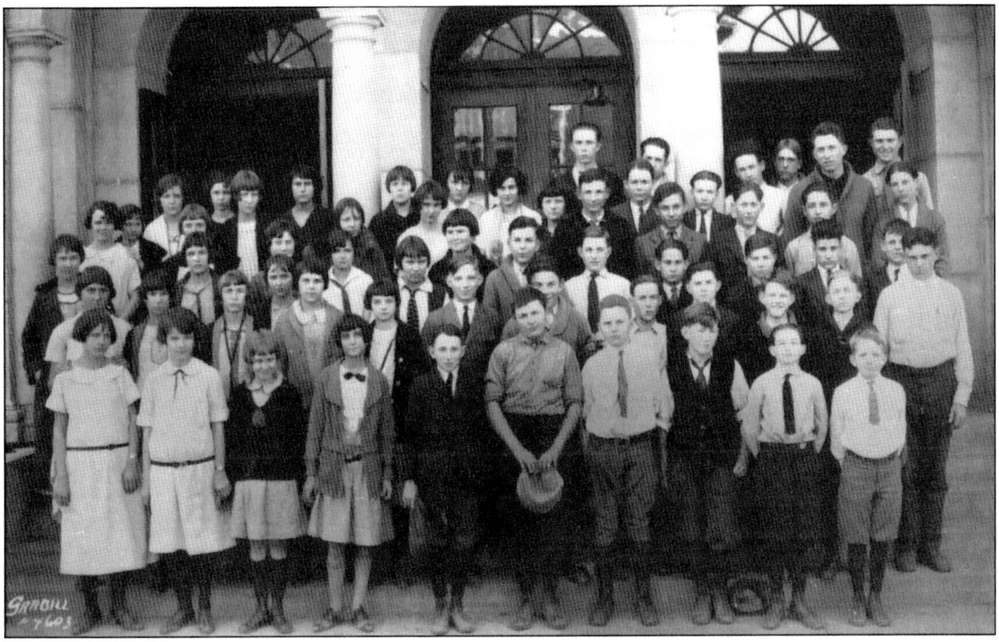

Famed Shreveport photographer Grabill took this image of students from the new Minden High School posed on the steps of the new school shortly after it opened. The age difference between the youngest and oldest students in this picture seems startling. (Courtesy of LSU-Shreveport Archives and Special Collections, Noel Memorial Library.)

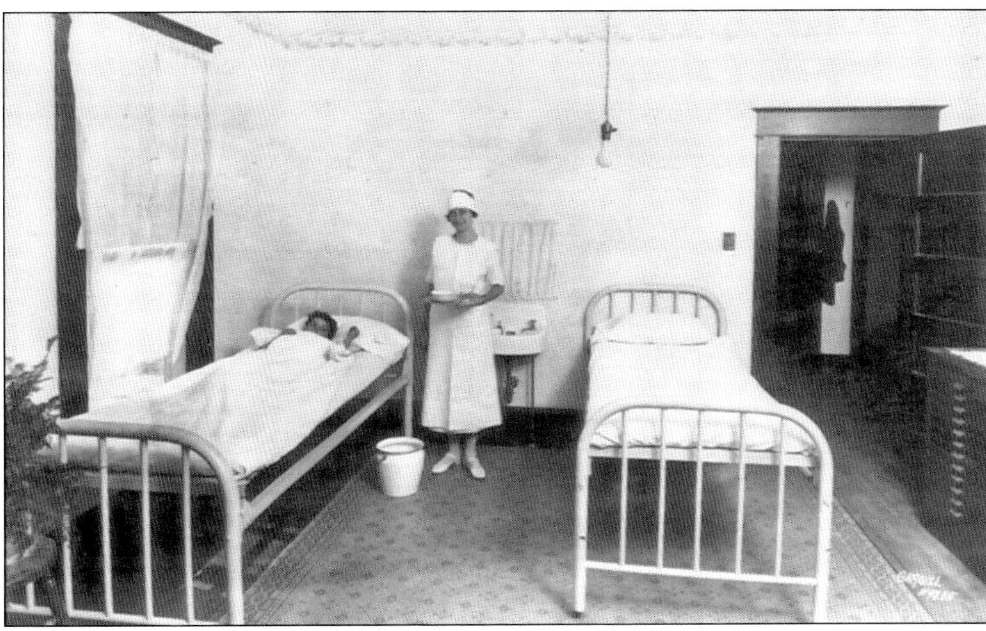

A unique feature to Minden at the new high school was the presence of a sickroom staffed with a nurse, as shown in this picture. Superintendent Richardson was mindful that the students who were bussed into town for school might need treatment before they would be able to return home. (Author's collection.)

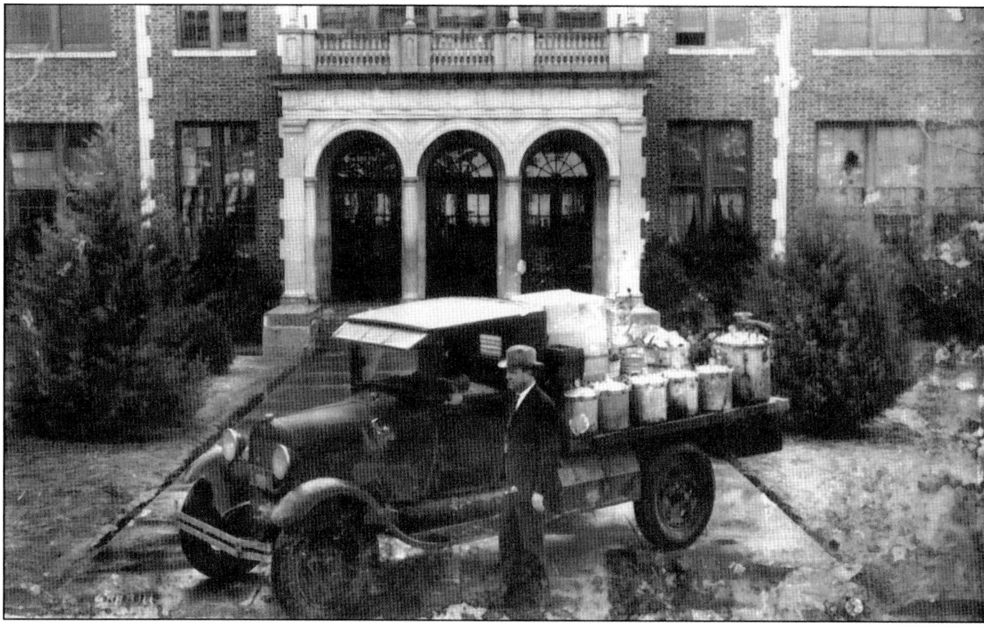

During the Great Depression, school facilities were used in all sorts of ways to aid in economic recovery. At Minden High School, a canning kitchen was set up under the auspices of the Works Progress Administration (WPA) to train local residents to better store and preserve food. This image shows the canning equipment being unloaded at the high school. (Courtesy of LSU-Shreveport Archives and Special Collections, Noel Memorial Library.)

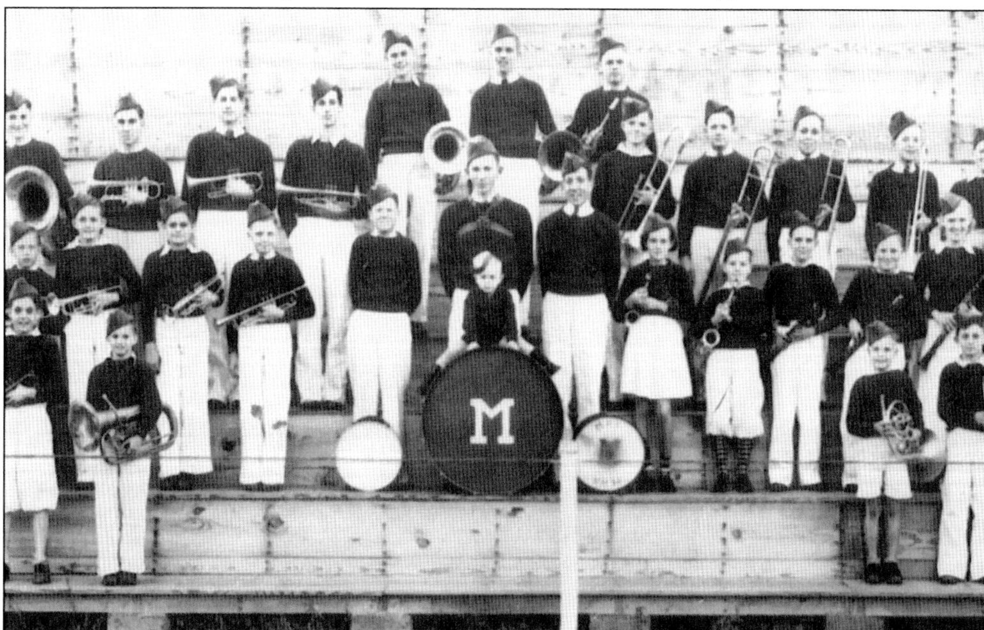

The Minden High School band of 1935 is shown in the football bleachers. While the band was most likely very good, the attention should have been focused on the little boy sitting on the bass drum who served as the mascot for the band. That is future moonwalking astronaut Alan Bean, whose family was temporarily living in Minden. (Author's collection.)

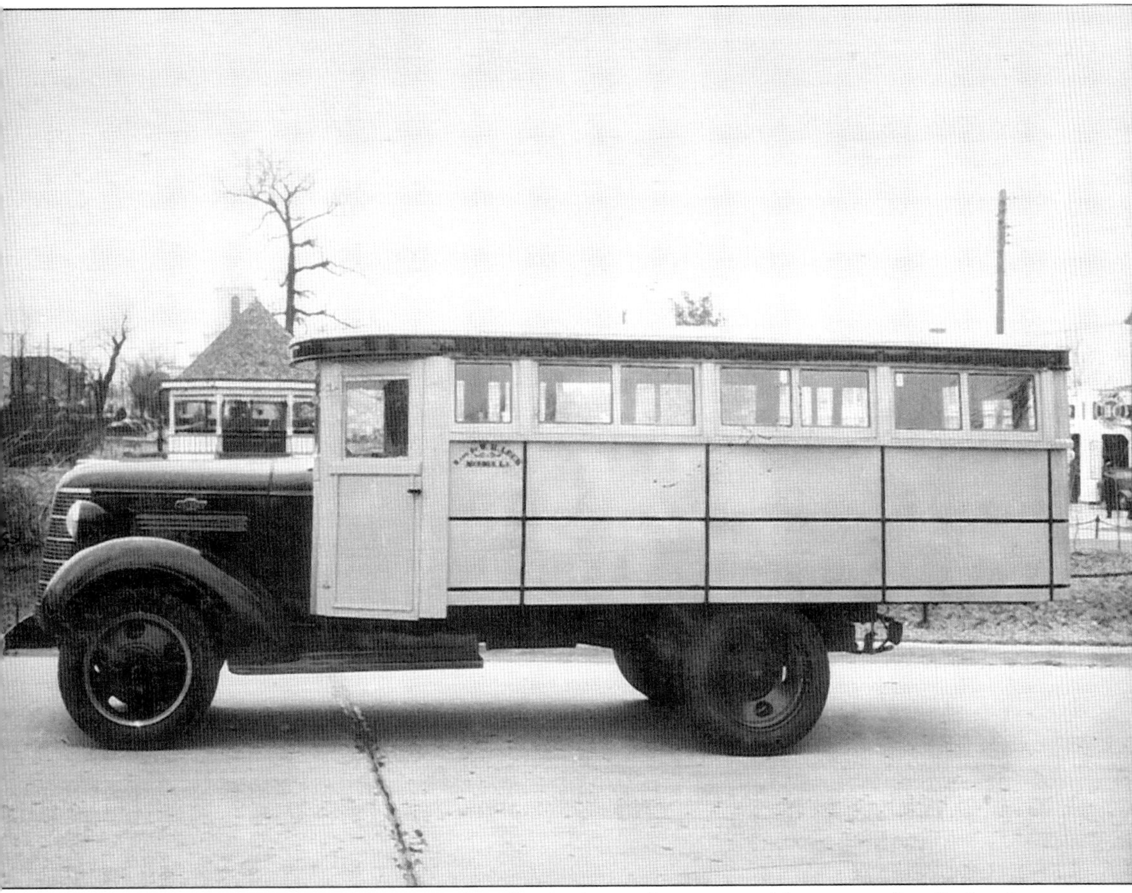

Minden blacksmith W.H. Luck began making bus bodies at the request of Superintendent Richardson and was able to turn that sideline into a prosperous business. Richardson had consolidated Webster Parish schools for white students down from 39 campus locations to 13 between 1920 and 1925, thus the students scattered across the parish needed a way to get to their new, more distant, schools. After studying the problem of the cost of the busses, Richardson approached Luck suggesting that a local man could manufacture the product at a cost less than the schools were paying and still make a profit. The partnership proved a success, and soon, Richardson was touting the local bus carriages everywhere he went to speak about his consolidation "miracle." The Luck busses, similar to the one in this picture, were used all across the nation. (Author's collection.)

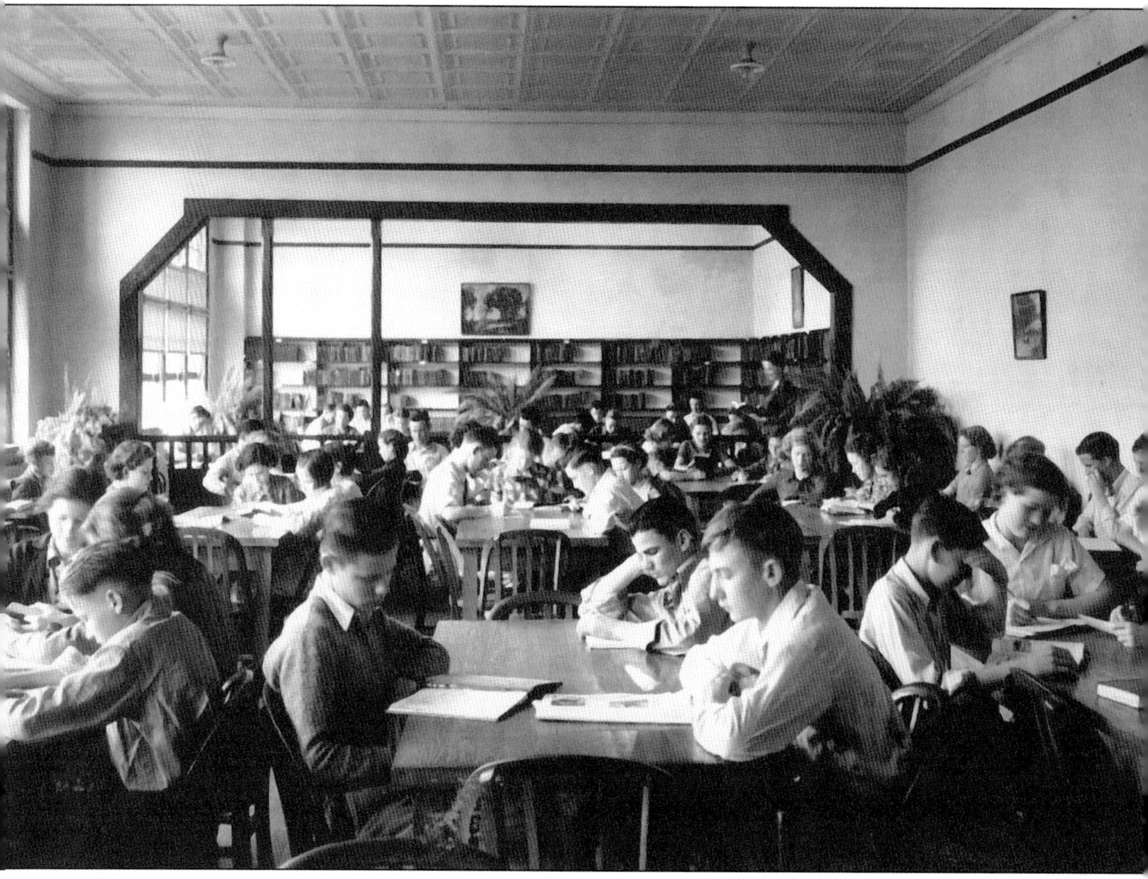

Students are shown during a study hall in the library at Minden High School library in 1937. Of particular interest to locals would be the two young men on the right side of the table at the front center of the image. Both of them would grow-up to make great impacts in the Minden community. The one closest to the camera is Henry Hobbs, later a successful Minden attorney and public servant. He served as city attorney, president of the Webster Parish School Board, and as member of the Webster Parish Library Board of Control for more than 50 years. The second young man is O.H. Haynes Jr., son of the then Webster Parish sheriff. The younger Haynes would quarterback Minden High School to its first state football championship the next season and then as an adult serve 12 years as Webster Parish sheriff. (Author's collection.)

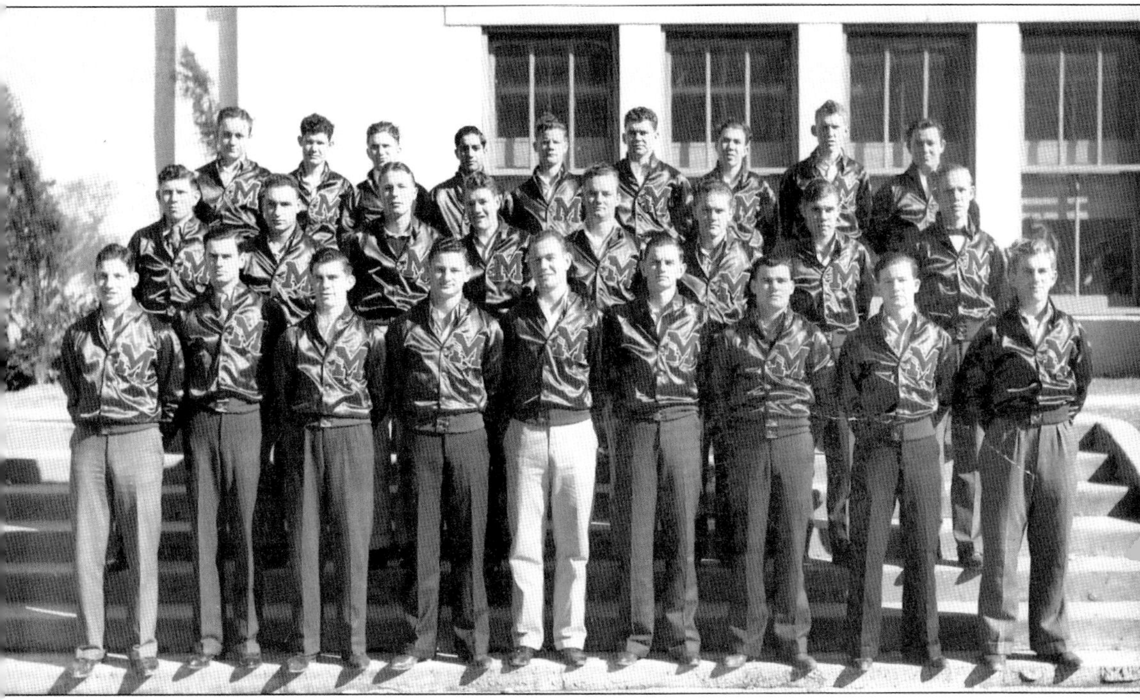

Minden High School won its first state football championship in the fall of 1938, and these are the young men who brought home that championship. They defeated Opelousas High School to gain the title of Class B Champions. MHS had come very close to winning a championship in 1921, but lost the championship game when the team gave up the only points they allowed all season. This 1938 championship would be the first of five that have been won by the Minden Crimson Tide, including in 1938, 1954, 1956, 1963, and 1980. During the 1950s, Minden won four state titles in three different sports in a two-year span—earning a new school motto, *Domus victorum*, which means "Home of the Champions." (Author's collection.)

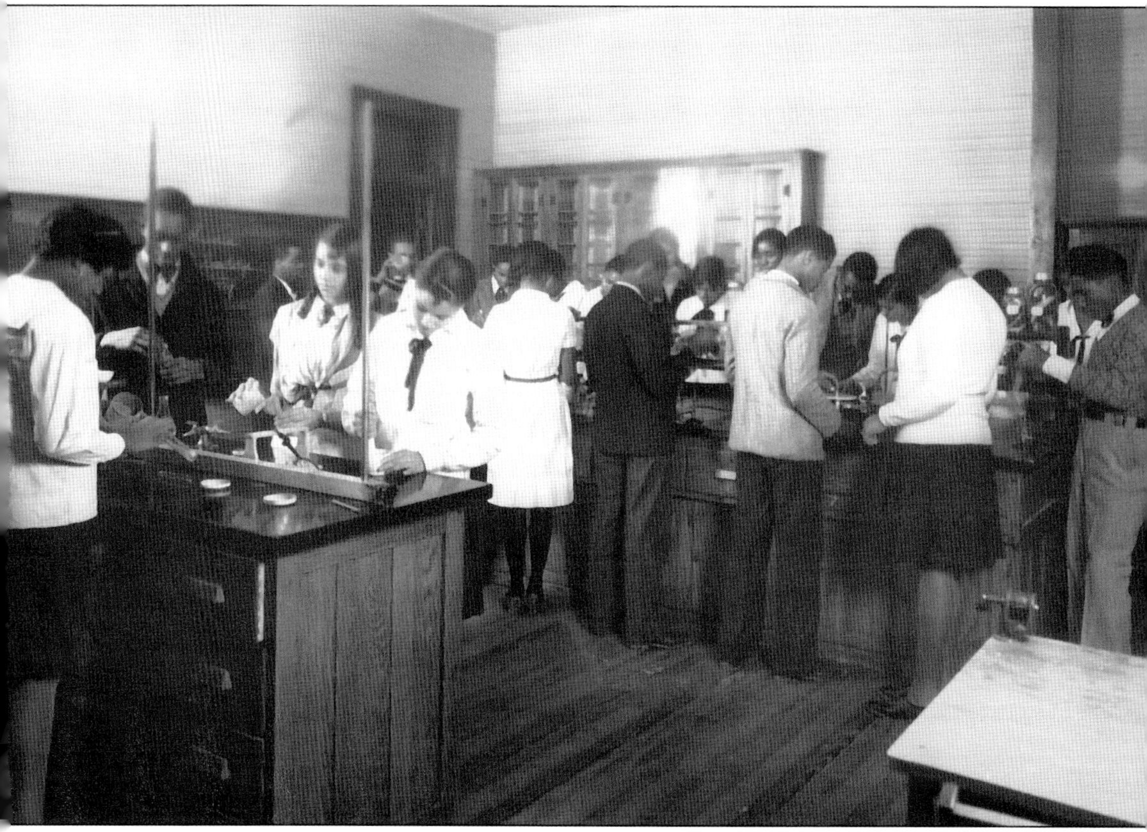

Minden in these years of segregation had a dual society, but images from the black community are difficult to find. The other public high school in town was for black students. After the first public schools were established in Webster Parish in 1900, the first schools for black pupils were housed in churches. No publicly funded buildings were erected until E.S. Richardson assumed control of the system in 1920. He established the Webster Training Institute in a wood-frame building on the eastern edge of town. It offered largely vocational training at first but soon evolved into an academic school called Webster High School. This is a chemistry lab at Webster during the 1930s. Despite the fact that Richardson was able to construct modern brick schools for all of the white campuses in Webster Parish, Webster High would remain in a wood-frame building until the mid-1950s. (Courtesy Dorcheat Historical Museum.)

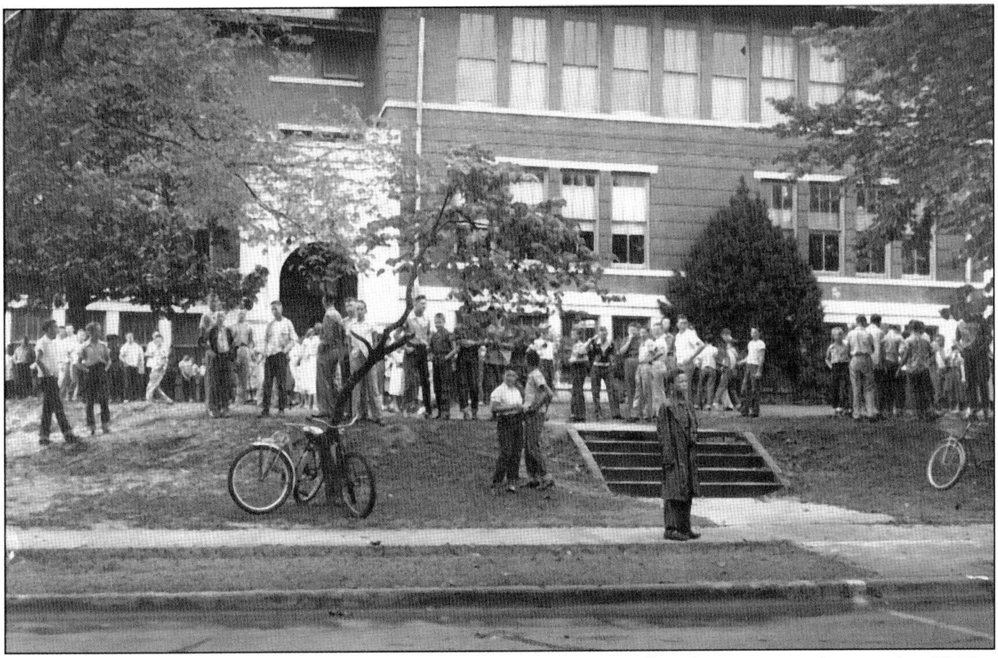

The campus at the Minden public school is shown during a break or recess during the 1940s. As Minden continued to grow, it became obvious to most that the two buildings on the campus would soon be inadequate to house the white students in the Minden school district. (Author's collection.)

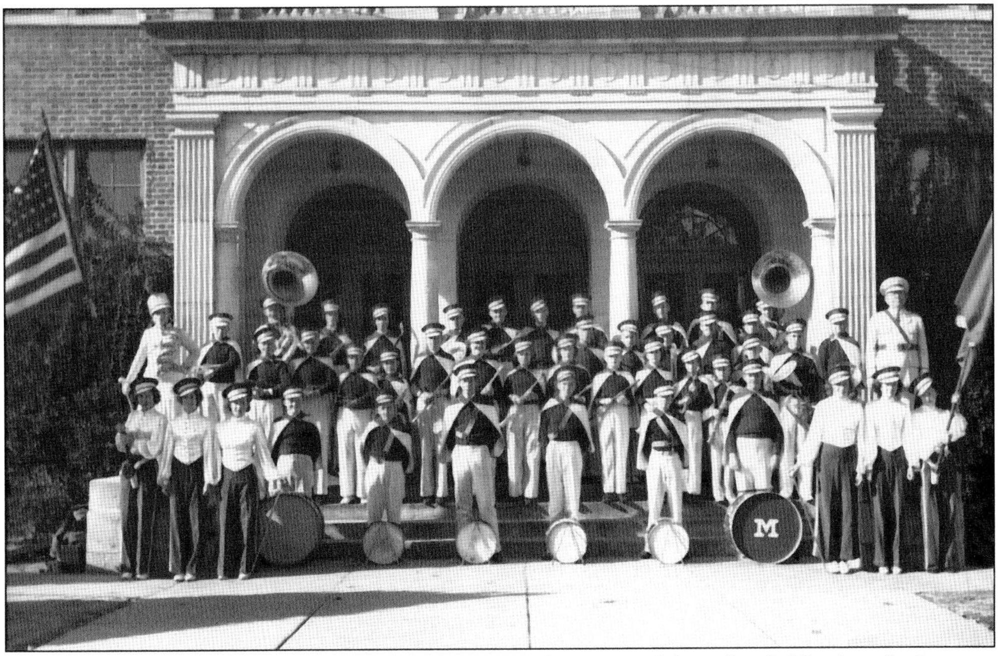

The 1940 Minden High School band is shown on the steps of the school. The band's director, Dwight Blake, is at the left-hand end of the back row in this picture. Blake had come to Minden with the L&A Railway, for which he led the band, and became the first band director for Minden High. (Author's collection.)

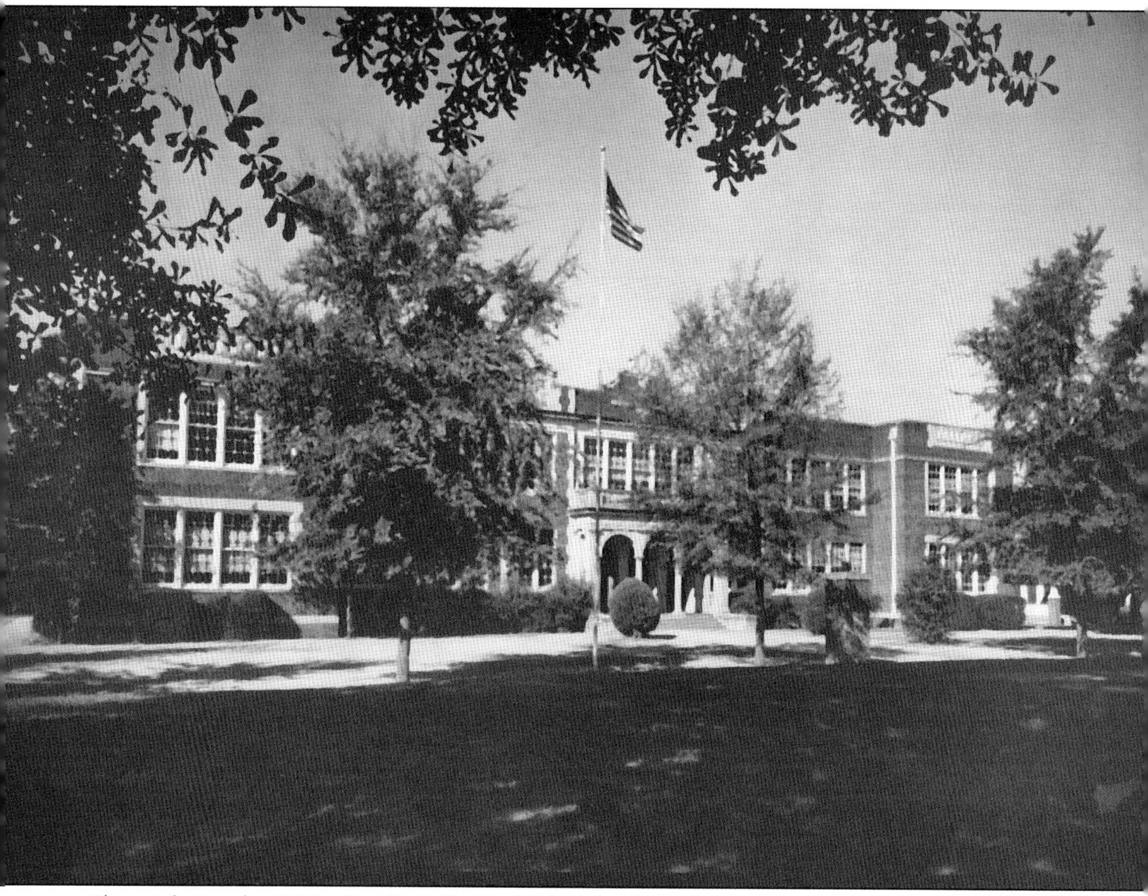

Shown during the 1940s, the 1924 Minden High School building was reaching its capacity while the 1910 building was proving difficult to adapt to modern needs. In the years since 1924, the coming of the Louisiana Ordnance Plant had boosted school populations by more than 25 percent. The 1910 building had not been designed to house classes of the size needed by the growing school. Shortly after the end of World War II, local voters approved funding to build new schools to fix the crowding problem in the white schools. However, the stunning rise in prices after the war and difficulty in determining where the new schools would be located created a nearly three-year delay while the problems at the two schools continued to grow. (Author's collection.)

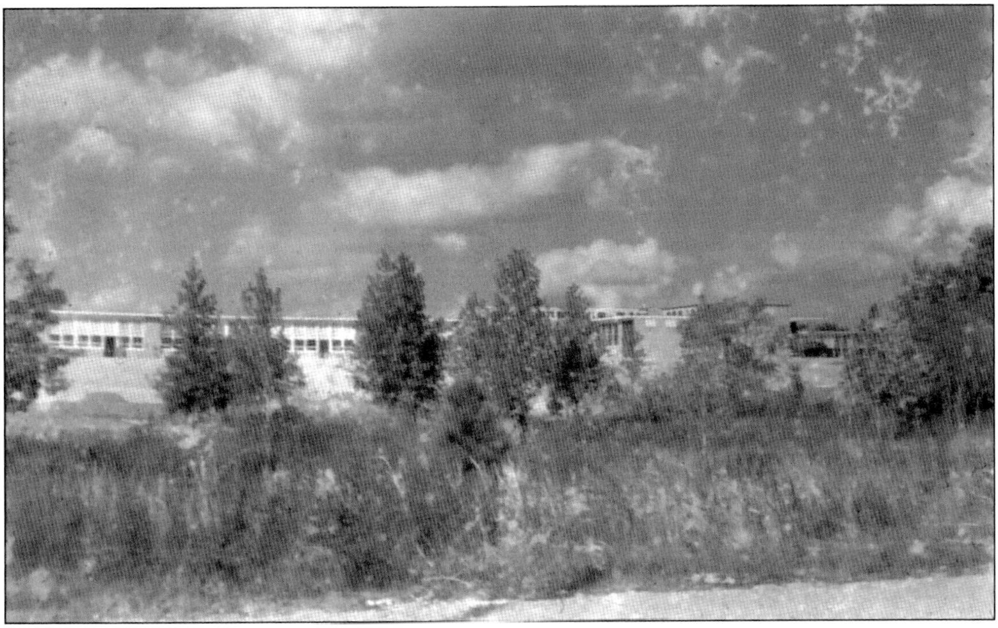

After several years delay, two new elementary schools were built on each side of Minden for white students in 1948. Originally, they were called Eastside and Westside Elementary Schools. This image shows Eastside at the time it was built. Later, the school would be renamed E.S. Richardson Elementary. (Courtesy of LSU-Shreveport Archives and Special Collections, Noel Memorial Library.)

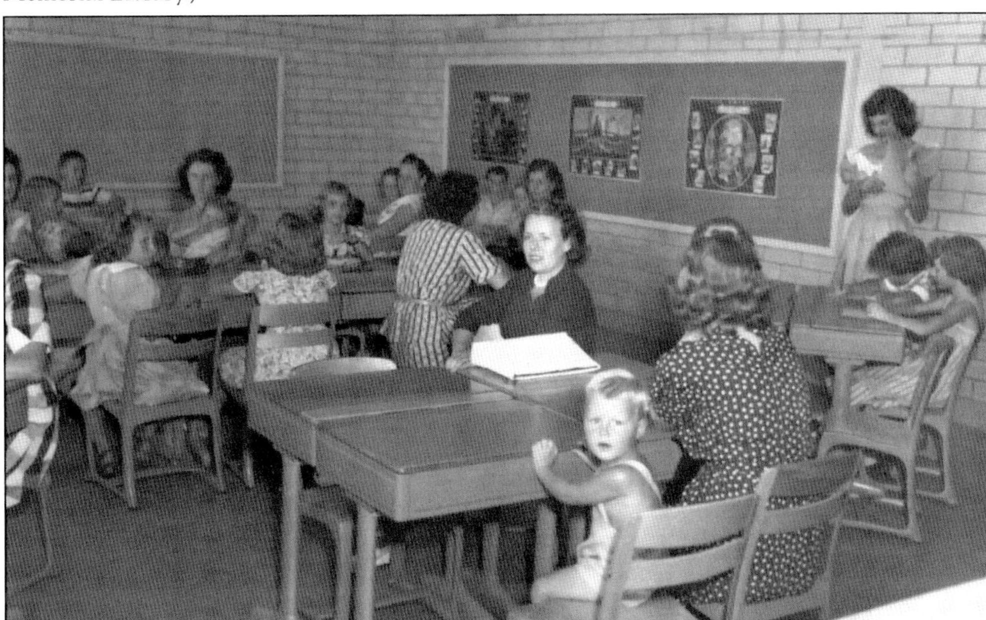

Shown in the 1950s, this is a classroom at Westside Elementary. Later, this school was renamed the W.G. Stewart Elementary School, in honor of the president of the school board who aided Richardson in the school consolidation. Richardson Elementary is still used today, while Stewart has been closed and demolished. (Courtesy of Dorcheat Historical Association Museum.)

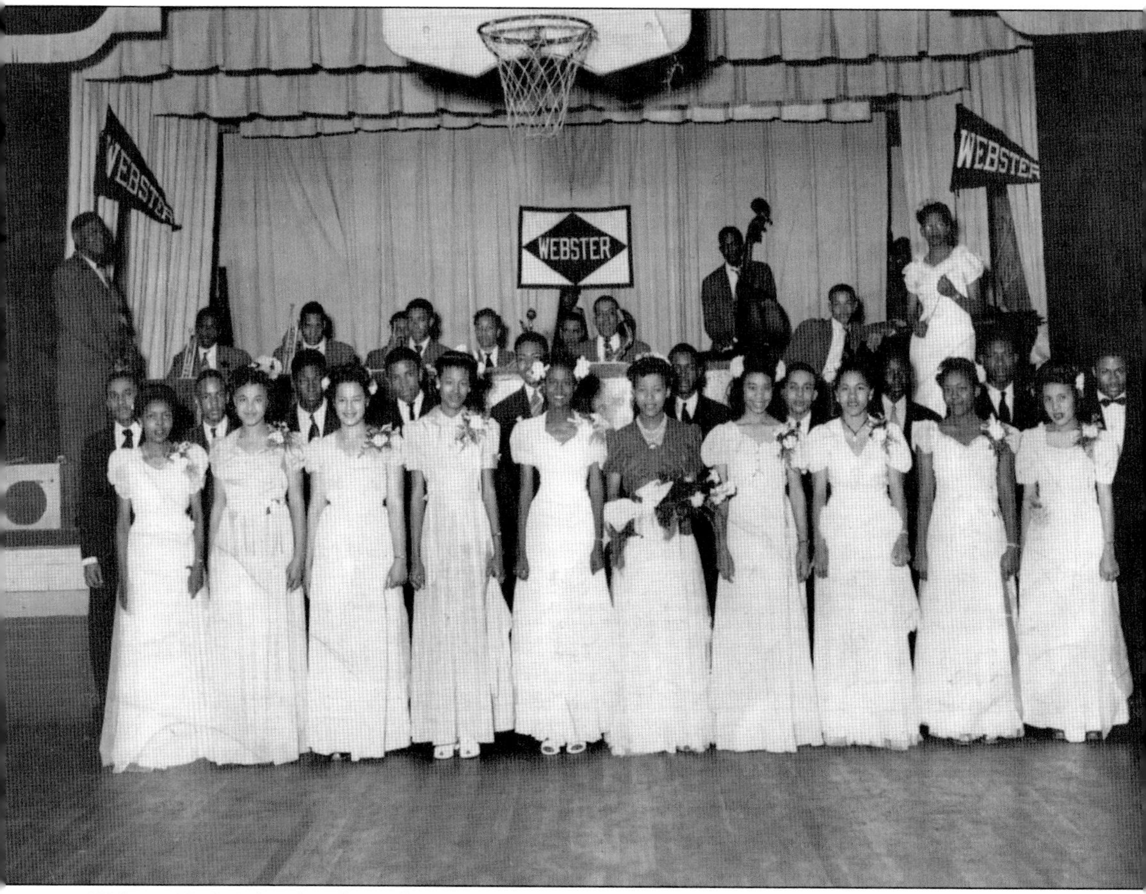

Webster High School and Minden High School both had new buildings constructed in the period between 1953 and 1955. As the national debate over segregation continued, many communities in the South began to recognize that it was obvious their facilities for black schools were clearly only separate and not equal. In Webster Parish, the response was a series of new tax issues that were passed to remedy that situation. One of those issues built a new Minden High School, replacing the old 1910 building. Another expanded athletic facilities at Minden High. The third built a new Webster High School and two new elementary schools for the black community. This image of a dance held at Webster High School was taken after the new buildings were constructed. (Courtesy of Dorcheat Historical Association Museum.)

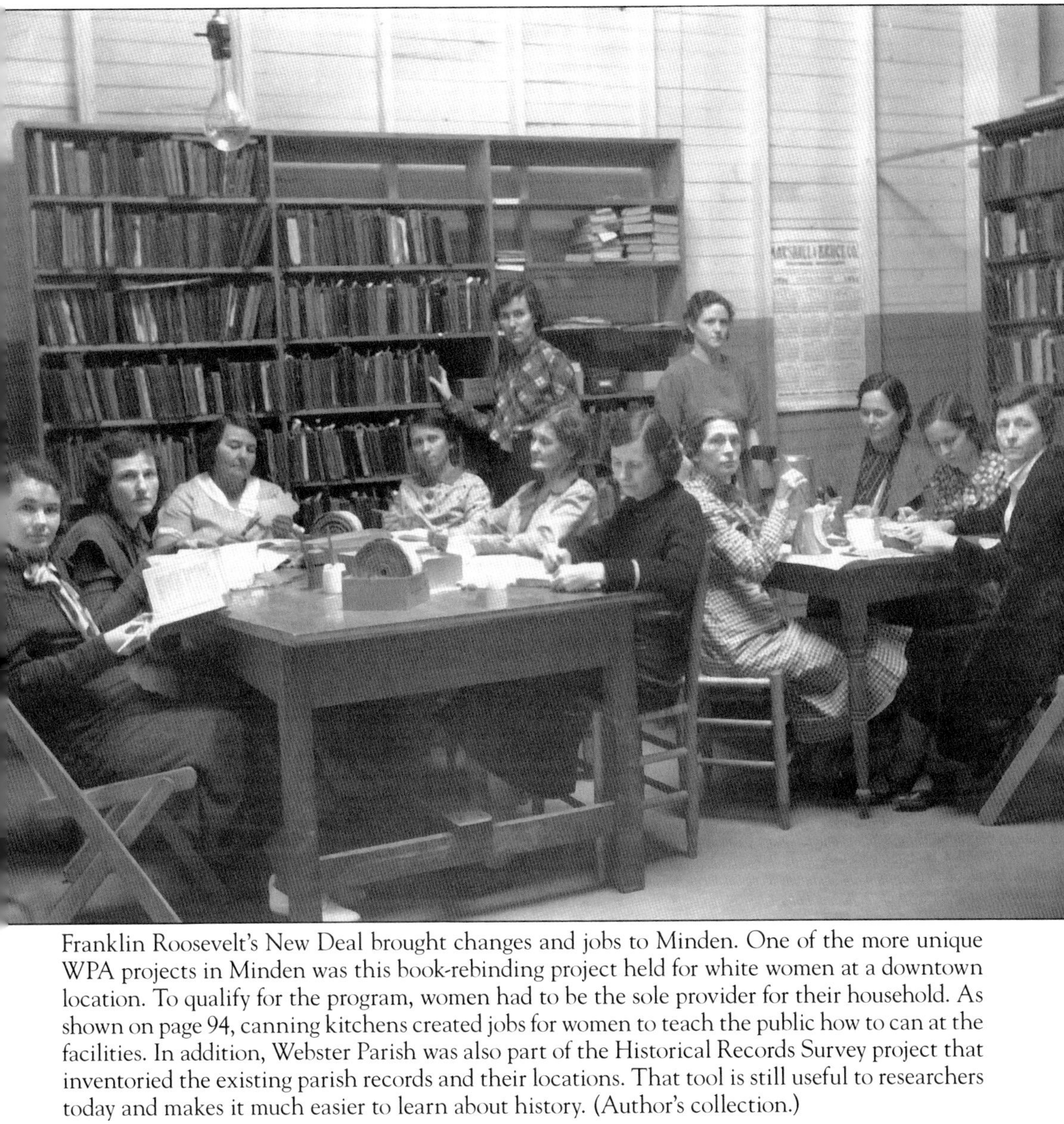

Franklin Roosevelt's New Deal brought changes and jobs to Minden. One of the more unique WPA projects in Minden was this book-rebinding project held for white women at a downtown location. To qualify for the program, women had to be the sole provider for their household. As shown on page 94, canning kitchens created jobs for women to teach the public how to can at the facilities. In addition, Webster Parish was also part of the Historical Records Survey project that inventoried the existing parish records and their locations. That tool is still useful to researchers today and makes it much easier to learn about history. (Author's collection.)

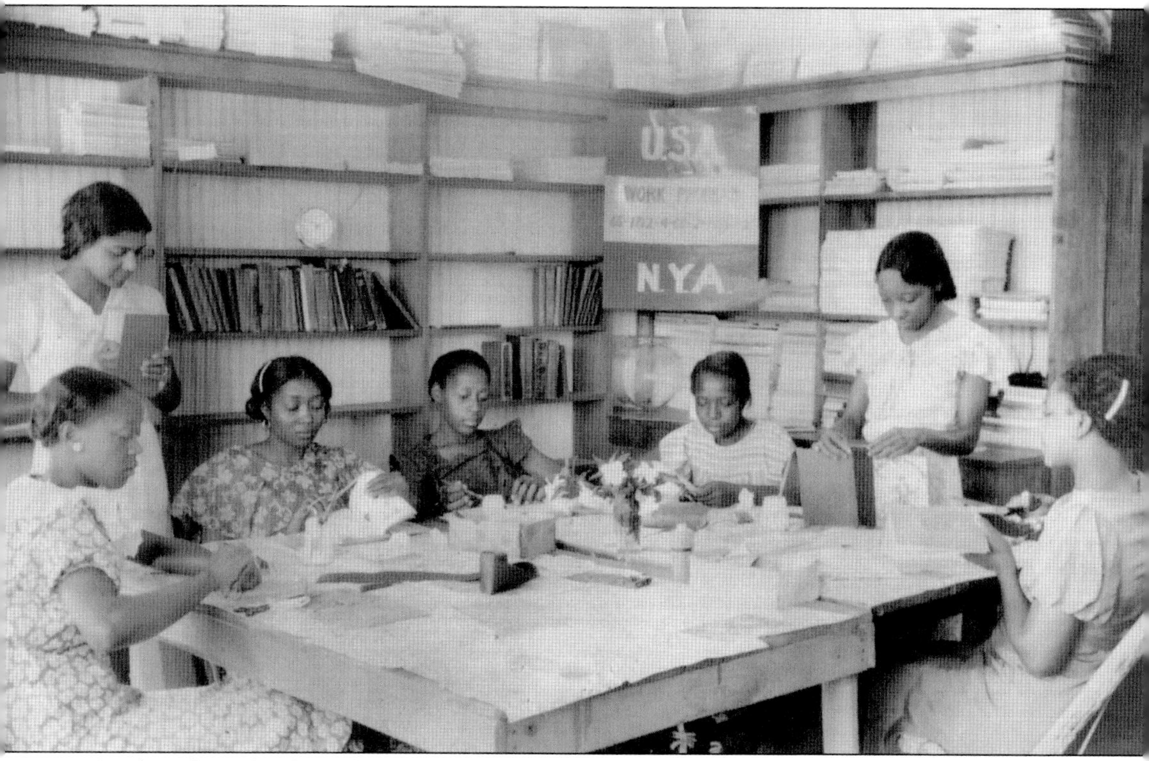

On the other side of Minden, the National Youth Administration (NYA), a branch of the WPA, operated a similar book-rebinding project for young black women between the ages of 16 and 25. In those years, most young women had either completed school or dropped out by the age of 16, and they were largely without work options other than as a domestic. The NYA project was hosted at Webster High School, as seen in this image. Unfortunately, most of the programs sponsored in the South were segregated, because of the laws of the states and the wishes of Southern lawmakers in Congress. So, the programs in the black community were not as well funded and not as successful, despite the fact that the economic problems of the day were equally, if not more, severe in the black community. (Author's collection.)

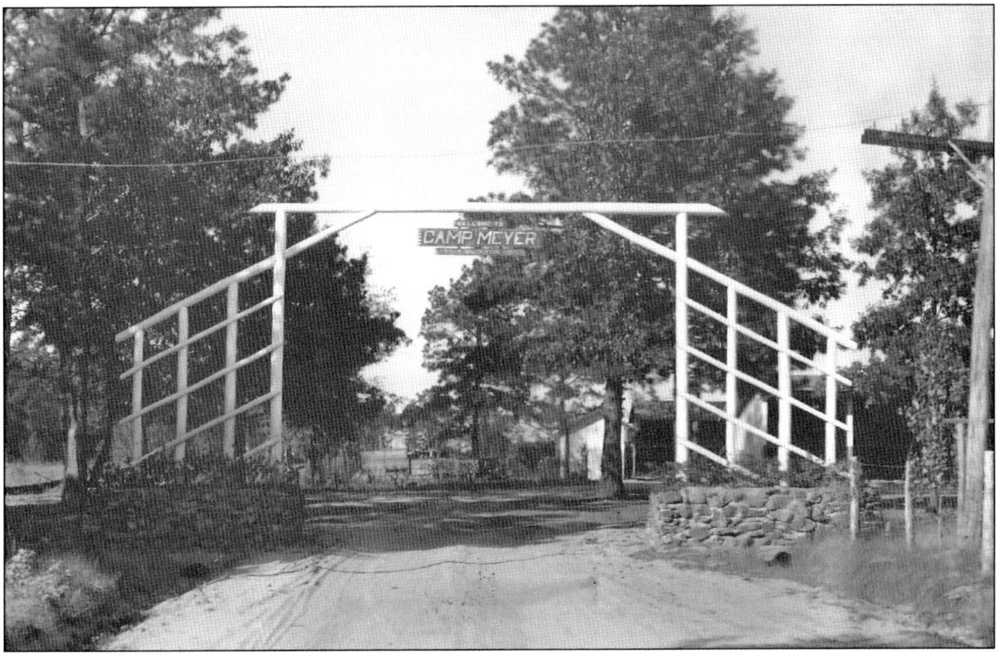

Another New Deal initiative that reached Minden was the Civilian Conservation Corps (CCC). The federal government was heavily involved in soil conservation projects in the Minden area and even constructed a lake. The CCC cadets, housed behind these gates at Minden's Camp Meyer, worked on the projects. (Author's collection.)

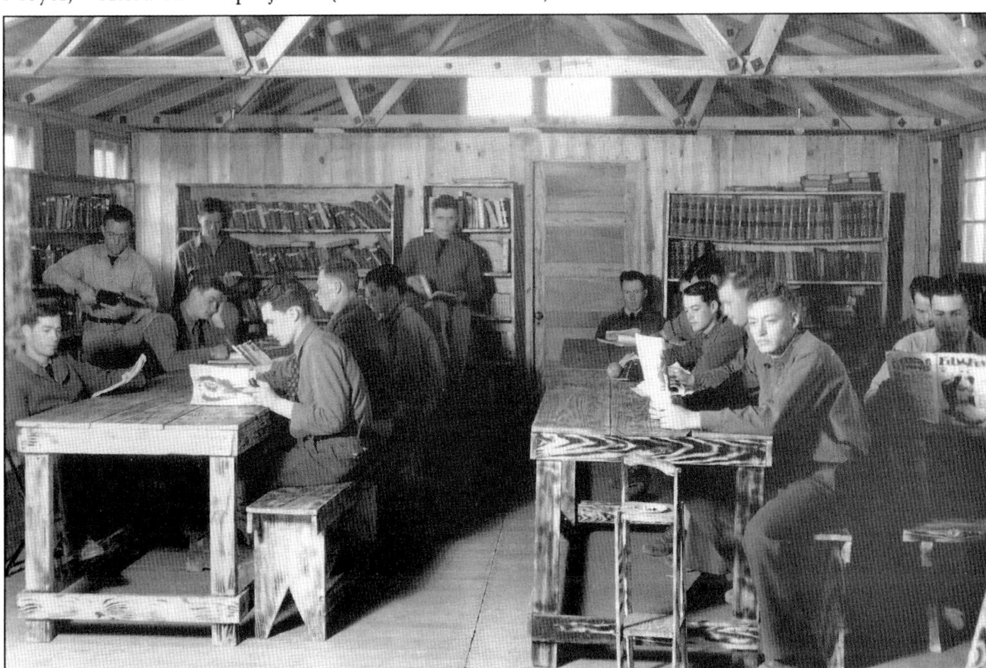

Cadets are shown relaxing in the reading room at Camp Meyer. Most of the young men assigned to the camp came from either Georgia or New Jersey. In accordance with the laws of the times, all cadets sent to Camp Meyer were white. (Author's collection.)

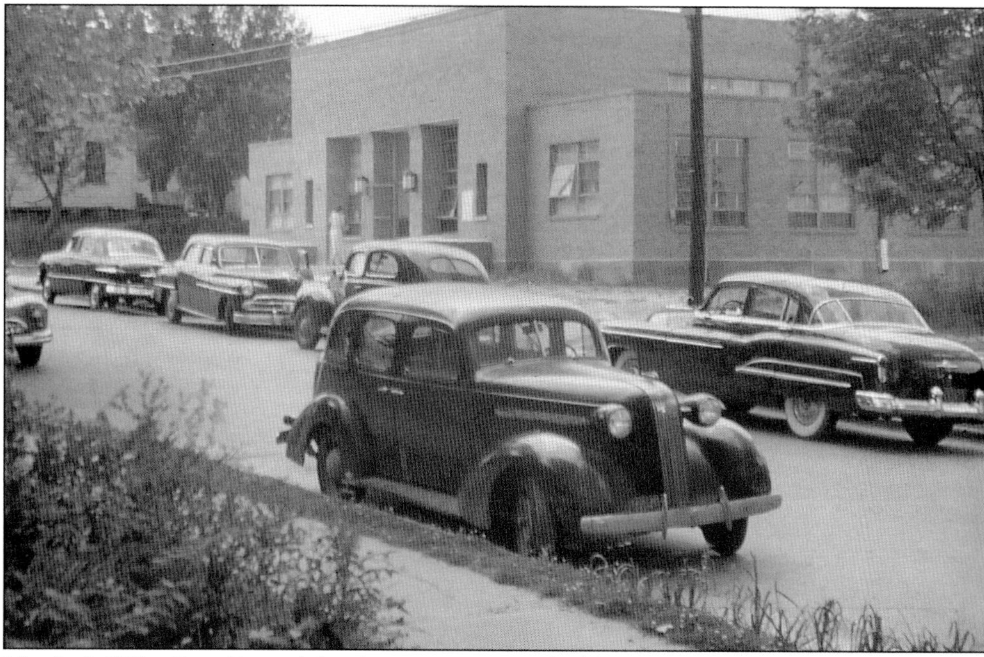

Minden's Wiley-Pevy Post of the American Legion had been founded in 1919 and was a very active chapter; however, members had no permanent meeting spot, rotating between several local business locations before building this post hall in the early 1950s. Today, it is still in use. (Courtesy of LSU-Shreveport Archives and Special Collections, Noel Memorial Library.)

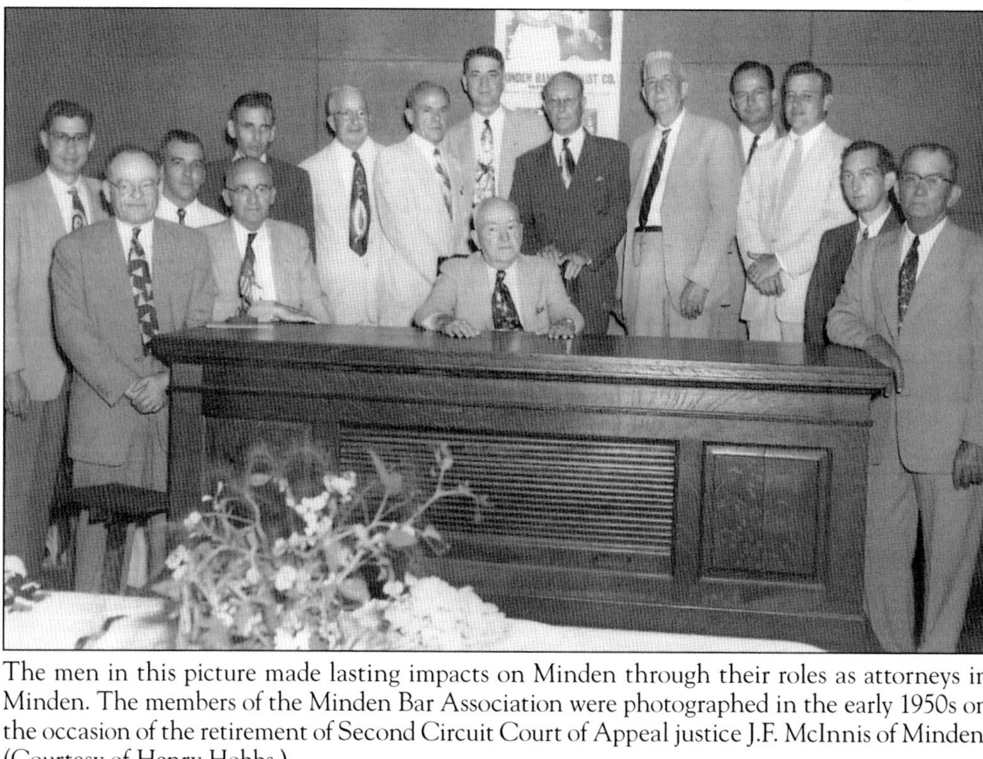

The men in this picture made lasting impacts on Minden through their roles as attorneys in Minden. The members of the Minden Bar Association were photographed in the early 1950s on the occasion of the retirement of Second Circuit Court of Appeal justice J.F. McInnis of Minden. (Courtesy of Henry Hobbs.)

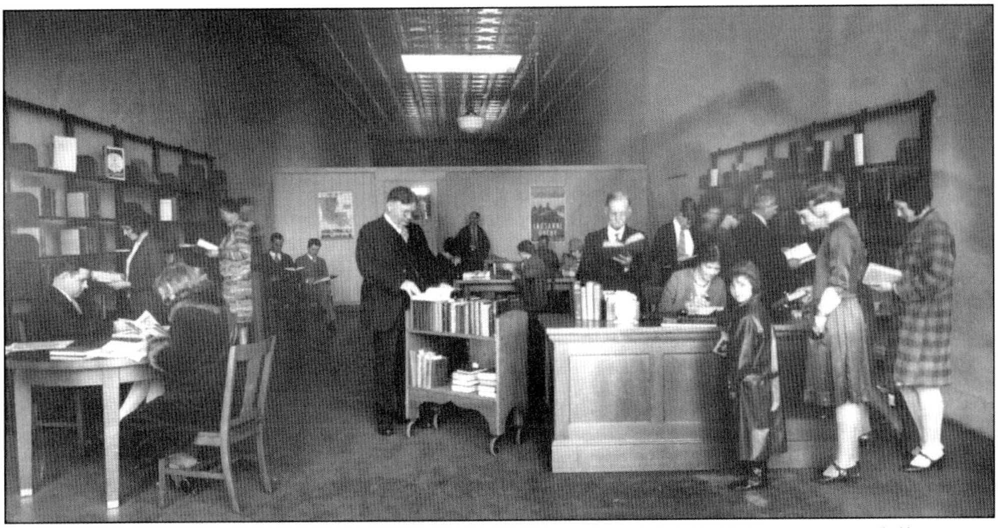

In 1929, Webster Parish became only the fourth parish in Louisiana to open a full-service public library. This picture was taken at the grand opening in October 1929. The gentleman looking over the book cart at the center of the picture is Superintendent E.S. Richardson. (Author's collection.)

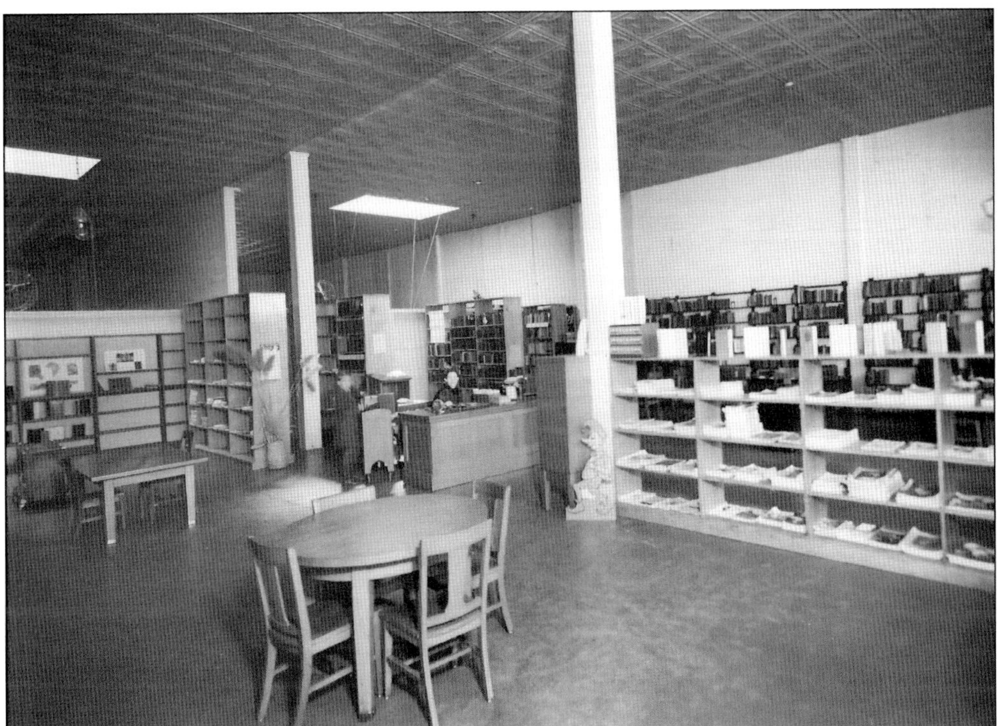

The new library had extended hours making it available for working patrons to stop by after their jobs to read. A movement had been started to bring a library to Minden as early as the 1880s but it took more than 40 years to make the service a reality. (Author's collection.)

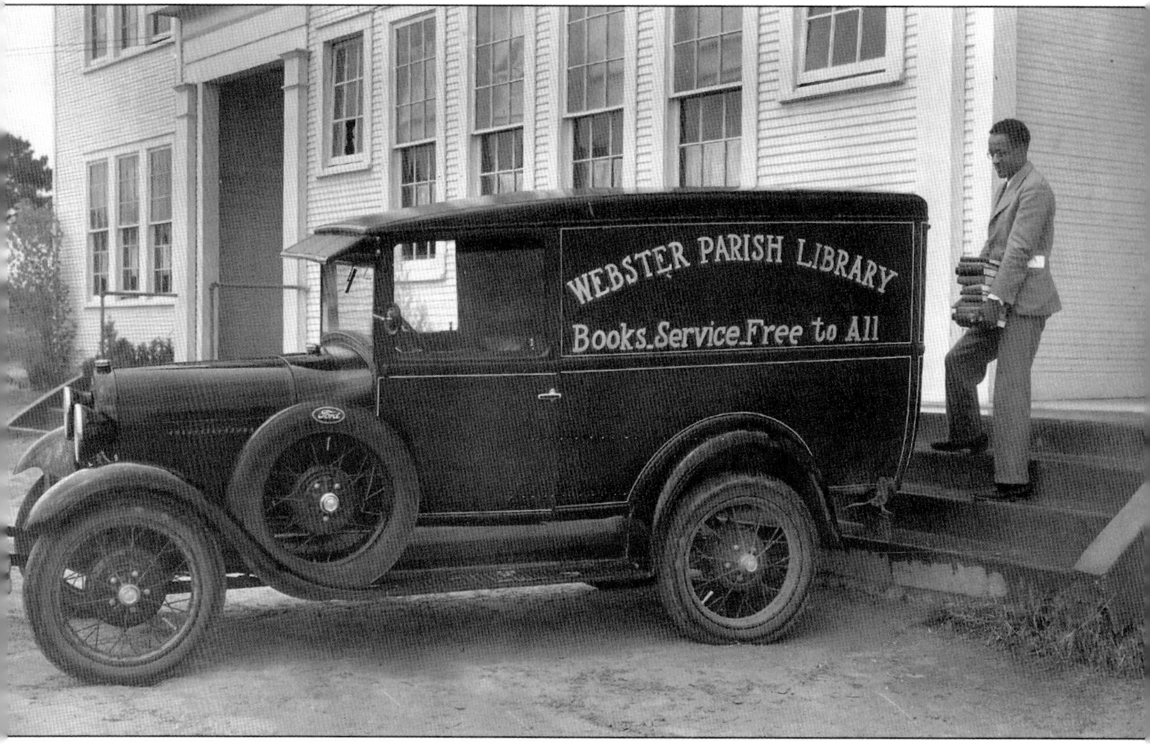

For the first decades of its existence the Webster Parish Library partnered with Webster Parish Schools to provide books to the schools, both black and white. During the summer, the library system used the school facilities for branches in the smaller communities, allowing the students to read during a period when in the past they would have not been able to get any books. Here is the library truck unloading books at the Webster Training Institute in Minden. The library system was one of the few entities in Minden and Webster Parish that truly attempted to provide equal access and opportunity to the parish residents regardless of race. Because of the economic hardship and the lack of quality schools in the black community, this access to reading materials provided by the library made a tremendous difference in the lives of many residents. (Author's collection.)

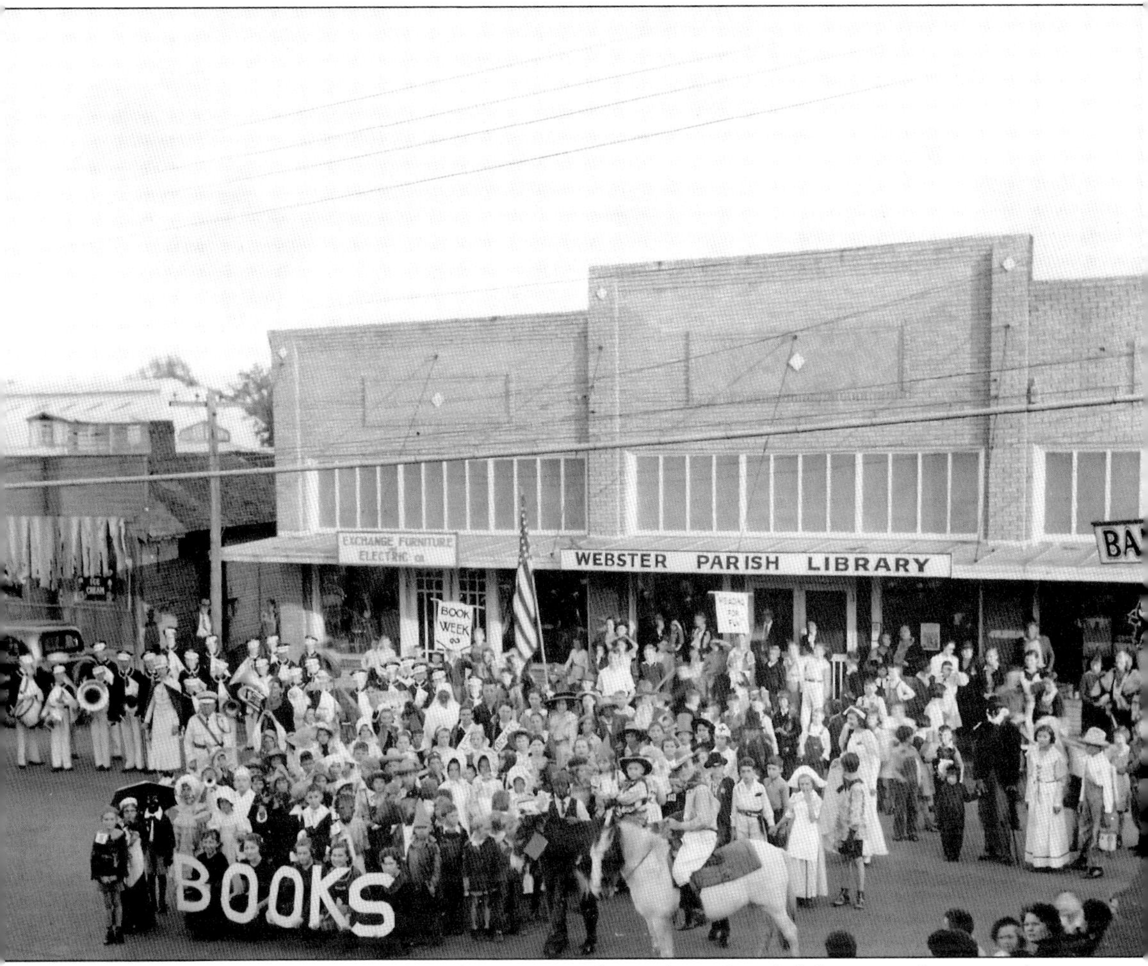

Book Week was clearly a cause for celebration at the Webster Parish Library, as shown in this image from 1937. The library sponsored reading programs for all ages from the time it opened, and those programs always focused most on improving reading skills of students. Accordingly, this celebration, like most other library activities, was held in conjunction with the parish schools, and school students were transported to the library for the special event held on the last day of that week. Contests were held among the students who came in costume, dressed as characters from their favorite books, with winners selected from each grade. The school band played, and visiting entertainment was provided for all in attendance as reading and learning were celebrated. Minden seemed to truly embrace the asset of having an active, quality public library in the community. (Author's collection.)

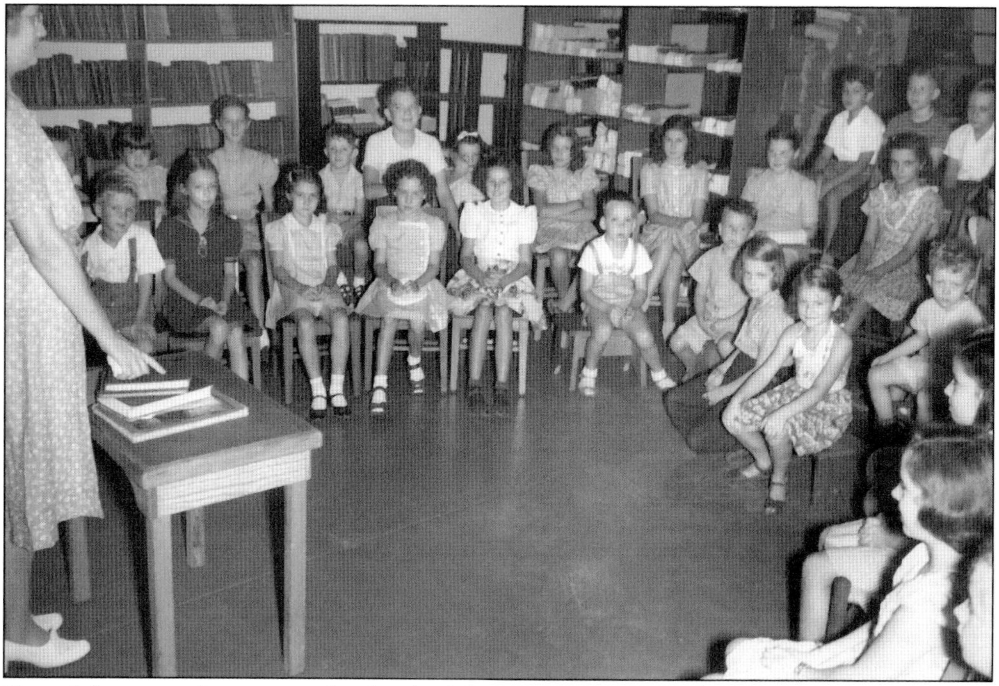

One of the outreach programs that has had the greatest success is the summer reading program and storytime at the library. Here is a picture of storytime from the early years of the library operation. (Courtesy of Webster Parish Library.)

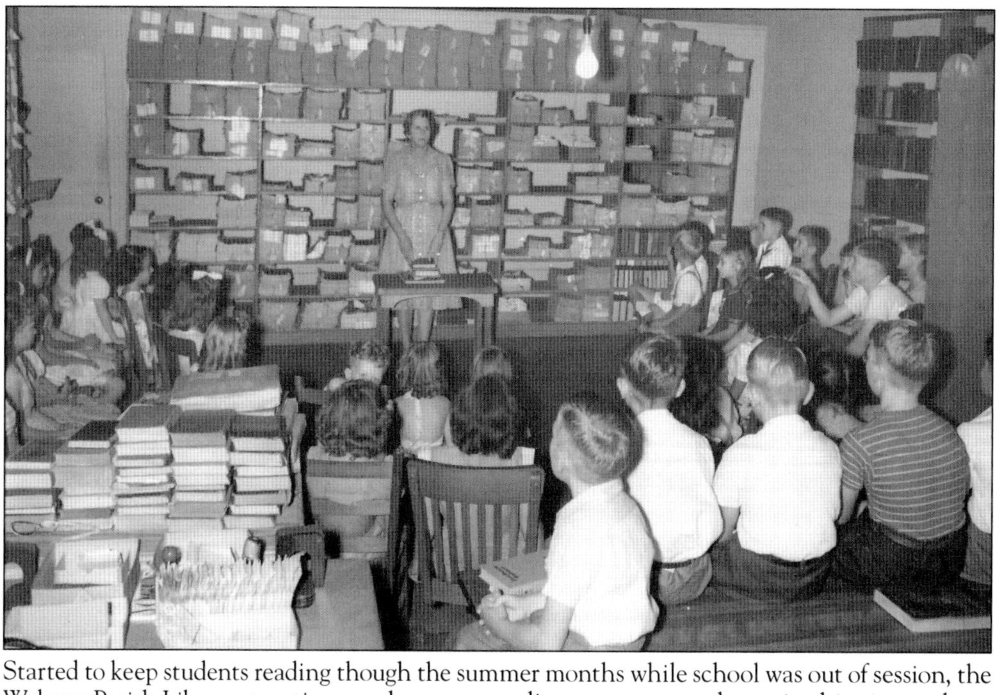

Started to keep students reading though the summer months while school was out of session, the Webster Parish Library storytimes and summer reading programs, as shown in this picture, have been enjoyed by thousands of youngsters over the 85 years the library has been in operation. (Author's collection.)

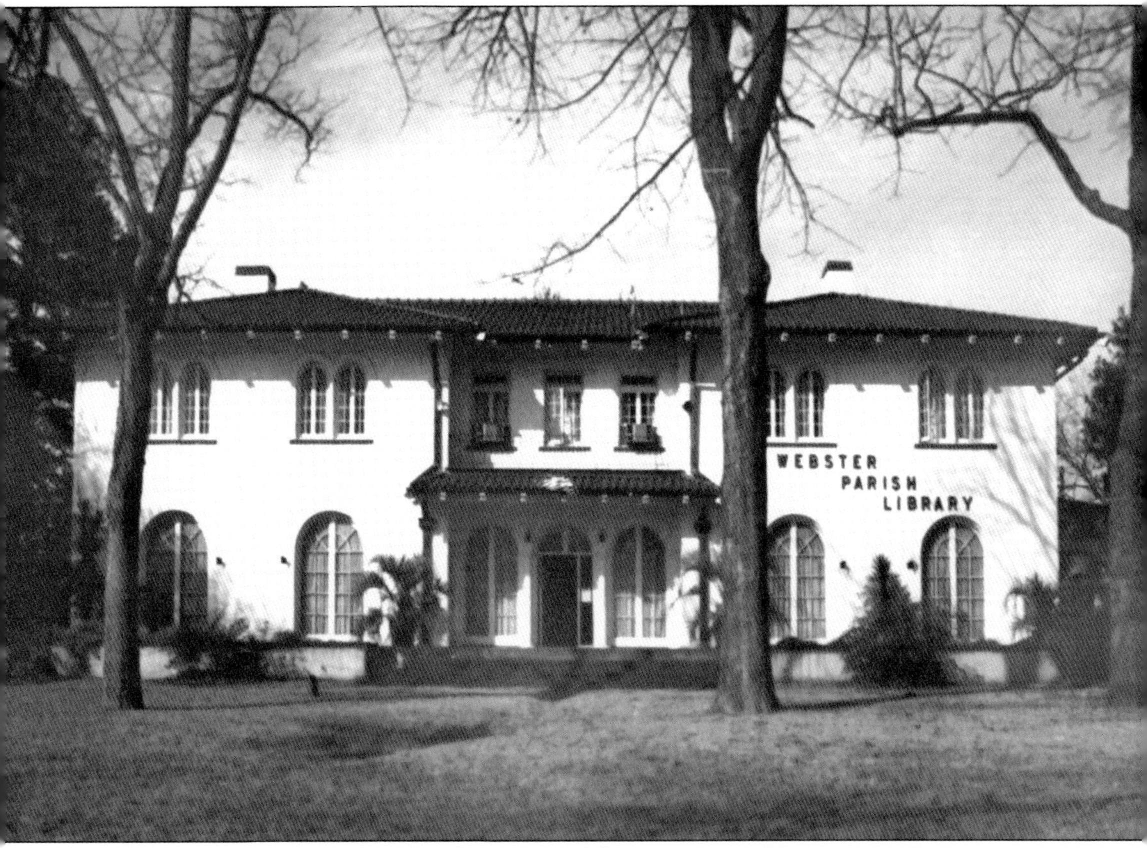

In 1964–1965, the Webster Parish Library moved from its original location to this structure, formerly the home of the Ferguson family. The home had been purchased by the Edomond Stewart family after the Ferguson heirs sold the property. Jim (Mrs. Edomond) Stewart served for many years on the library board of control and wanted to leave a legacy for the organization. In her will, she stipulates the home be given to the library, and her family, through her sister Dell Brown, carried out those wishes. Renovations began on the Stewart Home, and after 35 years in this location, the Webster Parish Library moved to this building in late 1964, formally opening in 1965. The old home served as the parish's main library for about 30 years, and today, it has been renovated again as the Stewart Center of the Library, hosting meetings and the administrative offices of the library system. (Courtesy of LSU-Shreveport Archives and Special Collections, Noel Memorial Library.)

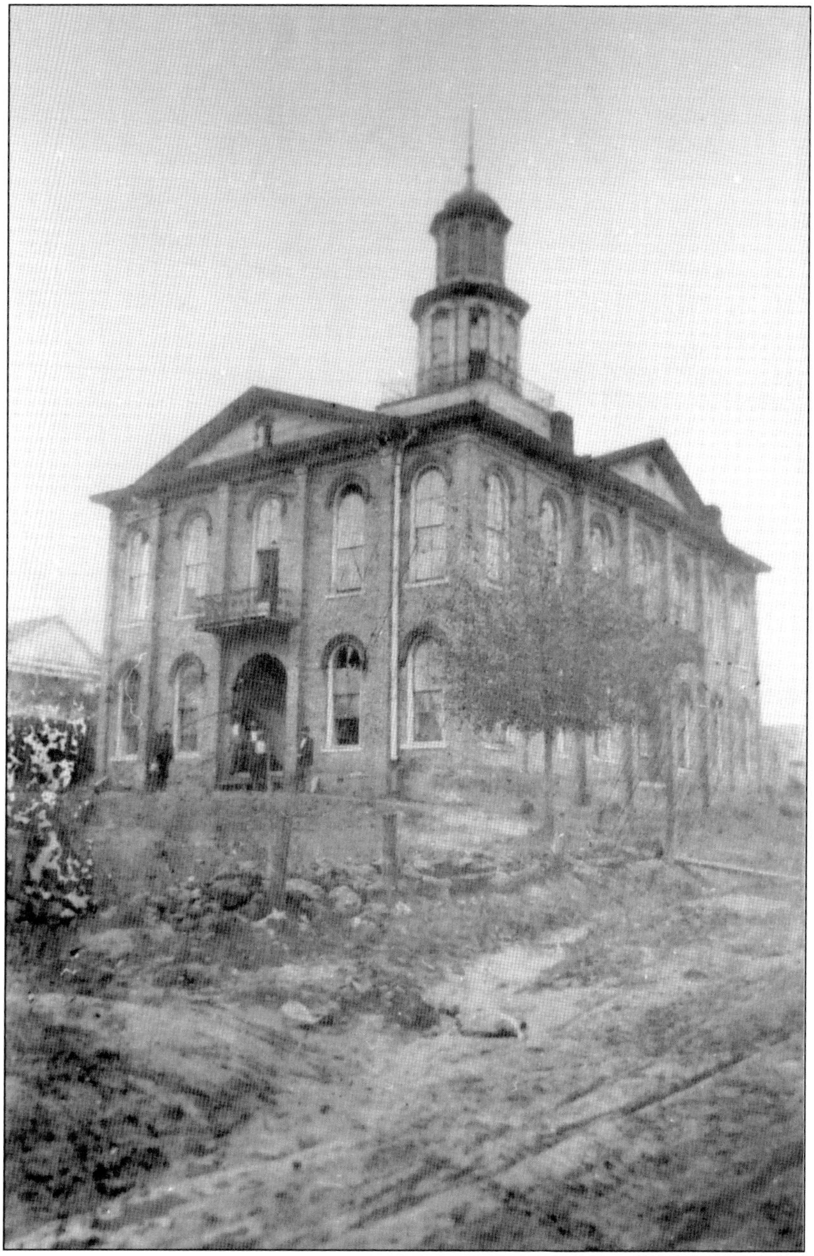

In February 1871, Minden became the parish seat of the newly formed Webster Parish. The next year, this courthouse was completed, at a total cost of just over $20,000, to house parish government. This courthouse would serve the parish for the next 33 years until foundation problems caused by poor drainage forced it to be replaced by a new structure. The erosion of the soil around the building, visible in this picture, indicates the major drainage problems encountered on the property. Becoming a parish seat had been the major goal of Minden's founder, Charles Veeder, but after trying for nearly 15 years, Veeder had left Minden for California in the Gold Rush of 1849. It took the political machinations of Reconstruction in Louisiana to lead to the creation of Webster Parish and Minden gaining the status of the government center of the new political subdivision. (Courtesy of LSU-Shreveport Archives and Special Collections, Noel Memorial Library.)

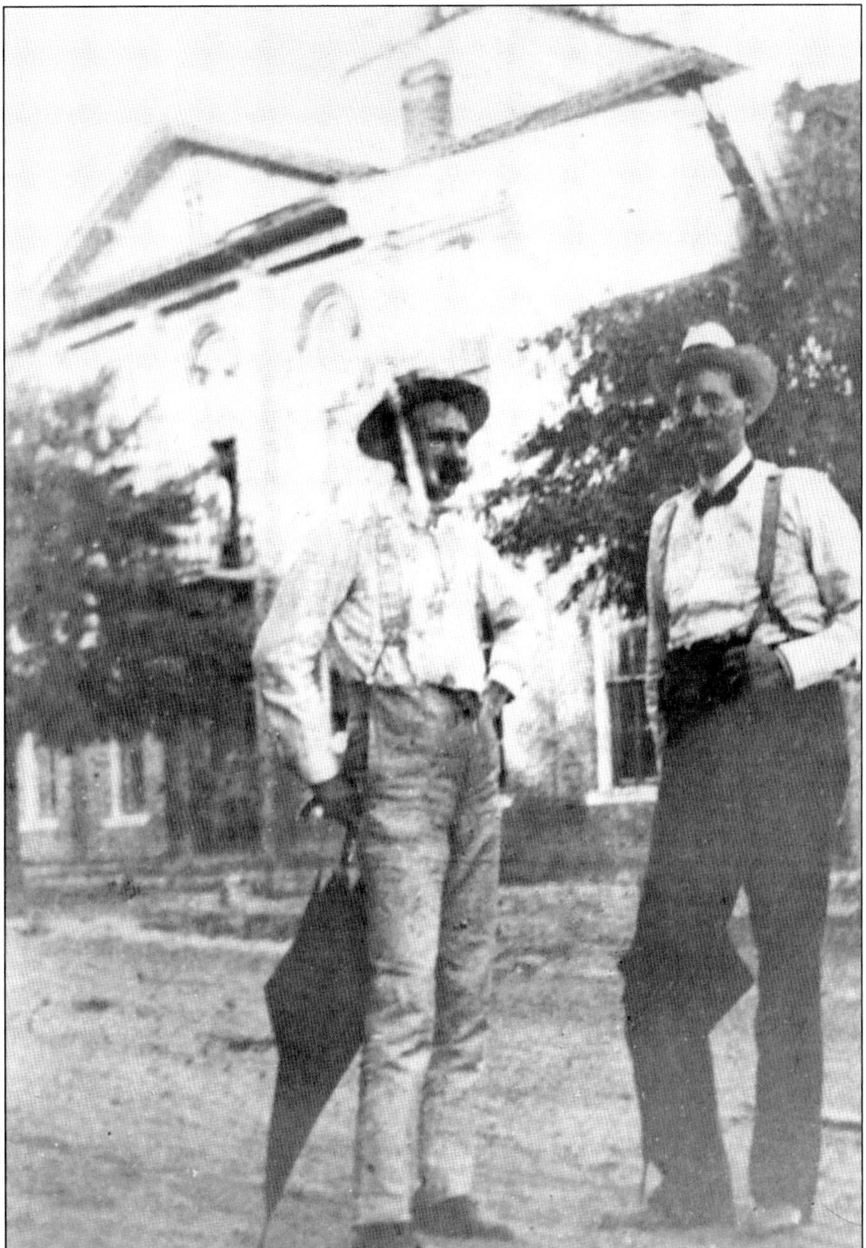

Two prominent Minden politicians are shown in front of the 1872 courthouse shortly before the building was replaced and demolished. On the left is Connell Fort, who served as a town alderman for many years and was elected mayor of Minden on three occasions. Fort is seen earlier as a younger man in the photograph of the German Club. He would preside over some controversial events in the local community. During his final term as mayor, a political feud to which he was a party led to the assassination of a member of the Minden City Council in 1933. After that tragedy, Fort was defeated when he sought reelection and never held office again. On the left is H.A. Barnes, who served two terms as mayor in the early years of the 20th century. The two men were political allies. (Author's collection.)

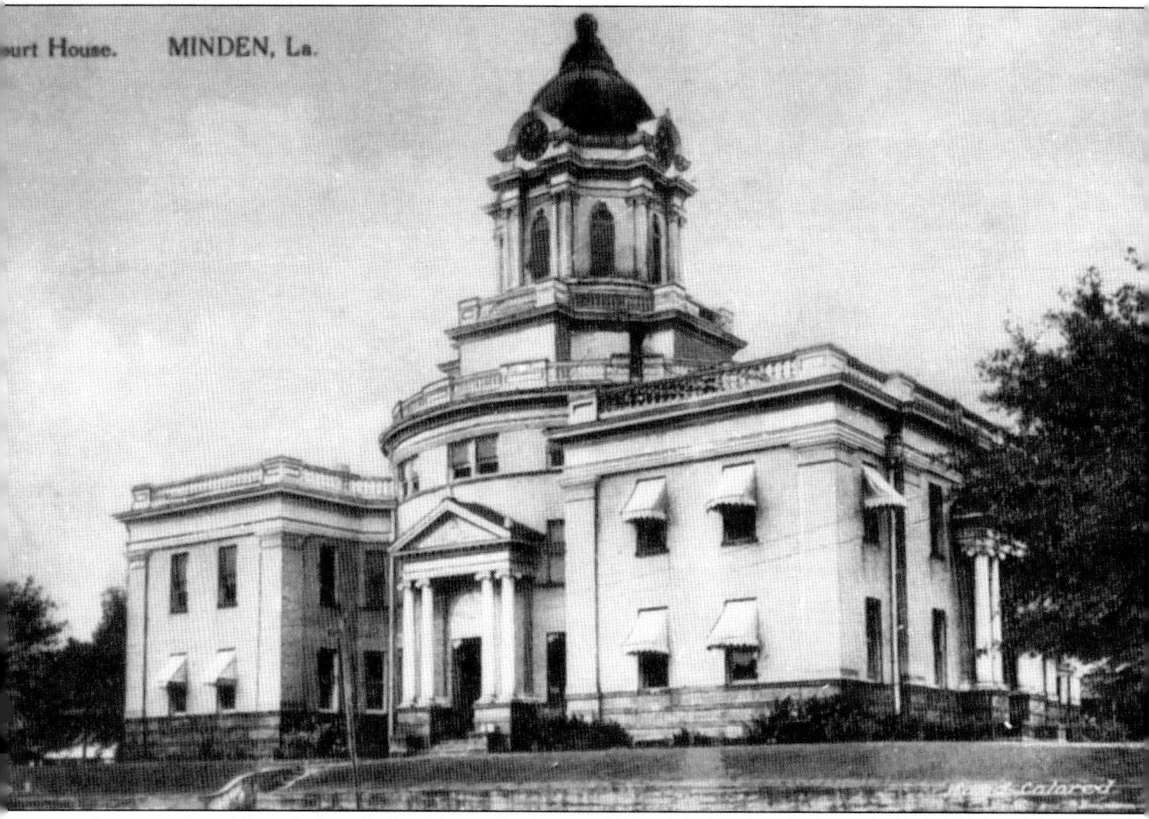

Structural problems led to the building of a new Webster Parish Courthouse in 1905. In its original condition, as seen here, this courthouse had a metal dome that included a four-faced clock. The inclusion of a clock in the tower of the courthouse had been quite a topic for public debate in Minden. There were two newspapers in Minden, and one took the position that a clock was needed to show the town was a forward-looking, progressive community, while the other held that such a clock was a waste of taxpayer money. Clearly, the pro-clock forces won that battle in the short term, but the dome and the clock would be plagued with problems over the years and, eventually, replaced. Inside the courthouse, there was a unique circular courtroom under the dome. (Courtesy of LSU-Shreveport Archives and Special Collections, Noel Memorial Library.)

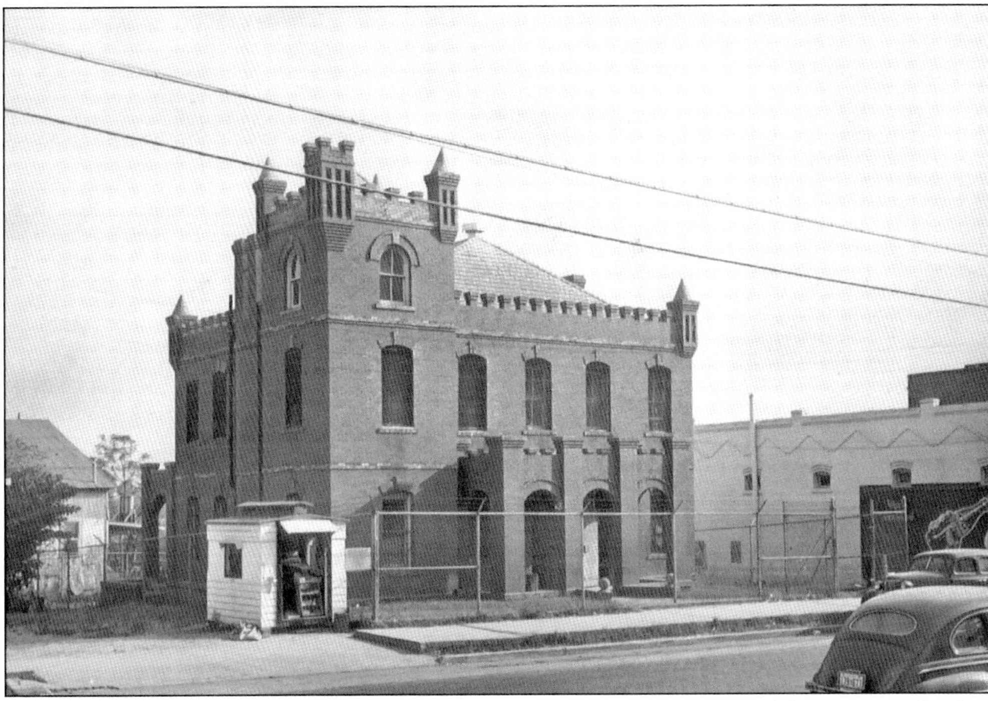

At the same time as the courthouse, a new parish jail was built replacing an older structure that had actually been condemned for more than a decade while still in use. This unique castle-like structure of the jail was a vast contrast from other buildings in the community. (Author's collection.)

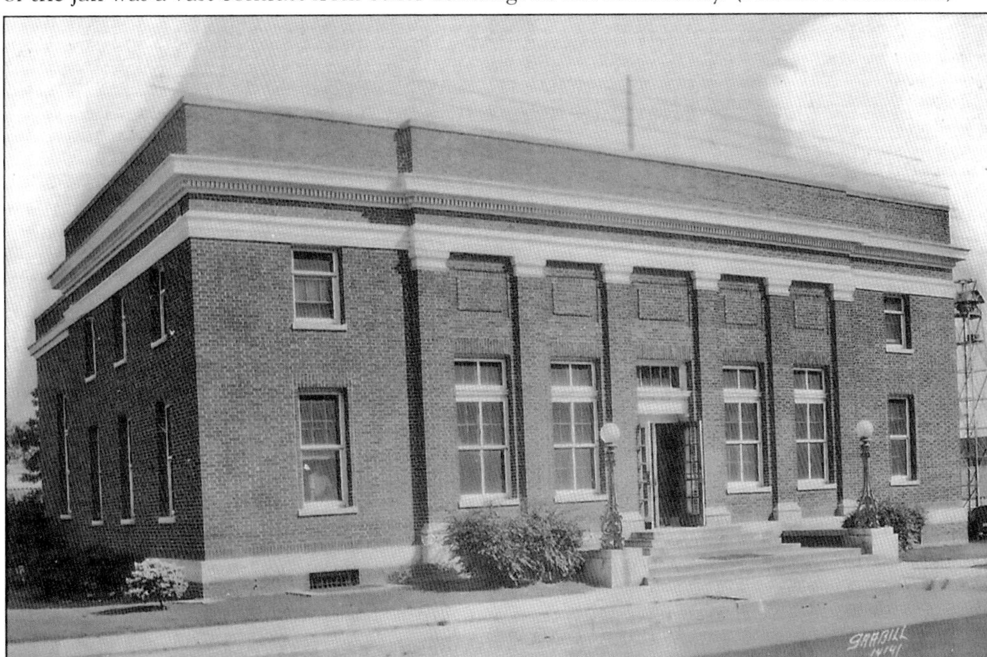

Another new edition to government buildings came in 1916 when Minden constructed its first post office. Before this time, the US post office rented space in local businesses to host the mail office. This building was located on the site of the old 1872 courthouse. (Author's collection.)

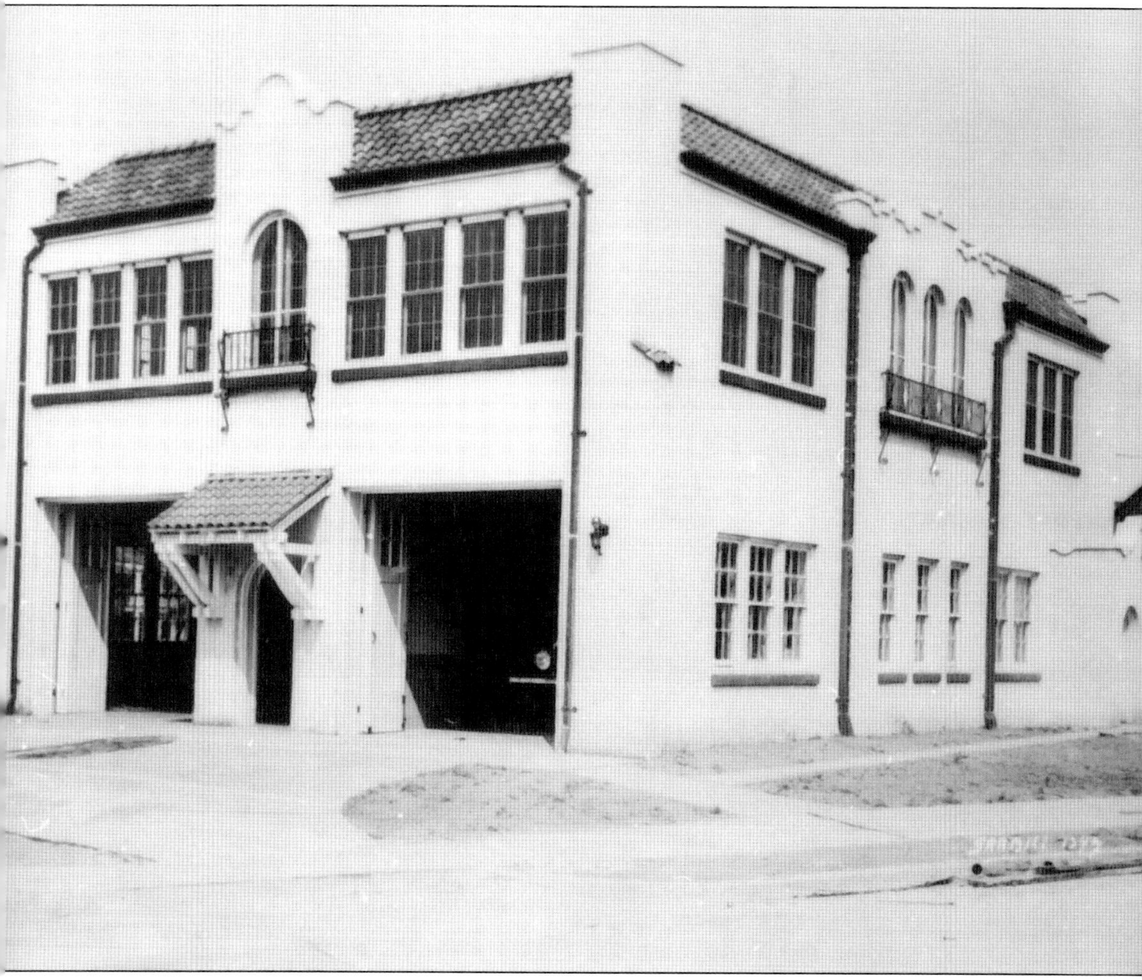

In 1926, after nearly 100 years of its existence, Minden finally constructed its first building dedicated to serve as the city hall. That same year, the town completed a new charter approved by voters. In addition, the population boom that occurred after the L&A shops arrived allowed the town to grow to where it, for the first time, met the standards for it to be officially classified as a city according to state law. This building housed all city offices and the station for the city's volunteer fire department. The city offices were eventually moved in the 1950s, but the fire station continued to be used into the 1970s, when the building was demolished. (Courtesy of LSU-Shreveport Archives and Special Collections, Noel Memorial Library.)

The largest section of the new government building was dedicated to the volunteer fire department. Minden organized its first volunteer fire company in 1860, but through the years, the town had been plagued by many disastrous fires. (Courtesy of LSU-Shreveport Archives and Special Collections, Noel Memorial Library.)

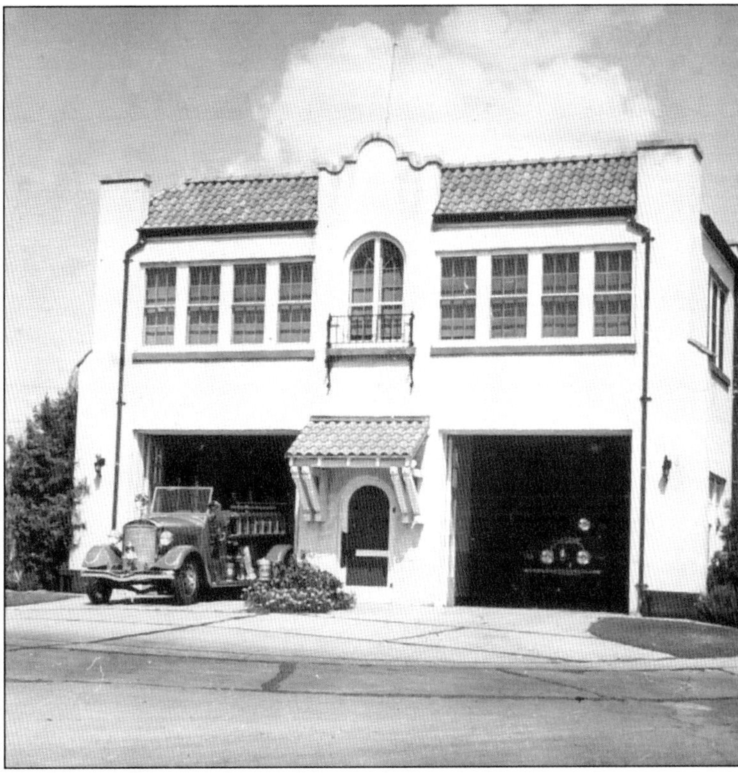

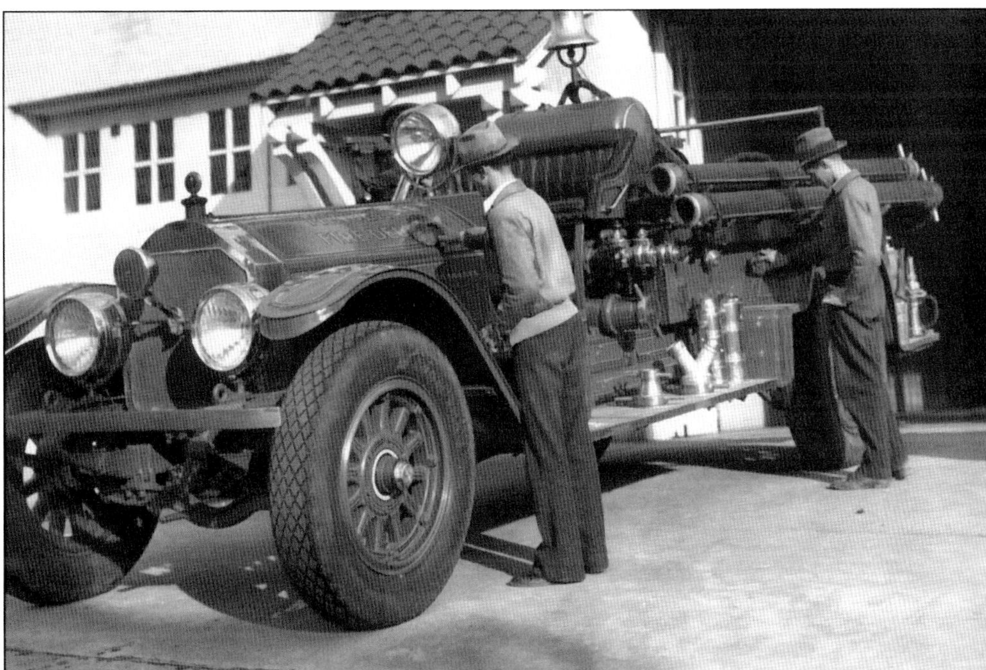

Because of the past fire losses, Minden became dedicated to providing some of the best firefighting equipment of any small town in the region. Items such as this American LaFrance fire truck helped provide more security to local residents and lowed insurance rates. (Author's collection.)

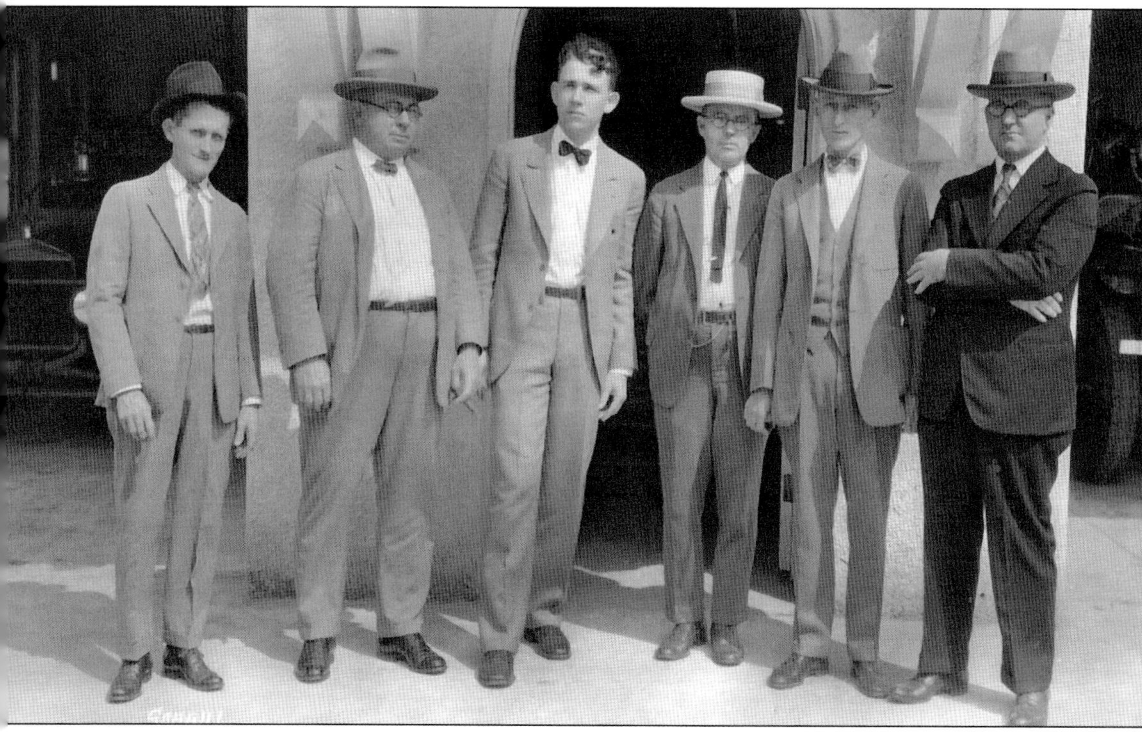

This is the elected governing body for Minden in 1926. With the town's change in status to a city, this was the first group to be called a city council under law. The men are posed standing in front of the new city hall, which also opened that year. Third from the left is Minden's "boy mayor," 24-year-old Robert F. Kennon. Kennon would go on to a distinguished career as a prosecutor, judge, and soldier. His political career culminated with his election as governor of Louisiana in 1952. Kennon had returned home to Minden from LSU Law School and, within a year, was elected to the city's highest office. Pictured are, from left to right, J. Ronald Murph, W.T. Burnett, Mayor Kennon, W.R. Garrison, Will Life, and S.H. McCrary. (Courtesy of Dorcheat Historical Association Museum and Douglas McCrary.)

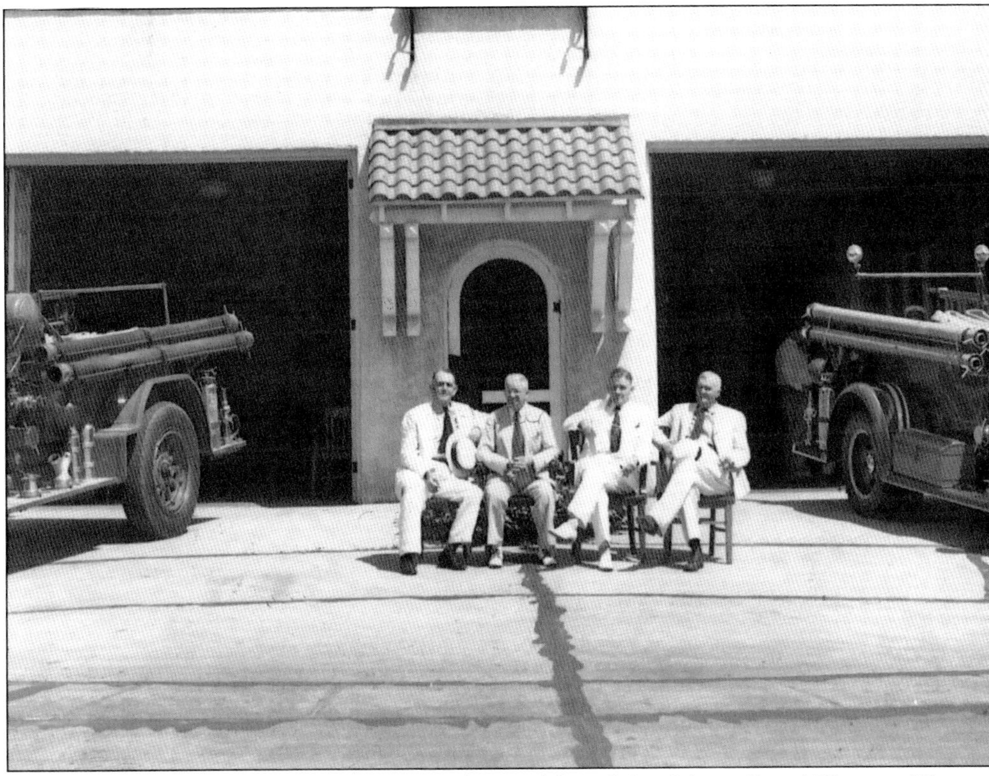

A later city council is shown in 1937. Seated second from left is Mayor David Thomas. Thomas was an immigrant from Wales who was an attorney, journalist, and professor and had many other roles during his time in Minden. (Author's collection.)

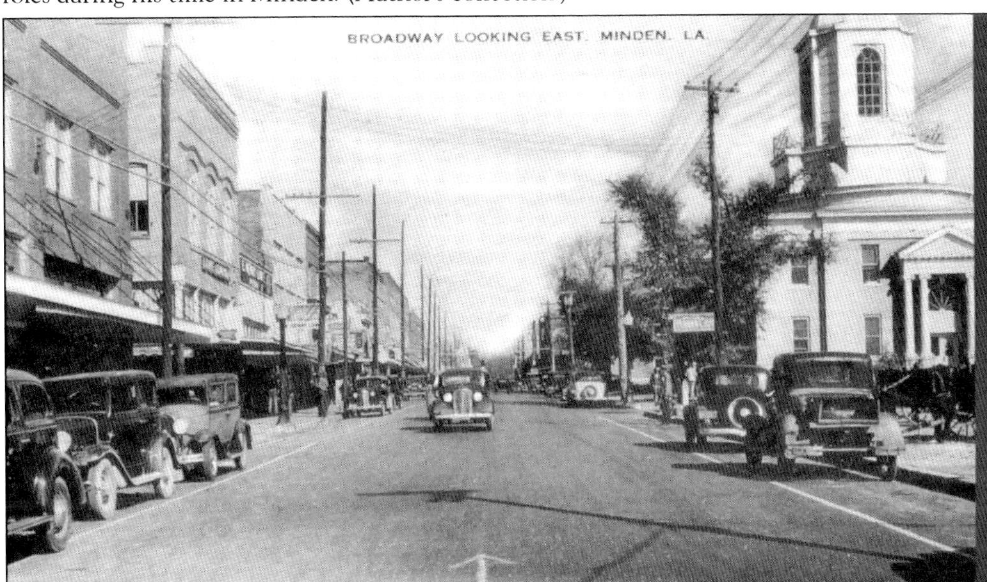

After the tornado of May 1, 1933, the Webster Parish Courthouse had remodeling done to the dome. The nonfunctioning clock was removed, and as seen in this image from the late 1930s, large windows were added to the now wooden dome. (Author's collection.)

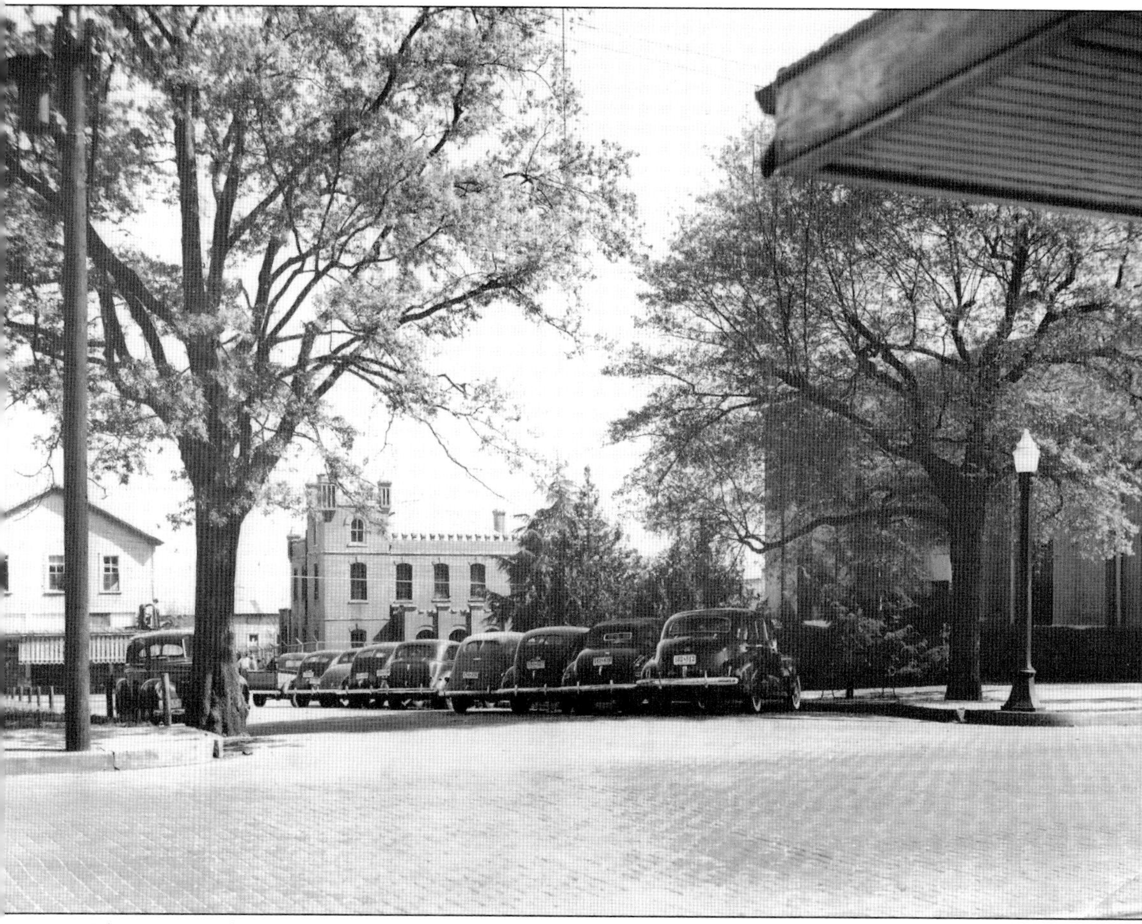

The view in this picture taken from Main Street during the 1940s looks toward the castle-like turrets of the Webster Parish Jail. The license plates on the vehicles are for 1941. From this angle, the bricks of Front Street are clearly visible. On the right is the Webster Parish Courthouse with the cars parked in the small street running to the east side of the courthouse. According to local tradition, this street runs though the area where the hanging tree used for executions was located during the middle portion of the 19th century. The last legal hanging in Minden took place in the 1880s, and after that date, prisoners were sent to the Louisiana State Penitentiary at Angola to be executed. To the left of the jail is Abraham Dow's store, which is featured earlier in this book and on the cover. It appears the store is undergoing painting or some other repairs. (Author's collection.)

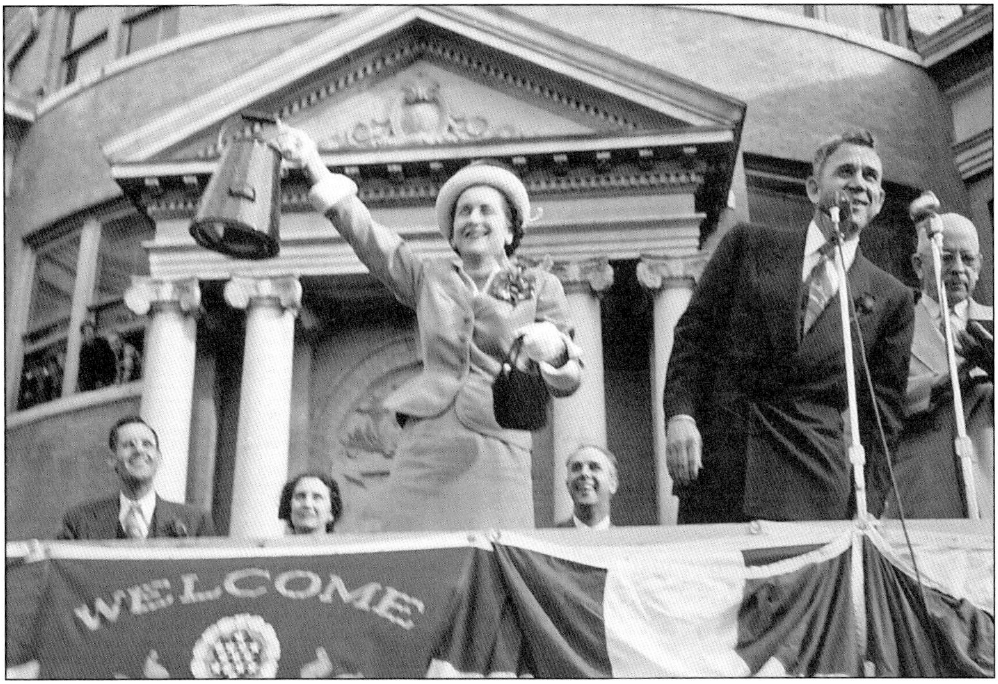

Former mayor Robert Kennon made the Webster Parish Courthouse a stop on his campaign for governor of Louisiana in 1952. Kennon would win the election and become the only governor of the state to claim Minden as home. (Author's collection.)

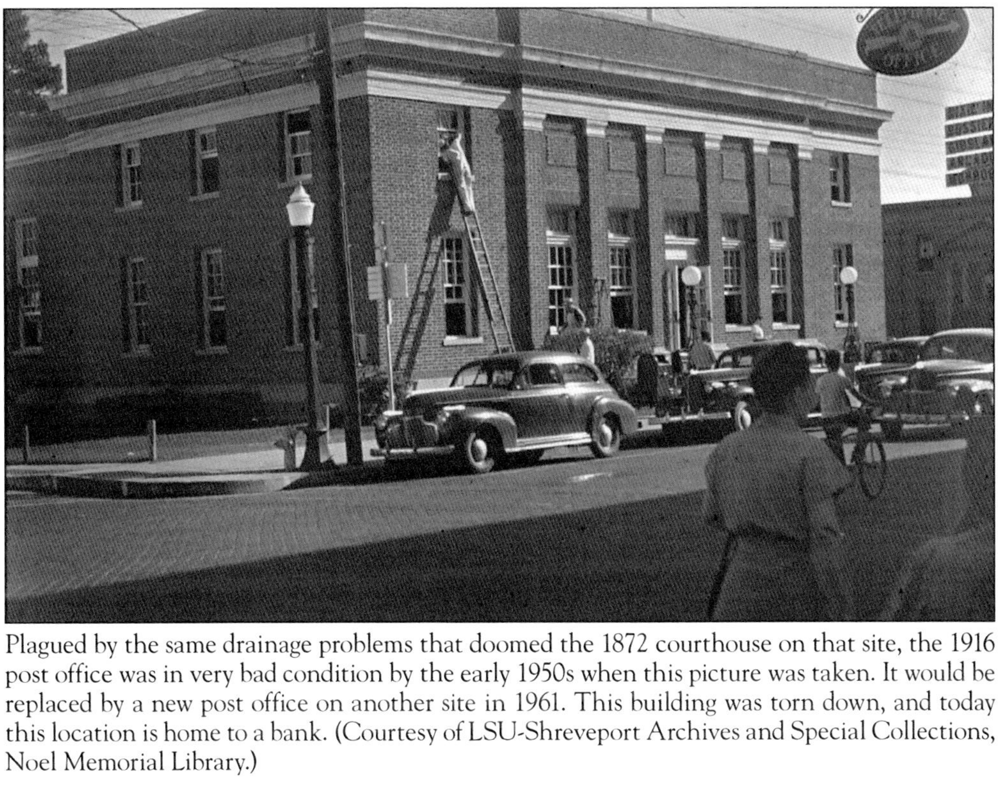
Plagued by the same drainage problems that doomed the 1872 courthouse on that site, the 1916 post office was in very bad condition by the early 1950s when this picture was taken. It would be replaced by a new post office on another site in 1961. This building was torn down, and today this location is home to a bank. (Courtesy of LSU-Shreveport Archives and Special Collections, Noel Memorial Library.)

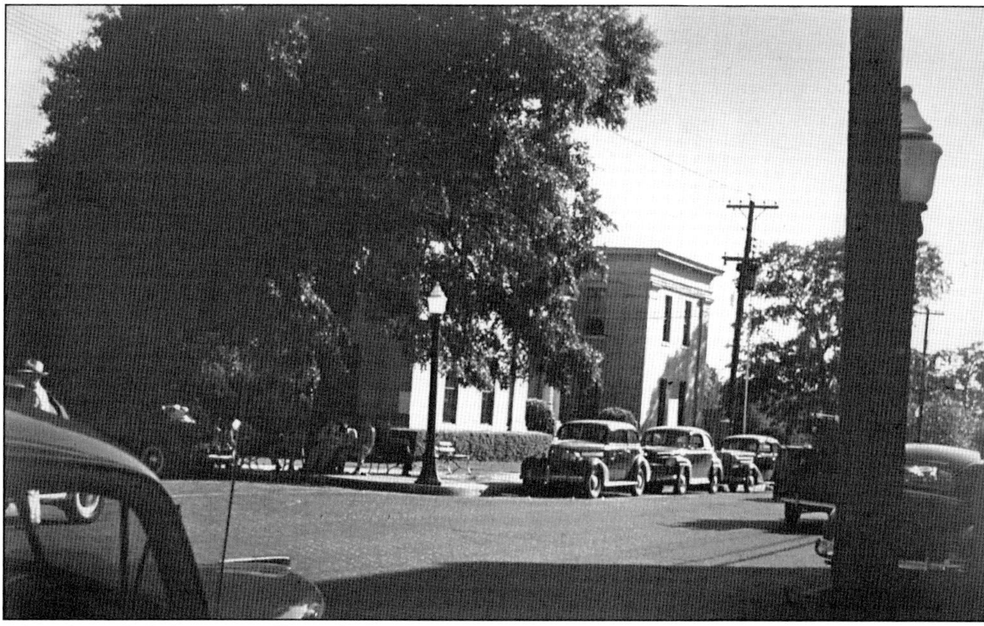

Jokingly called the "tree of knowledge" by local residents, this tree stood at the northeast corner of the Webster Parish Courthouse property. The name came from the older gentlemen of the town who, as seen in this picture, sat on the benches beneath the tree and "solved the problems of the world." The tree was destroyed in a storm in 1955. (Courtesy of LSU-Shreveport Archives and Special Collections, Noel Memorial Library.)

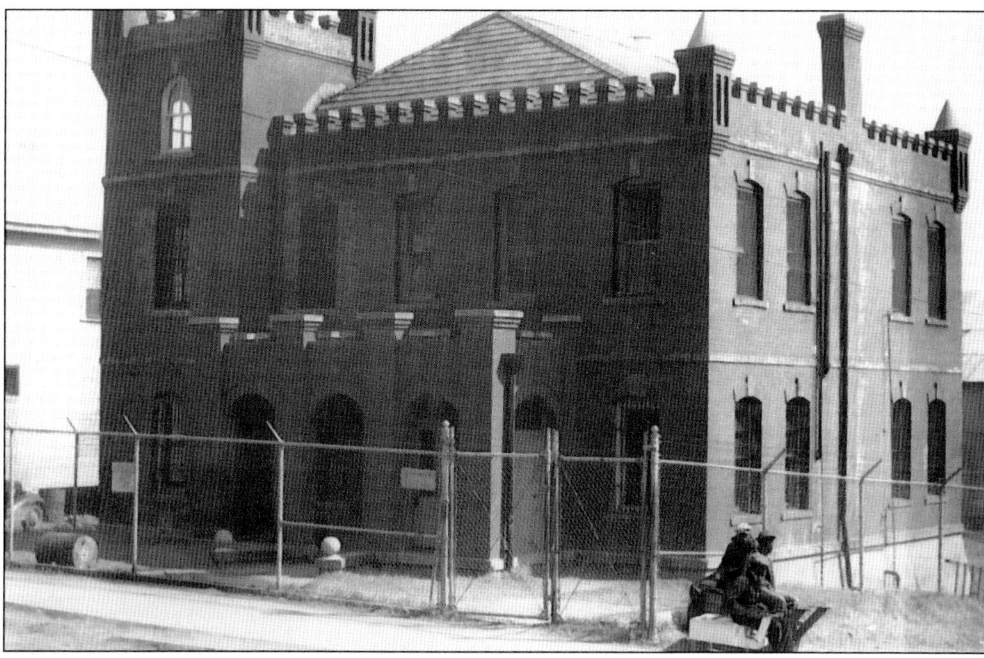

By 1952, growing pains and age were impacting city and parish structures. Both the Webster Parish Jail, shown here, and the Webster Parish Courthouse were showing signs of needing replacements. In addition, the city of Minden was outgrowing the city hall/fire station, and so community leaders got together and worked out a solution. (Author's collection.)

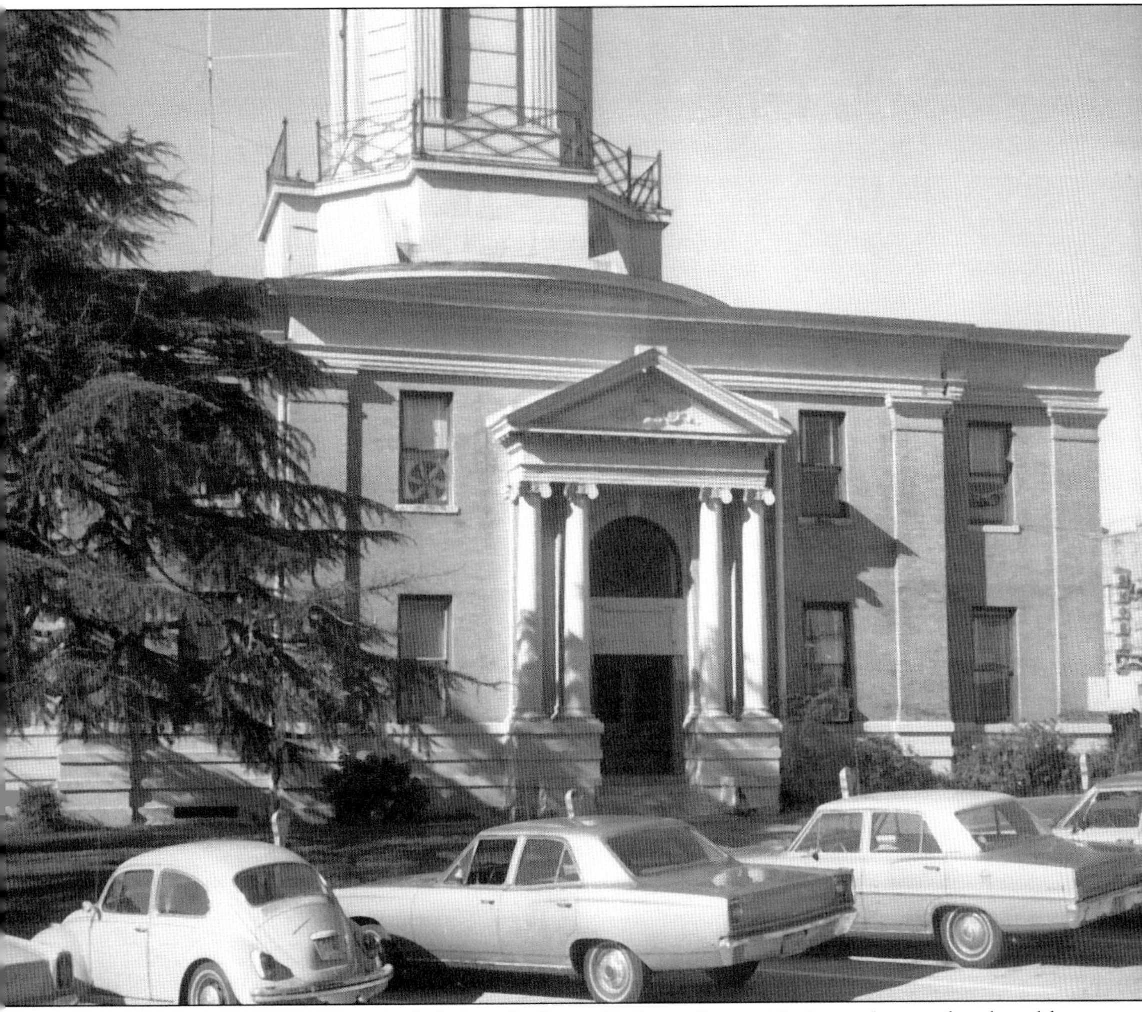

In 1953, the City of Minden traded the old Civic Park to the parish in exchange for the old parish jail and courthouse. A new courthouse was constructed on the site of the park, the jail was destroyed, and the old courthouse was converted to Minden City Hall. The 1905 courthouse would fill the role of Minden City Hall for the last 17 years of its existence. This image shows city hall during the 1960s. Note that the dome on the building has entered its third and final state. The windows added in 1933 have been removed, and the space has been boarded over by this point. The cars are parked in the same area as in the earlier picture from the 1940s, but the years of wear and tear on the building and that area of downtown are clearly visible in this image. (Author's collection.)

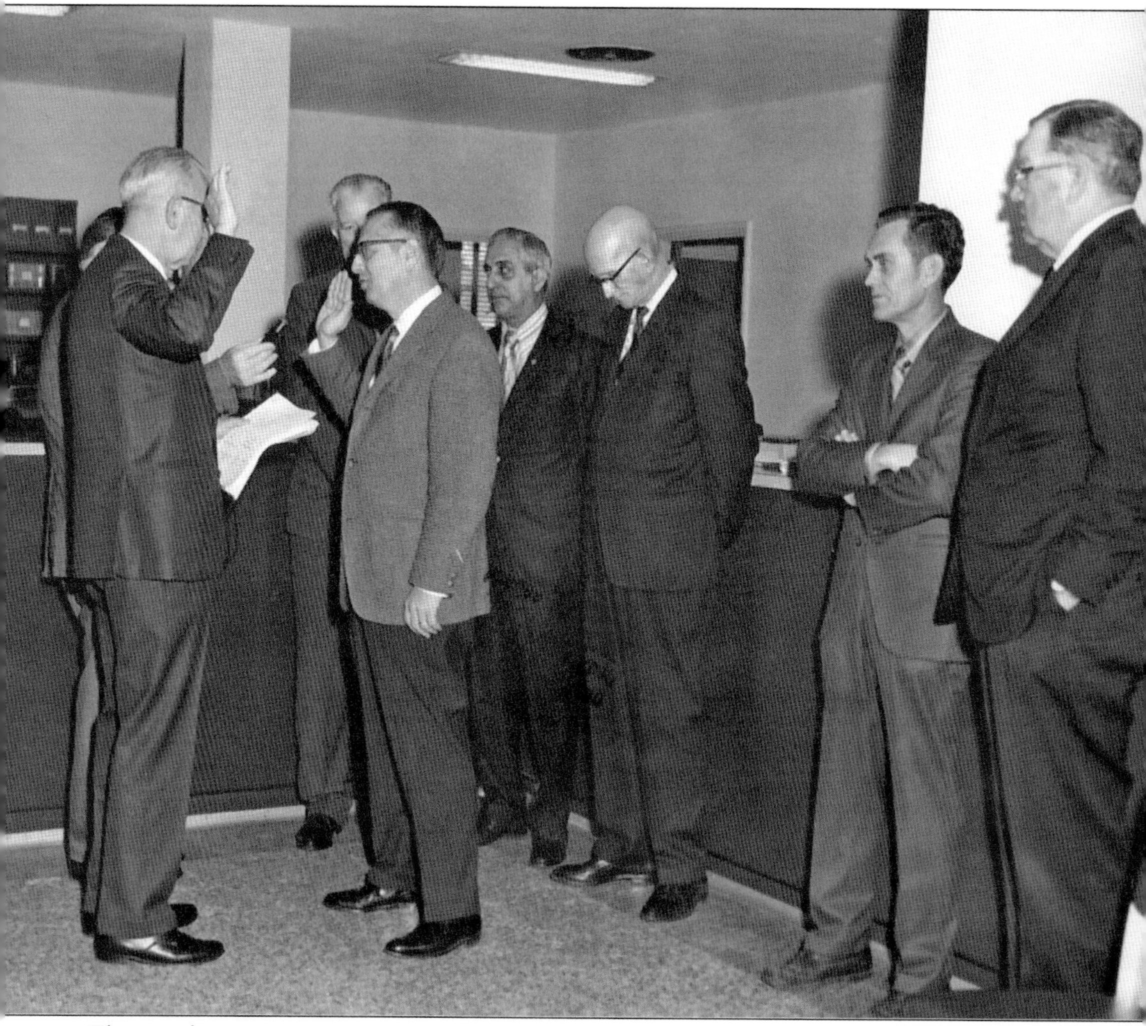

The race for mayor in 1966 was an indicator of great change coming to Minden. In that election, Tom Colten, shown along with members of the city council being sworn into office by Clerk of Court Clarence Wiley, became the first Republican ever elected mayor in Minden and one of the few since the years of Reconstruction in the entire state of Louisiana. Colten had come to Minden in the 1950s as editor and the publisher of the local newspaper and soon gained respect as a local leader and as a person with a vision for the town. Louisiana was still a one-party state as victory in the Democratic Primary normally was tantamount to winning election to office. The respect he earned in a community where Republicans were practically nonexistent was a great tribute to his character and abilities. Directly behind Mayor Colten, the head of councilman Jack Batton is visible. Then, from left to right, are council members Tony Elzen, Lonnie Cupples, Jack Crisler, and finally Police Chief Harvey McClung. (Courtesy of Tom Colten.)

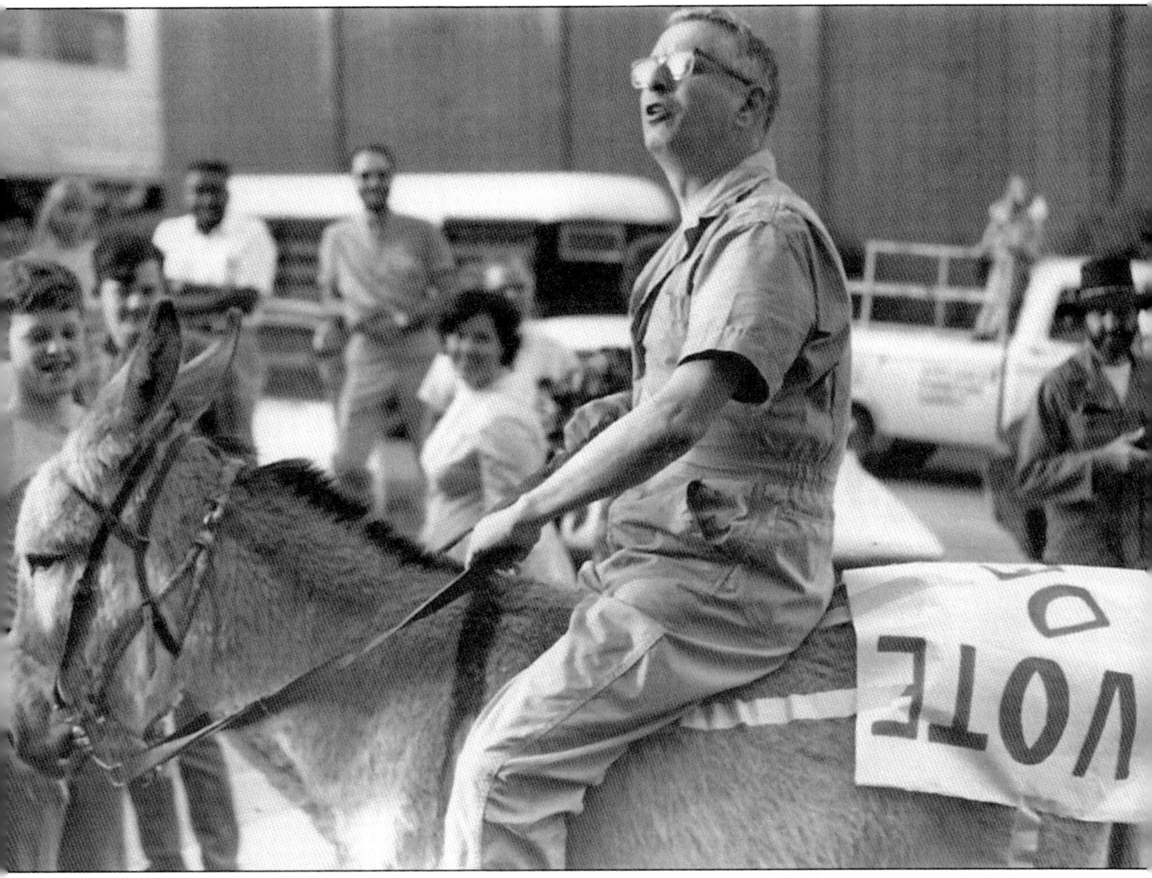

Colten brought a more businesslike approach to the office of mayor, which had largely been treated as part-time work in the past. He set out on a program of modernization that would bring many civic improvements. But, in addition, as seen in this picture, he had a sense of humor as a politician. This picture resulted from Colten losing a bet with some local residents, so in the spirit of goodwill, Colten appeared at a local parade with his unique mode of transportation, a "Democratic Donkey." It was yet another example that Colten, unlike many past mayors, recognized the need to project a friendly image for a town that labeled itself the "Friendliest City in the South." His efforts would do much toward keeping Minden moving ahead after the local economy took another hit when the Louisiana Army Ammunition Plant suffered from cutbacks. (Courtesy of Tom Colten.)

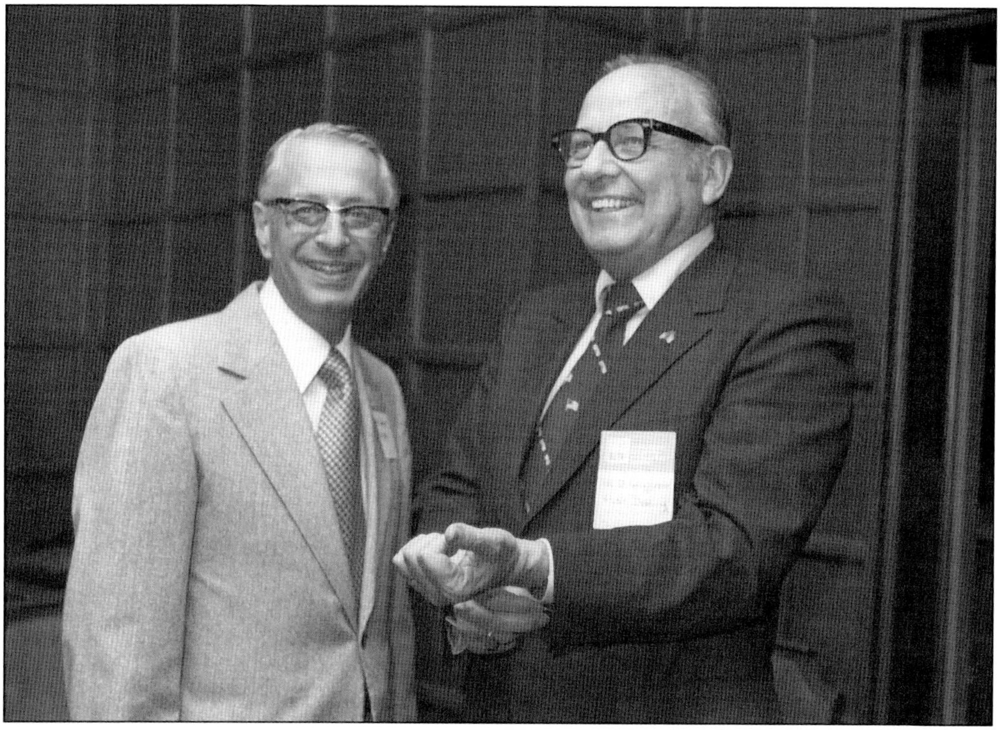

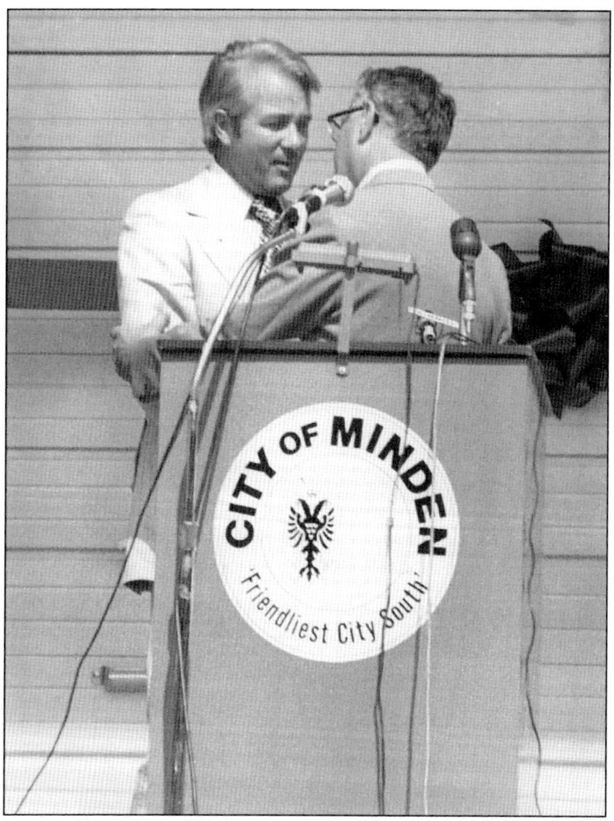

Colten (left) had the unique ability to reach across party lines to develop a close working relationships with Democratic politicians who still ran the state and dominated regional politics. He is shown here with Democratic congressman Joe D. Waggoner of the 4th District of Louisiana. (Courtesy of Tom Colten.)

While Waggoner was a conservative Democrat, Colten also worked well with more liberal Democratic politicians. In this picture, he is welcoming Louisiana governor Edwin Edwards (left) to a speaking engagement at the new Minden Civic Center's dedication in 1971. (Courtesy of Tom Colten.)

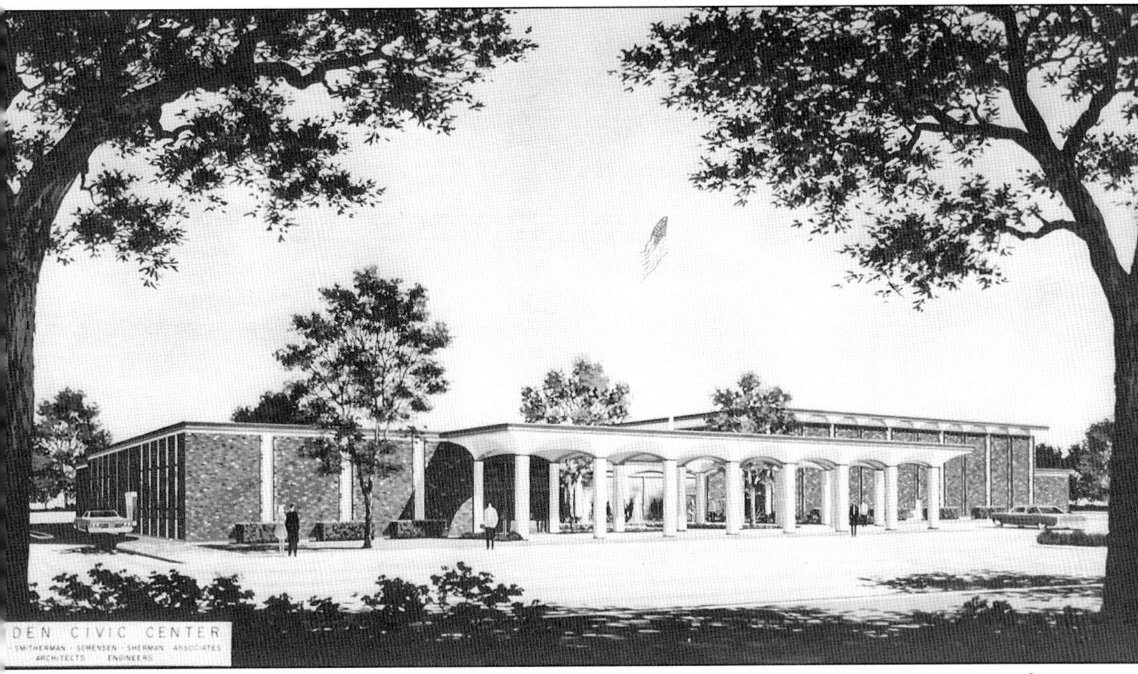

Probably the crown jewel of Colten's time in office was his direction of the construction of a new Minden Civic Center and City Hall Complex. This is an architect's sketch of the planned building shown to the public in 1968. When it was finished, the facility replaced the businesses formerly located on Back Street, such as Abraham Dow's and other stores shown earlier in this book. The old city hall was also demolished, and Pearl Street was extended through the area where the old building had stood. Today, more than 40 years later, this complex is still in full use by the city. The city offices have been expanded and remodeled, but the Minden Civic Center is still largely in the state it was in Colten's day and is host for most major events held in the Minden community. (Courtesy of Tom Colten.)